HARVARD-YENCHING INSTITUTE STUDIES
XIX

CH'ING ADMINISTRATION
Three Studies

BY
JOHN K. FAIRBANK
and
SSŬ-YU TÊNG

HARVARD UNIVERSITY PRESS
CAMBRIDGE, MASSACHUSETTS

© COPYRIGHT, 1960, BY
THE HARVARD-YENCHING INSTITUTE

Third Printing, 1968

DISTRIBUTED IN GREAT BRITAIN BY
OXFORD UNIVERSITY PRESS
LONDON

Library of Congress Catalog Card Number 60–7991

PRINTED IN THE UNITED STATES OF AMERICA

FOREWORD

This volume, the nineteenth of the Harvard-Yenching Institute Studies, is financed from the residue of the funds granted during World War II by the Rockefeller Foundation for the publication of Chinese and Japanese dictionaries. This series is distinct from the Harvard-Yenching Institute Monograph Series and consists primarily of bibliographical studies, grammars, reference works, translations, and other study and research aids.

AUTHORS' PREFACE

When we published these three studies of Ch'ing administrative institutions, almost twenty years ago, we regarded them as pioneer steps into virgin territory which many others would soon be exploring and exploiting more thoroughly. We expected our efforts to be quickly superseded. Instead, rather little further work has been done on these subjects. Important researches have been published in ancillary areas — the socio-political structure of late-Ch'ing China, its military history, diplomatic relations, foreign trade, early industrial growth, and domestic rebellions, even its intellectual history and (in Japanese) cultural relations. Yet the day-to-day processes of the bureaucratic machine of the Ch'ing period have commanded little attention, and on their respective subjects these articles have not yet been followed by more definitive work in English. No Chinese-English dictionary of Ch'ing administrative terminology has appeared, although a useful list of terms has been produced in Japanese at Tokyo University.* In general, almost no one has studied more fully the flow of official business to and from the emperor; few have explored the details of tribute missions and the trade connected with them.

While this explains why these articles are now reprinted without being reworked, it also raises a critical question about Western studies of modern China. Are we not trying in this field to go too directly into the big problems raised by contemporary social science — questions of social mobility, of entrepreneurship, of class and power structure and ideology, for example — without having first performed the factual, detailed foundation work

---

* See UEDA Toshio 植田捷雄, OGAERI Yoshio 魚返善雄, BANNO Masataka 坂野正高, ETŌ Shinkichi 衛藤瀋吉, and SOMURA Yasunobu 曾村保信, *Chūgoku gaikō bunsho jiten: Shimmatsu-hen* 中國外交文書辭典 (*Dictionary for Chinese Diplomatic Documents: Late Ch'ing*), Tōkyō Gakujutsu Bunken Fukyū Kai 東京學術文獻普及會, 1954, 7 + 139 + 3 pp.

On the use of late Ch'ing materials in research, and for recent bibliography, see also J. K. FAIRBANK, *Ch'ing Documents, An Introductory Syllabus*, 2nd revised edition, Harvard University Press, 1959, 2 vols.

which in other, more mature fields has facilitated the eventual asking of such big questions?

Is it not inefficient for Western sinologists either to plunge down into the maelstrom of piecemeal narrations of the events of nineteenth-century Chinese history or to soar up among the cloudbanks of carefully-formulated social-science analyses and conceptual frameworks without first having tied the special terminology of the Chinese documentary record to an established body of equivalent terms in English, traced out in these terms the day-to-day procedures and practices of the major institutions of administration, and so filled in with solid factual detail the now shadowy outlines of the official establishment? In other words, are we not unwisely led by our contemporary modern interests to neglect the study of traditional Chinese governmental processes and institutions?

One argument for such studies, whether of the salt administration, the Li Fan Yüan, the examination system, or the land tax, is that the voluminous records of the late Ch'ing period make possible a comparison of the official system, as formally set up, with its actual operation as seen in day-to-day documents. The latter have been, and remain, available in our libraries. We have no want of Chinese documentation, and in recent years, more and more American researchers have become capable of reading it. What we seem to have lacked is the patience, and indeed the courage, to ask small institutional, operational questions before asking big social ones. The present studies are reissued to assist primarily those who seek detailed and concrete mastery of finite institutional processes under the late Ch'ing government.

We are indebted to the Harvard-Yenching Institute for making these articles available in its *Studies* series, as well as for their original publication in the *Harvard Journal of Asiatic Studies*. They are here reprinted, in the same order, from *HJAS* 4(1939).12–46, 5(1940).1–71, and 6(1941).135–246. Since the reproduction is photographic, several typographical errors are carried over to this book. The only change that has been made is the addition of continuous pagination at the bottom of each

AUTHORS' PREFACE

page, and it is these new page numbers that are referred to in the following list of errata:

Page 7, note 17, line 4 from bottom: *for* Kiangsi, *read* Kiangsu.

Page 90, line 11 from bottom: for *I-wu shih-lo,* read *I-wu shih-mo.*

Page 94, line 10 from bottom: *for* SHÊN-CH'ÊNG 申呈 STATEMENT, *read* SHÊN-CH'ÊN 申陳 STATEMENT.

Page 154, line 4: *for* presered, *read* preserved.

Page 182, line 8: *for* LAN *Ting-yüan, read* LAN Ting-yüan.

Attention is called to the forthcoming publication by the Harvard University Press, in the Harvard East Asian Studies series, of a volume by E-tu Zen Sun, translator and editor, *Ch'ing Administrative Terms: A Translation of "The Terminology of the Six Boards with Explanatory Notes (Liu-pu ch'eng-yü chu-chieh* 六部成語註解). Although not a dictionary, this handbook of the Ch'ing period deals extensively with terms used in the administrative process.

JOHN K. FAIRBANK
SSU-YÜ TÊNG

January 1960

Note to the Third Printing

The account of the Ch'ing system of correspondence presented on page forty-one et seq. of this volume should now be modified in the light of recent work by Professor Silas Hsiu-liang Wu, "The Memorial Systems of the Ch'ing Dynasty (1644–1911)" in *The Harvard Journal of Asiatic Studies,* Vol. 27, 1967, pp. 7–75. Mr. Wu has found that *tsou-pen* and *tsou-che* are two distinct types of document.

In brief, the Ch'ing inherited from the Ming a system of routine memorials *(pen-chang)* which were of two kinds, namely *t'i-pen* and *tsou-pen*. Each had its distinctive uses, more or less as described in our original study; but the emperor in the late seventeenth century began to develop a new system of *tsou-che* or "palace memorials" as a means of greater speed and secrecy in communication. These documents were sent directly to the emperor by special couriers and so were seen by no one but the sender and the emperor, except as he showed them to his assistants. This new type of document came to be handled largely by the Grand Council, which began to take shape in 1729 as a new institution to assist the Yung-cheng Emperor. As this development continued during the Ch'ien-lung period, Mr. Wu finds that "the *tsou-pen* type of routine memorial was abolished as redundant in 1748." Eventually the ancient t'i-pen type of routine memorial was also abolished, in 1901.

Thus in the present volume references to *tsou-pen* after 1748 should generally be revised to read *tsou-che*; and statements identifying these two types of documents are in error (see below pages 43, 44, 57, 59–64, and pages 78ff. under *Che-tsou, Tsou-che,* and *Tsou-pen*). In general, Mr. Wu's study is now the most authoritative on this whole subject.

J. K. F.
S. Y. T.

CONTENTS

ON THE TRANSMISSION OF CH'ING DOCUMENTS . . . 1
  1. The Ch'ing postal system 3
      Table 1: Table of time limits for transmission of despatches to Peking, together with distances, from various provincial yamen . 10
      Table 2: Residences of provincial officials . . 17
  2. The actual speed of transmission in the period 1842–1860 26
      Table 3: Time consumed in transmission of memorials to the Grand Council, 1842–1861 . 28
      Table 4: Time consumed in correspondence between Peking and provincial officials, 1842–1860 30

ON THE TYPES AND USES OF CH'ING DOCUMENTS . . 36
  1. Introduction 36
  2. Procedure in the Grand Secretariat (Nei Ko) . . 40
  3. Procedure in the Grand Council (Chün Chi Ch'u) . 55
  4. Select list of published collections of Ch'ing documents 69
  5. Catalogue of types of documents 71

ON THE CH'ING TRIBUTARY SYSTEM 107
  1. The traditional role of tribute 107
  2. Tributaries of the late Ming 116
      Table 1: Ming tributaries c. 1587 123
  3. The Li Fan Yüan (Court of Colonial Affairs) under the Ch'ing 130
  4. Ch'ing tributaries from the south and east — general regulations 135
      Table 2: Regular Ch'ing tributaries 146
      Table 3: Frequency and routes of tribute . . 148
  5. European countries in the tributary system . . 150
      Table 4: European embassies to the Court of Peking 160

CONTENTS

6. Ch'ing tribute embassies and foreign trade . . . 162
   Table 5: Tribute embassies 1662–1911 . . . 165
   Table 6: Non-tributary trading countries 1818 . 174
7. A selected list of Ch'ing works 1644–1860 on maritime
   relations 178
8. Index of tributaries listed in six editions of the *Collected
   Statutes* 191
Appendix 1: Bibliographical note 210
Appendix 2: Additional lists of Ch'ing tributaries . . 215
Appendix 3: Author and title index to section 7 . . . 217

ON THE TRANSMISSION OF CH'ING DOCUMENTS

J. K. FAIRBANK and S. Y. TENG
HARVARD UNIVERSITY

Chinese documents relating to foreign affairs in the nineteenth century are now available in large number,[1] but many essential facts concerning them remain obscure. Compared with workers in other fields of diplomatic history, the student of Chinese foreign policy is in a peculiar position. He has a wealth of documents to study but no clear idea of how they came into being. For example, he knows the date on which a memorial was seen by the emperor, but not the date on which it was written. What organs of government drafted, transmitted, recorded, copied, and finally compiled the documents now available—all this has yet to be worked out. The object of this paper is to attack one part of the problem, namely, the manner in which documents relating to foreign affairs were transmitted by postal service between Peking and the provinces—particularly, the amount of time generally required for such transmission.

The postal arrangements here in question are those of the Ch'ing Dynasty before the days of extensive foreign intercourse,[2] and in this early modern period we are concerned only with the transmission of official documents and not with the "letter hongs" or Min Hsin Chü 民信局 (People's Letter Offices) which were de-

---

[1] The chief published collection is *Ch'ou-pan i-wu shih-mo* 籌辦夷務始末, Peiping 1930: photo-lithograph of the original compilations made by imperial command and presented, 80 *chüan* for the period 1836-50, in 1856; 80 *chüan* for the period 1851-61, in 1867; and 100 *chüan* for the period 1862-74, in 1880.

[2] The modern Chinese Postal Service was not developed until the creation after 1858 of modern organs of administration, particularly the Imperial Maritime Customs Service and the Tsungli Yamen, followed by the establishment in 1876 of the Wên Pao Chü 文報局 (Despatch Office) for the transmission of Chinese diplomatic documents abroad, the institution of the Shu Hsin Kuan 書信官 (Letter Office) by the Customs after 1878, and the final establishment of the national Postal Service under Sir Robert Hart in 1896. The latter was separated from the Customs in 1911, and China joined the International Postal Union in 1914. Cf. H. B. MORSE, *The International Relations of the Chinese Empire*, vol. 3, London, 1918.

veloped by private Chinese firms for the use of the general public.[3] Among the many types of official documents current in this period we are concerned primarily with those sent and received by the Chün Chi Ch'u 軍機處 (Council of State, or Grand Council, lit. Place of Plans for the Army) which at this time had general charge of relations with the western barbarians. Nearly all documents on foreign affairs appear to have passed through this body at the capital and to have been carried by horse in the provinces. Consequently we are less concerned with documents carried by foot in the provinces and passing chiefly through the Nei Ko 內閣 (Grand Secretariat, or Imperial Chancery, or Inner Cabinet) at the capital, and these divisions of the general system for the transmission of documents will be mentioned only secondarily.[4]

For ease in analysis, the following discussion relates, first, to certain official regulations, principally those given in the *Ta-ch'ing hui-tien* 大清會典 (Institutes of the Ch'ing Dynasty),[5] and second, to the actual working of the postal service so far as it can be viewed in the documents themselves.

[3] This popular service is said to have been inaugurated in the fifteenth century and to have spread chiefly from Ningpo among the coastal provinces, eventually extending even into the northwest. It included the sending of ordinary and of registered letters, transmission of parcels and of money orders, and even the transportation of baggage. In the nineteenth century before their supercession by the modern postal service, firms of this type commanded a wide network of several thousand offices in China with branches among the Chinese communities overseas. Cf. CHANG Liang-jên, Chung-kuo li-tai yu-chih kai-yao 張樑任, 中國歷代郵制概要 (A General Survey of the Postal System of Successive Dynasties), *Tung-fang tsa-chih* (*The Eastern Miscellany*) 32 no. 1, research section, 10b-12b.

[4] Translations of official titles follow H. S. BRUNNERT and V. V. HAGELSTROM, *Present Day Political Organization of China*, Shanghai 1912, trans. by A. BELTCHENKO and E. E. MORAN, cited below as BRUNNERT. W. F. MAYERS, *The Chinese Government*[3], Shanghai 1897, revised by G. M. H. PLAYFAIR, cited below as MAYERS, although less comprehensive is often more accurate for this early period. Place names follow the Chinese Postal Atlas when feasible, or G. M. H. PLAYFAIR, *The Cities and Towns of China*[2], Shanghai 1910 (Wade System).

[5] The various editions of the *Ta-ch'ing hui-tien* are referred to below by the reigns in which they appeared, as: *K'ang-hsi hui-tien* (imperial preface dated 1690), *Yung-chêng hui-tien* (imperial preface dated 1732), *Ch'ien-lung hui-tien* and *Ch'ien-lung hui-tien tsê-li* (both compiled under imperial auspices in 1748), *Chia-ch'ing hui-tien* and *Chia-ch'ing hui-tien shih-li* (both completed in 1818), *Kuang-hsü hui-tien* and *Kuang-hsü hui-tien shih-li* (both published in 1899).

1. The Ch'ing Postal System

The Chinese official postal service, called by western writers the I Chan 驛站 (lit. Postal Stages), had a long history, from which most of the Ch'ing arrangements were inherited. It may be noted in passing that for more than a thousand years there had been a distinction between carriage of the post by couriers on foot and by mounted couriers, and that both of these activities had been under the control of the Board of War (Ping Pu 兵部). There are references to a postal service (I 驛) from the Spring and Autumn period; under the Han there had been a distinction between ordinary despatches and express despatches carried by horse.[6] Under the T'ang the service was already well articulated. According to the *T'ang liu-tien* 唐六典 [7] (The Six Statutes of the T'ang), there were 1639 postal stations, including 1297 on land used by mounted couriers and 260 on waterways. These stations were in charge of postmasters (I Chang 長) with postmen (I Fu 夫) under them, and are said to have been usually about 30 li apart.[8]

Under the Yüan the service was called Chan Ch'ih 站赤 and was administered by the Board of War in the provinces of China; for the vast territory under Mongol control in the northwest there was another organ, the T'ung Chêng Yüan 通政院; a system of express stations (Chi Ti P'u 急遞舖) was also developed. The postal system of the Ming included, under the Board of War, a Remount Department (Ch'ê Chia Ch'ing Li Ssŭ 車駕清吏司) and under it a central office in Peking (Hui T'ung Kuan 會同館) and stations in the provinces for ordinary post carried by horse or by water (Shui Ma I 水馬), for transporting official baggage (Ti Yün So 遞運所) and for express service (Chi Ti P'u). As will appear below, the postal system of the Ming was copied almost as it stood by the Manchus, and before describing the special arrangements used for foreign affairs, we may begin with the main

---

[6] PAI Shou-i, *Chung kuo chiao-t'ung shih* 白壽彝，中國交通史 (History of Chinese Communications), Shanghai 1937, gives a brief summary on pp. 145-8, 179-90.

[7] Kuang-ya shu-chü edition 1895, 5.12.

[8] Cf. CH'ÊN Yüan-yüan, T'ang-tai i-chih k'ao 陳沅遠，唐代驛制考 (A Study of the Postal System in the T'ang Dynasty), *SHNP* 1, no. 5 (Aug. 1933) 61-92; a detailed analysis with maps and bibliography.

elements of the hereditary system, as provided for in the regulations of the early nineteenth century.[9]

The Ch'ing postal service was under the general charge of one of the four sub-departments of the Board of War, which may be called the Remount Department (MAYERS—" Cavalry Remount and Postal Department "). The Remount Department had charge both of the military stud and of the postal service. The regulations for the former make it plain that there was no lack of a supply of horses which could, if necessary, be used for the postal service.[10]

The backbone of the postal service was, of course, the series of stations which extended through the provinces in all directions from the capital. From the central station in Peking, the Huang Hua I 皇華, there were four main routes along which these stations were scattered: (1) the northeastern route, from Peking to Mukden and thence to Kirin and Heilungkiang; (2) the eastern route, to Shantung and thence to (a) Anhwei, Kiangsi, and Kwangtung, or (b) Kiangsu, Chekiang, and Fukien; (3) the central route, to Honan and thence to (a) Hupeh, Hunan, and Kwangsi, or (b) Kweichow and Yünnan; (4) the western route, to Shansi and Shensi and thence to (a) Kansu and Sinkiang, or (b) Szechwan and Tibet. There may also be added: (5) the northwestern route, to Kalgan and thence to Uliassutai, and Kobdo or Urga.[11]

Along these various routes there were several different types of stations, each with a different name. The chief distinction was between those called I 驛,[12] which were usually within the Wall

[9] Unless otherwise noted, the following account is drawn from *Chia-ch'ing hui-tien* 39, especially 17-34.

[10] For the military stud the bannermen at Peking were required to feed in stables a total of 2400 official horses (Kuan Ma 官馬). In addition there were to be 2000 kept horses (Shuan Ma 拴馬) maintained among the troops and various sections of government, 3188 horses maintained by bannermen in Chihli, and other similar arrangements of supply. At provincial cities and points of importance fixed numbers of horses were also to be kept, often by the thousand; at Nanking, for example, there were to be 359 maintained by the civil authorities and 5726 by the military, while nearby at Ching K'ou 京口 were to be another 143 and 2274 respectively.

[11] Cf. *Yung-chêng hui-tien* 142. 7; PAI Shou-i, *op. cit.* (see note 6) 188.

[12] The stations (I 驛) of each province are controlled by the sub-prefecture (t'ing 廳), department (chou 州), and district (hsien 縣) [officials]. Occasionally there are

and under the control of the local civil authorities, and those called Chan 站, which were usually beyond the Wall and under the control of the military authorities. The latter (probably derived from Chan Ch'ih of the Yüan) were established for purposes of military intelligence and were to be found chiefly on the two routes to the west and northwest.[13] At these stations military officers were in charge of the reception and transmission of the post, although the economic support came from the local civil authorities. The name Chan was also used in Kirin and Heilungkiang and for stations along the Great Wall and in Mongolia. T'ang 塘 were military courier stations beyond Chia Yü Kuan on the route to An Hsi and Hami, under military administration but supported by the civil authorities. T'ai 臺 (or Chün T'ai 軍臺) were military posts established along the routes to Uliassutai, Kobdo, and Urga. Another type of station was the So 所 (standing for Ti Yün So 遞運所) which were originally set up for the purpose of transporting baggage and other official property in the provinces; about the end of the eighteenth century, they were annexed to the I, except in Kansu. The relative distribution of these various types of stations is indicated in the subjoined table, from which the predominance of the I, particularly in the coastal provinces, will be obvious.[14]

specially established postal inspectors (I Ch'êng 驛丞) in charge of postal matters. The expenses and provisions, postmen, and horses [for these stations] come within the administration of the seal-holding officials [yin-kuan 印官]. All are subject to the direct investigation of the intendants and prefects, and also to the general superintendence of the financial commissioner of the province who is concurrently in charge of mounted courier affairs" (Chia-ch'ing hui-tien 39.17a). Although the station at Mukden was called I 驛, it was really a military station under the control of the Mukden Board of War 盛京兵部.

[13] Of these two routes, "one passes through Kalgan and along the Altai Military Post Road to transmit despatches to the North Road 北路. One skirts the Outer Wall and crosses over Shansi, Shensi, and Kansu, emerges through Chia Yü Kuan and connects with the military courier stations to transmit despatches to the West Road 西路." Ibid.

[14] Totals of post stations in the provinces, omitting stations in Mongolia and the northwest, from Chia-ch'ing hui-tien 39.18:

Province	I	I and Chan	Chan
Chihli	...	185	...
Shengching	29	...	...

All the stations mentioned above were designed for the rapid transfer of documents by horse or an equivalent means.[15] Quite aside from the stations so far mentioned, however, there existed another and subsidiary system of stations for unmounted couriers

Province	I	I and Chan	Chan
Kirin	...	...	38
Heilungkiang	...	...	36
Shantung	139	...	...
Shansi	...	125	...
Honan	120	...	...
Kiangsu	40	...	...
Anhwei	81	...	...
Kiangsi	47	...	...
Fukien	68	...	...
Chekiang	59	...	...
Hupeh	71	...	...
Hunan	62	...	...
Shensi	...	129	...
Kansu	total of I, Chan, T'ang, and So 331		
Szechwan	65	...	...
Kwangtung	10	...	...
Kwangsi	19	...	...
Yünnan	81	...	...
Kweichow	23	...	...
Totals	914	439 331	74

Grand total of above 1758
Grand total in *Chia-ch'ing hui-tien*, including 273 stations in Mongolia and the northwest 2031

(The So appear to have been abolished, except in Kansu, sometime between the compilation of the *Ch'ien-lung hui-tien* and the *Chia-ch'ing hui-tien*, i.e. before 1818.) It should be noted that among the various editions of the *hui-tien*, the total number of stations listed was greatest in the Chia-ch'ing edition.

Period	Total stations listed
K'ang-hsi (1662-1722)	842
Yung-cheng (1723-1735)	899
Ch'ien-lung (1736-1795)	792
Chia-ch'ing (1796-1820)	2031
Kuang-hsü (1875-1905)	1777

Cf. *K'ang-hsi hui-tien* 100.2b, 101.26b; *Yung-chêng hui-tien* 141.4b, 142.7; *Ch'ien-lung hui-tien tsê-li* 120.1-9b; *Chia-ch'ing hui-tien* 39.18; *Kuang-hsü hui-tien* 51.2.

[15] It is stated that horses, or donkeys, were used in all the provinces except Fukien, Kwangtung, and Kwangsi; oxen and camels were used in Manchuria and Mongolia, respectively; and carts and boats were used in appropriate places, the latter particularly in the south. *Chia-ch'ing hui-tien* 39.18b-21b; *Kuang-hsü hui-tien* 51.2b-4.

who transmitted official despatches on foot only. These stations were called P'u 舖 and were to be found in all the provinces, under control of the local authorities. Where the I were some 100 li apart, the P'u were usually from 10 to 30 li apart.[16] For purposes of this discussion they are relatively unimportant, and we may confine our attention, for the time being, to the I, through which nearly all documents concerning foreign affairs were sent from the coastal provinces to Peking.

The use of these post stations was regulated by a system of tallies (yu-fu 郵符), which were given to riders going over the route and allowed them to use certain horses or other conveyances and supplies on their way. These tallies were of two kinds: (1) k'an-ho 勘合, which were given to official express riders (kuan ch'ih-i chê 官馳驛者); and (2) huo-p'ai 火牌, which were given to military express riders (ping-i ch'ih-i chê 兵役馳驛者). The latter were also given to candidates for the public examinations coming from Yünnan, Kweichow, and Kansu west of Chia Yü Kuan. Every year the Governors-General and Governors, Provincial Commanders-in-chief and Brigade Generals of the Chinese army, and Tartar Generals and Lieutenant-Generals of the Manchu forces were given huo-p'ai and sometimes also k'an-ho by the Board of War. These tallies could be used whenever mounted couriers needed to be sent.[17]

---

[16] "Within every province the sub-prefectures, departments, and districts all establish station masters (p'u-ssŭ 舖司). Those from the capital to the various provinces are also called Ching T'ang 京塘. Each uses postmen and post-soldiers on foot to transmit public documents. Their rations are accounted for from the land tax reported to the Board of Revenue." *Chia-ch'ing hui-tien* 39.18a; *Kuang-hsü hui-tien* 51.1-2. Cf. list of the P'u in *Chia-ch'ing hui-tien shih-li* 523-557.

[17] The number of post tallies, of both types, distributed for annual use was as follows:

Officials	huo-p'ai	k'an-ho
Governors-General of Liang Kiang, Hu-Kwang, Yün-Kwei, Shên-Kan, Liang Kwang, Min-Chê, Szechwan, and Director-General of Grain Transport, each	20	..
Governor-General of Chihli, Directors-General of the Yellow River and Grand Canal Conservancy (one in Kiangnan, one in Shantung), Governors of Kiangsi, Anhwei, Chekiang, Hupeh, Hunan, each	18	..
Governors of Shantung, Shansi, Honan, Kiangsi, Fukien, Kwangtung, Kwangsi, Yünnan, Kweichow	16	..
Provincial Commander-in-chief of Kansu	4	10

But these tallies were used also in a much more general way by all officials moving from place to place in their official capacity, and they secured for the holder the service not only of horses but also of attendants, carts, boats, and other facilities. The extent of these facilities depended upon the rank of the official, the route, and the nature of the journey, all of which was minutely specified in the regulations. Thus officials despatched from the capital on a land journey were given tallies for saddle horses, pack horses, and others, in number corresponding to their rank; and on a water journey they were given boatmen. If they did not use horses, they were allowed three men for every horse they would have had. Certain government rations were also allowed them. In addition to government officials, these facilities were extended to tribute bearers from foreign countries. Finally, the I were used for the carriage of public goods. For this purpose again the regulations were most detailed. For example, in the transfer of the land tax silver in Chekiang, for a sum up to Tls. 160,000 a t'ai-p'ing 太平 boat should be used, for a sum between Tls. 160,000 and Tls. 200,000 a sha-fei 沙飛 boat should be used, and so on.[18] From this it is apparent that the post stations (I) were really used for a good deal more than the transmission of official correspondence, and constituted in effect a service of transport and communication rather than a mere postal service in the western sense. Its im-

Officials	huo-p'ai	k'an-ho
All other Provincial Commanders-in-chief, each	4	..
All Brigade Generals, all Salt Comptrollers, each	2	..
Mukden Prefect, all Literary Chancellors, each	4	..
Mukden Board of War	20	20
Tartar Generals of Kirin and Heilungkiang	10	10
All other Tartar Generals, each	4	4

Provincial Financial Commissioners in charge of posts, number not fixed.

The officials last named were to estimate their annual needs and request tallies from the Board of War. Cf. *Chia-ch'ing hui-tien* 39.22b. They were not given a fixed number of tallies because they were themselves in general charge of the provincial postal service. All tallies actually used were to be reported to the Board of War at the end of each year.

[18] *Chia-ch'ing hui-tien* 39.23a-27a. These extensive regulations provide also for annual reports, punishment for misuse of postal facilities, and the general upkeep and use of the service.

portance was mirrored in the large amounts of revenue set aside for its maintenance.[19] The transmission of official documents was therefore only one of the activities carried on at the post stations; but for present purposes the other activities may be disregarded.

In transmitting a document by horse post the first necessity was an express warrant (huo-p'iao 火票). The regulations state that " to all public documents for transmission by horse there are to be attached warrants of the Board of War ordering the various post stations along the route to receive and transmit them. On documents coming from the provinces to the capital, or passing back and forth among the provinces, there are pasted way-bills (p'ai-tan 排單). It is the rule that along the route the exact time (shih-k'o 時刻) of arrival at each station shall be noted on the way-bill." [20] This regulation appears to have applied to all documents sent by horse post, and was elaborated in a number of rules and requirements for the keeping of records and the proper sealing of the documents en route.[21]

---

[19] With certain exceptions, the stations were maintained from the land tax. Their total cost, although said to have been reduced, was estimated at Tls. 3,000,000 in the middle of the nineteenth century. CHANG Shou-yang, *Huang-ch'ao chang-ku hui-pien* 張壽鏞, 皇朝掌故彙編 (A Compilation on Governmental Affairs of the Reigning Dynasty), 1902, *nei-pien* 51.7b. With this may be compared the amounts authorized for the upkeep of the service in *Chia-ch'ing hui-tien* 39.21, which totalled in the neighborhood of Tls. 2,000,000 in silver alone, not counting allowances of rice, beans, and fodder (totals given *op. cit.* 12.6a-7a and *Chia-ch'ing hui-tien shih-li* 558.18b differ, but do not fall below this round figure). At this period (about 1818) the estimated annual yield of the land tax totalled Tls. 32,845,474. Cf. *Chia-ch'ing hui-tien* 11.16b. The regulations show an obvious desire to limit expenditure, specifying the rates at which the populace might be paid when their services were enlisted, requiring that only a certain proportion of the post horses, usually thirty or forty per cent, could "fall down and die" 倒斃 in one year, and fixing the prices payable for new horses. These prices varied between Tls. 6 in Heilungkiang and Tls. 18 in Kweichow. *Chia-ch'ing hui-tien* 39.19b.

[20] *Chia-ch'ing hui-tien* 39.27a.

[21] " As to all important public documents from the provinces,—on the one hand they are to be transmitted by horse at express speed 飛遞, and on the other hand, there is to be prepared a report to the provincial government for their records. Each yamen which receives documents for express transmission and each departmental and district postal station which forwards them along the route is to inform the said yamen in charge of the post stations, for its examination and information, as to the year, day, and month of receiving and transmitting [the documents] and as to the yamen concerned in the matter." Trimonthly reports to the provincial authorities and

In addition it was possible, in the case of important or secret memorials, to send them by a special messenger who would make use of a tally of the type described above (huo-p'ai 火牌).[22] It was apparently in such cases as this that the provincial officials made use of the tallies given to them each year.

Once a document had been started on its way at express speed, it was expected to travel at the rate of 300 li a day; "but if documents are urgent, then the warrant may state that they are to be transmitted by express at the limit of 400 li, 500 li, or 600 li."[23] In other words, official intelligence during the period of the Taiping Rebellion and the wars with England was expected, by law, to travel at most only some 200 miles a day. The question as to the rapidity with which documents were actually sent is both interesting and important.

Light is shed on this question by developments in the eighteenth century. In 1708 the maximum speed for urgent despatches was given as 500 li a day.[24] By 1742 this maximum had been raised to 600 li; but in 1748-9 an exception was made for the provinces of Fukien and Kwangtung, where despatches ordered to proceed at the rate of 600 li were allowed to travel only 300. In 1750 it was ordered that the rate of 600 li a day should be resorted to

annual reports to the Board of War were then to be made. Documents were to be sent sealed in despatch boxes 報匣, or sealed in boards 夾版, or sealed in cloth or paper. *Ibid.* 27b-28a.

[22] "As to all memorials 題奏 on important matters, such as impeachments of officials, . . . sent forward by special messenger, it is permitted to use one huo-p'ai filled in for two horses. If there are documents being sent on the same day by officials stationed at the same place, they may be put together under one tally but it may only be filled in for two horses." *Ibid.* The categories of documents to be regularly transmitted by horse are given by another source as follows: (1) documents despatched by the Grand Council, (2) important documents sent from the boards and other offices at the capital to the provinces, (3) important documents in the opposite direction, (4) memorials and tablets of congratulation to the Emperor from civil and military officials in the provinces, sent on the occasion of imperial birthdays, big festivals, and the like, (5) memorials of an urgent nature from the Director-General of the Yellow River Conservancy. *Ping-pu chung-shu chêng-k'ao* 兵部中樞政考 (A Study of the Central Administration of the Board of War), compiled under imperial auspices, preface dated 1825, 33.25-27.

[23] *Ibid.* 27a.

[24] *Ch'ien-lung hui-tien tsê-li* 121.30.

only in case of urgent necessity,[25] and we may conclude that the increase of speed, which may not have been unconnected with the campaigns in Central Asia, had been found expensive, as well as impossible in certain areas. According to the regulations for the Chia-ch'ing and Kuang-hsü periods, at the beginning and end of the nineteenth century, the normal distance per day by horse remained 300 li, and the express rate remained limited to 400, 500, or 600 li.[26] In the mountainous areas of Chihli, Honan, Hupeh, Kwangsi, and Kwangtung, where horses could not be used, the maximum of 600 li per day was reduced to 400, 300, 240, or even 200 li, according to the circumstances.[27] In short, in the five different editions of the Institutes of the Ch'ing Dynasty there is no mention of a rate of speed higher than 600 li a day. By 1842, however, this rate was being occasionally exceeded in practice, and imperial orders were given, and obeyed, for the transmission of documents at the rate of 800 li a day, as will be noted below.

The following table (1) is given for purposes of comparison, since it does not refer directly to documents sent by express, as were most of those concerning barbarian affairs. Under A are given the time limits for ordinary documents sent by unmounted courier (p'u-ti); under B are given the time limits for documents sent by horse, such as ordinary memorials (t'i-pên 題本). A third table, for documents sent by express at the rate of 300 li or more, can be constructed by inference, from the distances listed, but cannot be regarded as certain because in such calculations numerous allowances must be made for certain areas where, because of the terrain, the distance required per day was reduced by regulation to less than the normal stint. No doubt this qualification would apply with increasing force to the rates of speed higher than 300 li a day.[28]

---

[25] *Ibid.* 37-8.

[26] *Chia-ch'ing hui-tien* 39.27a; *Kuang-hsü hui-tien* 51.10b, 12.

[27] *Chia-ch'ing hui-tien* 39.28b-39b; *Kuang-hsü hui-tien* 51.12; *Kuang-hsü hui-tien shih-li* 700.11-13b.

[28] Cf. list of exceptions in *Chia-ch'ing hui-tien* 39.28b and *Kuang-hsü hui-tien* 51.12. The more important may be summarized as follows, all distances being substitutions for the rate of 600 *li*: in the region of Luan P'ing, Chengteh, and Süanhwa in Chihli, 300 *li*; in the region of Tê Hua on the border of Kiangsi, Fukien, and Chekiang, 400 *li*;

Hours, where given, are calculated at the rate of 2 hours for 1 shih 時.

* indicates water route, when distinguished from land route.

Distances, in most cases, are given in sources (1), (3), (4), (5), (8), and (9). Except where noted, distances in source (9) agree with those in (3), and distances in (8) agree with those in (4).

Time limits, in most cases, are given in sources (2), (4), (7), (8), and (9)—all of which agree, except where noted, on the number of days given under B for transmission by horse; and in sources (3), (4), (6), (8), and (9), all of which agree, except where noted, on the number of days given under A for transmission " on foot " (p'u-ti).

The variation in the distances recorded in different publications arises from different methods of calculation in each case, measuring sometimes to the yamen itself, sometimes to the city walls, and sometimes only to the border of the province.

This table and the one following (Table 2) include data (1) for all high provincial authorities and (2) for all taotais likely to be in contact with foreigners in the period 1842-60.

TABLE 1 [28a]

TABLE OF TIME LIMITS FOR TRANSMISSION OF DESPATCHES TO PEKING, TOGETHER WITH DISTANCES, FROM VARIOUS PROVINCIAL YAMEN

Note: This table is arranged alphabetically by cities and is based on the following sources, which are cited by number except in cases of general agreement.

(1) *Ch'ien-lung hui-tien* 66. 5b-6b.
(2) *Ch'ien-lung hui-tien tsê-li* 121. 31-34.

---

from Tung Hu to Siangyang in Hupeh, 400 *li*; in the mountainous area of Kwangsi, 300 *li*; in the mountainous area of Kweichow, 240 *li*; from Canton along the West River or to Hunan and Kiangsi, 200 *li*; from Canton to Fukien, 240 *li*; in Szechwan generally, 400 *li*; in Fukien generally, 300 *li*; from Hengchow in Hunan to the Kwangtung border, 240 *li*. It may be noted that there are no exceptions on the route between Kiangsu and the capital.

[28a] For explanatory remarks see the preceding paragraphs in the text.

(3) *Tsê-li t'u-yao pien-lan* 則例圖要便覽,
    original compiler SHIH Chung-yin 石中隱,
    revised edition by WANG Yu-huai 王又槐 (1792) 10.5-6.
(4) *Chia-ch'ing hui-tien* 39.29-30; 54.14-15.
(5) *Chia-ch'ing ch'ung-hsiu i-t'ung-chih* 嘉慶重修一統志 (1842).
(6) *Ping-pu ch'u-fên tsê-li* 兵部處分則例 (1823) 4.32-33b.
(7) *Ping-pu chung-shu chêng-k'ao* (1825) 兵部中樞政考 35.1-7b.
(8) *Kuang-hsü hui-tien* 51.12b-13b, 69.13b-15.
(9) *Kuang-hsü hui-tien shih-li* 700.1-4, 8b-11.
(10) *Kuang-tung t'ung-chih* 廣東通志 (1864) 84-88.
(11) *Chi-fu t'ung-chih* 畿輔 (1884) 48-55.
(12) *Shan-tung t'ung-chih* 山東 (1915) 1A.
(13) *Chê-chiang t'ung-chih* 浙江 (1899) 3.
(14) *Fu-chien t'ung chih* 福建 (1868) 4.
(15) *T'ung-an hsien-chih* 同安縣志 (1875) 1.3.
(16) *Shang-hai hsien-chih* 上海 (1871) 1.5.

Cities (and officials)	Distances to Peking in *li*	Time limits (days) for despatches carried A, on foot; B, by horse	
		A	B
Amoy	7380 (15)	..	30
An-shun (Kweichow)	7820 (5)	..	30
Anking (Anhwei governor)	2526 (3), 2624 (4), 2615 (1), 2700 (5), *3441 (4), *3430 (1)	25	15
Canton (Gov.-Gen., Governor, and Tartar General)	5570 (3), 5604 (4), 5670 (1), 7570 (5)	56	32
Chang-chou (Fukien)	7525 (5)	..	31
Ch'ang-chou (Chekiang)	2535 (5)	..	..
Changsha (Hunan Governor)	3757 (3), 3590 (4), 3670 (1), 3585 (5), *5081 (4), *5090 (1)	37	18 days and 18 hours
Chang-yeh (see Kan-chou)		..	..
Chao-ch'ing (Kwangtung)	7402 (10)	..	..
Chao-chou (Chihli)	720 (11)	..	..
Ch'ao-chou (Kwangtung)	9063 (10), (15)		38 days and 12 hours
Chapu	3120 (13)	31 (6)	16
Ch'ên-chou (Hunan)	3650 (5)		20 (7)
Chengteh	420 (11)	..	..
Cheng-ting (Chihli)	610 (11)	..	..
Chengtu (Szechwan Gov.-Gen.)	4770 (3), 4750 (4), 4675 (1), 5710 (5)	48	24

13

Cities (and officials)	Distances to Peking in *li*	Time limits (days) for despatches carried A, on foot; B, by horse	
Chi-ning (Shantung)	1145 (3), 1200 (5)	11 (3)	7 (7)
Chia-ying-chou (Kwangtung)	8763 (3)	..	..
Chiao-chou (Shantung)	1600 (12)	..	..
Chungking	6670 (5)	..	29
Chinkiang	2300 (3, 5)	23 (6)	13 (7)
Ch'ing-chiang-p'u (Kiangnan conservancy)	1975 (3)	20	10-12 (7)
Ch'ing-chou (Shantung)	1300 (12)	..	8 (8)
Ch'iung-chou (Kwangtung)	9715 (10)	..	44 (8)
Ch'u-chou (Chekiang)	4580 (13)	..	25 (7)
Ch'üan-chou (Fukien)	7255 (5)	..	29 (7)
Ch'ung-ming (Kiangsu)	....	..	14 (7)
Foochow (Gov.-Gen., Governor, and Tartar General)	4775 (3), 4848 (4), 4862 (1), 6130 (5)	48	27
Formosa, Tai-wan-fu	7332 (14)	..	30 (3)
Fu-ming (Fukien)	7200 (5)	..	33 (3)
Hai-chou (Kiangsu)	1700 (5)	..	..
Hangchow (Chekiang Governor)	3050 (3), 3133 (4), 3117 (1), 3300 (5), *3531 (4), *3486 (1)	30	17
Heilungkiang (Tartar General)	3983 (3), 3317 (4), 4127 (1), 3300 (5)	40	18
Ho-chien (Chihli)	410 (11)	..	..
Hsing-hua (Fukien)	6403 (14)	..	..
Hsü-chou (Kiangsu)	1165 (5)		8 days and 22 hours (7)
Hu-chou (Chekiang)	4300	..	27 (7)
Hwaian (Director-General of Grain Transport)	1995 (3), 1975 (5)	20	12
Hui-chou (Kwangtung)	8485 (5, 10)	..	34 (7)
Hui-yüan Ch'êng, see Ili			
Ili	10044 (4, by I Chan), 193 (9) 10820 (5), 9220 (4, by Chün T'ai), 14549 (9)		43
Jehol (Military Lt.-Governor)	420 (3), 430 (9), 450 (4)	5 (8)	4 (7)

Cities (and officials)	Distances to Peking in *li*	Time limits (days) for despatches carried A, on foot; B, by horse	
Kaifeng (Honan Governor)	1545 (3), 1490 (1), 1495 (4), 1540 (5)	15	8 days and 14 hours
Kalgan (Military Lt.-Governor of Chahar)	410 (3), 390 (11)	4	4 (7)
Kao-chou (Kwangtung)	8647 (10, 5)	..	37 (8)
Kashing	4020 (13)	..	..
Kan-chou (or Chang-yeh, Kansu)	5080 (5)	..	28 (8)
Kirin	2882 (3), 2880 (1), 2245 (4), 2300 (5)	29 (6,3)	12 (7)
Kiukiang	4600 (5)	..	16 days and 8 hours
Kiungchow, see Ch'iung-chou			
Kobdo	6280 (9)	105 (9)	..
Ku-yüan	3480 (5)		
Kwei-hua (Shansi)	1160 (5)	..	6 (8)
Kweilin (Kwangsi Governor)	5469 (3), 4654 (4), 4909 (1), 7460 (5)	55	24
Kweiyang (Kweichow Governor)	4900 (3), 4755 (4), 4775 (1)	49	28
Lai-chou (Shantung)	1600 (12)	..	..
Lanchow (Shên-Kan Gov.-Gen.)	4115 (3), 4009 (4), 4040 (5), 4035 (1)	41	17, 18 (4)
Lei-chou (Kwangtung)	9505 (10)	..	44 (8)
Liu-chou (Kwangsi)	7830 (5) 1470 (5)	..	26 days, 20 hours and a half
Lo-ting (Kwangtung)	7860 (10)	..	37 (8)
Lung-yen (Fukien)	7120 (14)	..	..
Mowming, see Kao-chou			
Mukden (Shengking)	1500 (3), 1460 (4), 1470 (5)	15	8
Nanchang (Kiangsi Gov.)	3196 (3), 3184 (4), 3225 (1), 4850 (5), *4081 (4), *4090 (1)	32	18
Nanking (Gov.-Gen. of Liang Kiang)	2261 (3, 7), 2319 (4),	23	13 days and 8 hours

15

Cities (and officials)	Distances to Peking in *li*	Time limits (days) for despatches carried A, on foot; B, by horse	
Ninghsia (Tartar General)	4050 (3)	40	23
Ningpo	4640 (5)	..	20
P'an-yü, see Canton			
Paotingfu (Chihli Gov.-Gen.)	360 (3, 9), 330 (4)	4	3
Shanghai	2899 (16)	..	17 (7)
Shengking (see under Mukden)			
Shanhaikuan	670 (3)	7	4 (7, 8)
Shaohing (Chekiang)	4458	..	..
Sianfu (Shensi Governor, and Tartar General)	2550 (3), 2540 (4), 2475 (1), 2650 (5)	25	13
Siang Yang (Hupeh)	2620 (5)	..	..
Soochow (Kiangsu Governor)	2670 (3), 2743 (4), 2737 (1), *3141 (4), *3091 (1), 2720 (5)	27 ..	14 days and 8 hours
Suchow, see Hsü-chou			
Suiyüan (Shansi)	1125 (3, 9), 1145 (4)	11	6
Süanhua	340 (11)	..	..
Sungkiang	2950 (5)	..	14 (8)
Swatow, see Ch'ao-chou			
Tatung (Shansi)	720 (5)	..	4 (8)
T'ai-an (Shantung)	1200 (12)	..	..
T'ai-chou (Chekiang)	4778 (13)	..	..
T'ai-ts'ang-chou (Kiangsu)	2480 (5)	..	..
Tai-wan-fu, see Formosa			
Taiyüan (Shansi Governor)	1250 (3, 9), 1200 (5), 1150 (4), 2095 (1)	12	6
Talifu (Provincial Commander-in-chief)	11450 (5)	..	45
Tarbagatai	9624 (9)	161 (9)	..
Têng-chou (Shantung)	1000 (5)	22 in 5th, 6th, 7th, 8th mos. 16 (7) all other mos.	(7)
Tientsin	250 (5)	4 (7)	3 (7, 8, 9)
Ti-hua, see Urumtsi			
T'ing-chou (Fukien)	5226	..	28 (7)
Tinghai	4960 (13)	..	22
To-lun-no-êrh	700 (11)	..	..

16

Cities (and officials)	Distances to Peking in *li*	Time limits (days) for despatches carried A, on foot; B, by horse	
Tsinan (Shantung Gov.)	920 (3), 930 (4), 800 (5)	9	5
Tsitsihar, see Heilungkiang			
T'ung-chou (Kiangsu)	3695 (5)	..	13 (7)
Tushihkow	420 (11)	..	..
Uliassutai	4960 (9)	83 (9)	..
Urga	2880 (4, 9)	48 (9)	..
Urumtsi	8890 (5)	..	..
Wenchow (Chekiang)	4690 (13)	..	27 (7)
Wuchang (Hukwang Gov.-Gen., and Hupeh Governor)	2827 (3), 2690 (4), 2770 (1), *4321 (4), *4330 (1), 3150 (5)	28	14 days and 12 hours
Yangchow (Kiangsu)	2275 (5)	16 (7)	13 (7)
Yenchow	1230 (5)	16 in 5th, 6th, 7th, 8th mos. 12 (7) all other mos.	(7)
Yung-ch'un (Fukien)	7145 (14)		
Yünnanfu (Yün-kwei Gov.-Gen., and Yünnan Gov.)	6025 (3), 5910 (4), 5930 (1)	60	40

The time limits given in this table were used in the following manner. When a document left its point of origin, the day on which it should reach its destination, according to the regulations, was noted " on the face of the cover " 於封面上. When the document was received at its destination, the day of arrival was compared with the day already noted. If the transmission had fallen behind schedule, it was ascertained where the delay had occurred, and the officers in charge at that point were fined.[29]

From the table it will be seen that the distance to be covered by postmen on foot averaged with great regularity 100 li a day, say 33 miles, while the distance to be covered at the ordinary horse rate averaged a little less than 200 li a day, say 190 li or 63 miles. Thus, on foot, despatches would move at the rate of about two and three-quarters miles per hour during a twelve-hour

---

[29] *Ping-pu ch'u-fên tsê-li* 4.33, which also states that the penalty for each case of delay was one year's salary.

day. By horse they would move at the rate of about five and one-quarter miles an hour during a twelve hour day. Since documents sent by express were required to be forwarded both day and night, the rate of 300 li should not have been difficult of attainment.

Table 2 has been compiled as an aid to the use of Table 1. When provincial officials appear in the *I-wu shih-mo* documents or elsewhere as memorialists, their titles are given but there is usually no other indication as to the place where their memorials were written. We have, therefore, listed by provinces the normal residence of each official likely to have memorialized on foreign affairs, the distance of which from Peking can be found by reference to Table 1. This table 2 is arranged alphabetically by provinces and shows the cities from which the officials listed normally conducted their correspondence. The table is based on *Ch'ing-shih kao* (*chih-kuan chih* 職官志 3-4, *ti-li chih* 地理志 1-27), *Chia-ch'ing hui-tien* 4.2b-4b, *Kuang-hsü hui-tien* 4.2b-5, G. M. H. PLAYFAIR, *The Cities and Towns of China* (Shanghai 1910). The officials listed include:

governors-general (or "viceroys," tsung-tu, BRUNNERT no. 820);
governors (hsün-fu, BRUNNERT no. 821) [except where noted, the
financial commissioners (or "lieutenant-governors," or "treasurers," pu-chêng-shih, BRUNNERT no. 825), and the
judicial commissioners (or "provincial judges," an-ch'a-shih, BRUNNERT no. 830), reside at the same places as the governors of their provinces];
taotais (or "intendants," tao-t'ai, of various kinds, BRUNNERT no. 838, usually in charge of one or more prefectures (fu), also listed; those listed below have been selected as most likely to be concerned with foreign affairs);
tartar generals (or "Manchu generals-in-chief," chiang-chün, BRUNNERT no. 744),
provincial commanders-in-chief (or "generals-in-chief," t'i-tu, BRUNNERT no. 750).

It should be noted, of the two most widely used manuals of official titles, that BRUNNERT's pictures the situation after numerous reforms at the end of the Manchu period, so that all its details are not accurate for the mid-nineteenth century, while MAYERS' work does not give the details of residence here desired.

TABLE 2
RESIDENCES OF PROVINCIAL OFFICIALS

Province	Official	Residence
Anhwei	Governor-General of the Liang Kiang (Anhwei, Kiangsu, and Kiangsi)	Nanking, Kiangsu
	Governor, with the duties also of Provincial Commander-in-chief	Anking
Chekiang	Governor-General of Fukien and Chekiang (Min-Chê), with the duties also of Governor of Fukien	Foochow, Fukien
	Governor	Hangchow
	Hang-chia-hu Taotai (for Hangchow 杭州, Kashing 嘉興, and Hu-chou 湖州)	Hangchow
	Ning-shao-t'ai Taotai (for Ningpo 寧波, Shaohing 紹興, and T'ai-chou 台州)	Ningpo
	Wên-ch'u Taotai (for Wenchow 溫州 and Ch'u-chou 處州)	Wenchow
	Tartar General	Hangchow
	Provincial Commander-in-chief	Ningpo
Chihli	Governor-General, with the duties also of Governor; after 1870 with the duties also of Superintendent of Trade for the Northern Ports (Pei-yang ta-ch'ên, BRUNNERT no. 820B).	Paoting; after 1870, Tientsin, except in midwinter.
	Financial Commissioner	Paoting
	Judicial Commissioner	Paoting
	Superintendent of Trade for the Three Ports (Tientsin, Chefoo, and Newchwang, San-k'ou t'ung-shan ta-ch'ên, BRUNNERT no. 820B).	Tientsin, 1861-1870 only
	Ch'ing-ho Taotai (for Paoting, Ho-chien 河間, Chengting 正定, I-chou 易州, Chao-chou 趙州)	Paoting

ON THE TRANSMISSION OF CH'ING DOCUMENTS

Province	Official	Residence
	Jehol Taotai (for Chengteh 承德, Ch'ao-yang 朝陽)	Chengteh
	K'ou-pei Taotai (for Süanhwa 宣化, Kalgan, Tushihkow 獨石口, Tolunor 多倫諾爾廳)	Süanhwa
	Tientsin Customs Taotai (no territorial jurisdiction)	Tientsin, after 1870.
	Military Lieutenant-Governor of Jehol (Jê-ho tu-t'ung, see BRUNNERT no. 897)	Chengteh
Fengtien	Shengching (Mukden) Tartar General	Mukden
Fukien	Governor-General of Fukien and Chekiang (Min-Chê), with the duties also of Governor of Fukien	Foochow
	Governor of Formosa (Taiwan)	Foochow until 1875, then T'ai-pei fu
	Fu-ning Taotai (for Foochow 福州, Fu-ning 福寧)	Foochow
	Hsing-ch'üan-yung Taotai (for Hsing-hua 興化, Ch'üan-chou 泉州, Yung-ch'un 永春)	Ch'üan-chou
	T'ing-chang-lung Taotai (for T'ing-chou 汀州, Chang-chou 漳州, Lung-yen 龍巖)	Chang-chou
	Tartar General, with the duties also of Superintendent of Maritime Customs	Foochow
	Provincial Commander-in-chief	Foochow
Heilungkiang	Tartar General	Tsitsihar
Honan	Governor, with the duties also of Provincial Commander-in-chief	Kaifeng
Hu-Kwang	Governor-General of the Liang Hu (Hunan and Hupeh)	Wuchang
Hunan	Governor-General of Hunan and Hupeh, as above	Wuchang, Hupeh
	Governor	Changsha

20

Province	Official	Residence
Hunan	Provincial Commander-in-chief	Ch'ên-chou 辰州
Hupeh	Governor-General of Hunan and Hupeh as above	Wuchang
	Governor	Wuchang
	Provincial Commander-in-chief	Siangyang 襄陽
Jehol	(See under Chihli, of which southern and central Jehol formed a part)	
Kansu	Governor-General of Shensi and Kansu (Shên-Kan), with the duties also of Governor of Kansu	Lanchow
	Tartar General	Ningsia 寧夏
	Provincial Commander-in-chief	Chang-yeh 張掖
Kiangnan	(originally one of the Liang Kiang provinces divided in the K'ang-hsi period into Anhwei and Kiangsu, q. v.; the name was preserved thereafter in several official titles: e. g. Kiangnan ...	
	Tartar General	Nanking
	Provincial Commander-in-chief	Sungkiang
	Superintendent of Maritime Customs	Shanghai
	These officials are the same as those listed under Kiangsu)	
Kiangsi	Governor-General of the Liang Kiang (Kiangsi, Anhwei, and Kiangsu)	Nanking, Kiangsu
	Governor, with the duties also of Provincial Commander-in-chief	Nanchang
Kiangsu	Governor-General of the Liang Kiang (Kiangsu, Anhwei, and Kiangsi) with the duties also of Superintendent of Trade for the Southern Ports (Nan-yang ta-ch'ên, BRUNNERT no. 820B) after 1866	Nanking
	Governor	Soochow
	Ch'ang-chên-t'ung-hai Taotai (for Changchow 常州, Chinkiang 鎮江, T'ungchou 通州, Hai-mên 海門)	Chinkiang

21

ON THE TRANSMISSION OF CH'ING DOCUMENTS 33

Province	Official	Residence
	Hsü-hai Taotai (for Suchow 徐州 and Haichow 海州)	Suchow
	Huai-yang Taotai (for Hwaian and Yangchow)	Hwaian
	Su-sung-t'ai Taotai (for Soochow 蘇州, Sungkiang 松江, and T'ai-ts'ang-chou 太倉州) with the duties of Superintendent of Maritime Customs	Soochow
	Chiang-ning Taotai (for Kiangning)	Nanking
	Director-General of Grain Transport (ts'ao-yün tsung-tu, BRUNNERT no. 834)	Hwaian (Ch'ing-chiang-p'u)
	Tartar General, for Kiangnan	Nanking
	Provincial Commander-in-chief, for Kiangnan	Sungkiang
Kirin	Tartar General	Kirin
Kwangsi	Governor-General of the Liang Kwang (Kwangtung and Kwangsi)	Canton, Kwangtung
	Governor	Kweilin
	Provincial Commander-in-chief	Liu-chow 柳州
Kwangtung	Governor-General of the Liang Kwang (Kwangtung and Kwangsi)	Canton
	Governor	Canton
	Hui-ch'ao-chia Taotai (for Hui-chou 惠州, Ch'ao-chou 潮州, Chia-ying-chou 嘉應州)	Swatow
	Kao-lei-yang Taotai (for Kao-chou 高州, Lei-chou 雷州, Yeungkong 陽江)	Mowming
	Ch'iung-yai Taotai (for Kiung-chow on Hainan Is. 海南島 and Yai-chow 崖州)	Kiungchow
	Kuang-chao-lo Taotai (for Canton, Chao-ch'ing 肇慶, Lo-ting 羅定, Fo-kang 佛岡, Ch'ih-ch'i 赤溪)	P'an-yü
	Tartar General	Canton
	Provincial Commander-in-chief	Hu-mên
	Superintendent of Maritime Customs	Canton

22

Province	Official	Residence
Kwangtung	(Yüeh hai-kuan chien-tu, the "Hoppo" 粵海關監督 BRUNNERT no. 833A)	
	Superintendent of Maritime Customs (Ch'iung hai-kuan chien-tu 瓊海關監督)	Kiungchow
Kweichow	Governor-General of Yünnan and Kweichow (Yün-Kuei)	Yünnan-fu, Yünnan
	Governor	Kweiyang
	Provincial Commander-in-chief	An-shun
Liang Hu	(see Hu-Kwang)	
Liang Kiang	Governor-General of the Liang Kiang provinces (Kiangsi, Anhwei, and Kiangsu)	Nanking
Liang Kwang	Governor-General of the Liang Kwang provinces (Kwangtung and Kwangsi)	Canton
Min-Chê	Governor-General of Fukien and Chekiang (Min-Chê)	Foochow
Mongolia	Military Governor of Uliassutai (wu-li-ya-su-t'ai chiang-chün, BRUNNERT no. 879)	Uliassutai
	Imperial Agent at Urga (K'u-lun pan-shih ta-ch'ên, BRUNNERT no. 879A)	Urga
Shansi	Governor, with the duties also of Provincial Commander-in-chief	Taiyüan
Shantung	Governor, with the duties also of Provincial Commander-in-chief	Tsinan
	Têng-lai-ch'ing-chiao Taotai (for Tengchow 登州, Lai-chou 萊州, Ch'ing-chou 青州, and Kiaochow 膠州)	Ch'ing-chou
Shên-Kan	Governor-General of Shensi and Kansu	Lanchow
Shensi	Governor-General of Shensi and Kansu, as above,	Lanchow
	Governor	Sian
	Provincial Commander-in-chief	Ku-yüan
Sinkiang	Governor	Lanchow
	Provincial Commander-in-chief	Urumtsi (Ourumtsi, or Ti-hua)

23

ON THE TRANSMISSION OF CH'ING DOCUMENTS

Province	Official	Residence
	Tartar General and Military Governor of Ili (I-li chiang-chün, BRUNNERT no. 866)	Hui-yüan ch'êng 惠遠城
Szechwan	Governor-General	Chengtu
	Provincial Commander-in-chief	Chengtu
Tibet	Imperial Resident in Tibet (Chu-tsang ta-ch'ên, BRUNNERT no. 907)	Lhasa
Yün-Kwei	Governor-General of Yünnan and Kweichow	Yünnan-fu
Yünnan	Governor-General of Yünnan and Kweichow, as above	Yünnan-fu
	Governor	Yünnan-fu
	Provincial Commander-in-chief	Tali

For the administration of the express service, as distinct from the ordinary horse post, there were strict regulations. Ordinary despatches were not to be sent by express.[30]

It now remains to note the organs of government which intervened between the postal facilities outlined above and the central authority in Peking. How were edicts started on their journeys over the post routes? How did memorials reach the Emperor after their arrival in Peking?

Beginning with the ordinary and routine documents, it may be said in general that the foot-courier service was managed at its Peking end by the Superintendents of Courier Posts (T'i T'ang

---

[30] Violations of this rule were punishable by degradation three ranks in the Ch'ienlung period or two ranks in the later Chia-ch'ing period. Cf. *Ch'ien-lung hui-tien tsê-li* 121. 35b; *Ping-pu ch'u-fên tsê-li* 24. 11. " Ordinary despatches of the Governors-General and Governors of the various provinces are all to be sent by the soldiers of the foot-courier stations; it is not permitted to use the horse post without authority. For all documents issued by the Grand Council (Chün Chi Ch'u), which are all to be forwarded by horse at express speed, the limit fixed per day is 300 *li*. If there is a matter of extra emergency, then the formula may be added ' daily to go 400 *li*, 500 *li*, or 600 *li*.' As to memorials of provincial Governors-General and Governors 奏摺 which ought to be transmitted by special messenger, they ought not unauthorizedly to use the horse post." The regulations enjoined care in keeping the use of the express to a minimum, e. g. an edict sent out at the 600 *li* rate need not necessarily be replied to at that same rate. *Chia-ch'ing hui-tien* 39.31a.

Kuan 提塘官). There were sixteen of these officials resident at Peking representing provincial administrations.[31] Acting as agents of the provincial governments with which they were connected, they were charged with the work of transmitting documents from these governments to the boards or departments in Peking for which they were intended, and of despatching documents from the boards in Peking to the provinces; they also managed the issue of the *Peking Gazette* (*T'ang pao* 塘報) for the provinces.[32] Similarly, there were sixteen superintendents residing at provincial capitals (Chu Shêng T'i T'ang 駐省提塘) who had charge of the opposite end of the service, transmitting documents to Peking and distributing to provincial authorities the documents and copies of the *T'ang pao* received from Peking.[33]

Of the sum total of ordinary and routine documents received at the capital by the Superintendents of Courier Posts, only a portion would consist of memorials for imperial consideration. For memorials on ordinary or routine subjects the procedure was that which had been inherited from the Ming period, and since this does not concern us directly, it will be referred to only briefly.

[31] Namely, Chihli, Shantung, Shansi, Honan, Kiangnan, Kiangsi, Fukien, Chekiang, Hupeh, Hunan, Shensi and Kansu, Szechwan, Kwangtung, Kwangsi, Yünnan and Kweichow, Director-General of Grain Transport and Director-General of Yellow River Conservancy (one for the last two). These men were metropolitan military graduates (wu chin-shih) or officers of similar grade, nominated by the high provincial authorities of the areas which they represented, and under the general control of the Board of War. *Chia-ch'ing hui-tien* 39.33b.

[32] In greater detail, their duties included the following: (1) transmission of official documents from the Heads of Departments (Pu-yüan i.e. Presidents of the Six Boards and of the Superior Courts) to the provincial governments, and from the provincial governments to the Heads of Departments; (2) the sending of imperial decrees and of seals 勅印 to the provincial authorities with whom each superintendent was particularly connected; (3) the publication of all documents of which copies were to be distributed,—this included imperial edicts and orders, and memorials on ordinary subjects. The superintendents were by regulation to go in person to the Liu K'o or Imperial Supervisorate (Office of Scrutiny, MAYERS no. 188), and have copies of the documents made, printed, and distributed. This publication was known as the *T'ang pao* (Courier News) and was the fundamental form of the famous Peking Gazette (*Ching pao* 京報). Manuscript copies were sent to the high provincial authorities. Printed copies were also made, and reprints were made in the provinces. *Chia-ch'ing hui-tien* 39.33-34; cf. also S. COULING, *Encyc. Sinica* 429.

[33] BRUNNERT no. 435B; Ko Kung-chên, *Chung-kuo pao-hsüeh shih*[2] 戈公振，中國報學史 (A History of Chinese Journalism), Shanghai 1928, 41.

Such documents, generally known as t'i-pên 題本,[34] were delivered to the Transmission Office (T'ung Chêng Ssŭ 通政司), located on Hsi Ch'ang-an Chieh,[35] which since the Ming period had had the duty of receiving all such memorials to the throne, examining them to see whether they were in proper form, deliberating upon punishments in case of irregularities or omissions, or if they were in proper form, delivering them to the Grand Secretariat (Nei Ko 內閣).[36] Since the Grand Secretariat had been generally eclipsed in importance by the Grand Council (Chün Chi Ch'u) established in 1730, it dealt with few if any of the important documents on foreign affairs, and its manner of dealing with documents need not be gone into.

Documents of importance, transmitted by express and dealt with by the Grand Council, including those on barbarian affairs, were handled at Peking by several different agencies in cooperation. Under the Remount Department of the Board of War there was at the capital a sub-office called Hui T'ung Kuan 會同館 (Imperial Despatch Office),[37] which had charge of the Central postal station in Peking (Huang Hua I).[38] Also under the Remount Department of the Board of War was a sub-office called the Couriers Office (Chieh Pao Ch'u), which had the special function of receiving documents sent by express, and transmitting them inward and outward from the court. Memorials received from the provinces by express were sent by it to the Tsou Shih Ch'u 奏事處 (Chancery of Memorials to the Emperor). This latter office (also called by MAYERS the Privy Cabinet Office) examined memorials to see if they were in proper form and, if so, handed them over to the Grand Council for presentation to the Emperor.[39]

[34] The subject of the various forms of documents used in the imperial correspondence is an intricate one, with which we propose to deal in a later article.

[35] *Shun-t'ien fu-chih* 順天府志 (1884), 7.8.

[36] *Li-tai chih-kuan piao* 歷代職官表 (1783), Ssŭ-pu pei-yao ed., 21.3a.

[37] To be distinguished of course from the *Hui T'ung Ssŭ I Kuan* 會同四譯館 under the control of the Board of Rites and in charge of barbarian tribute missions.

[38] Here were maintained 500 post horses, 250 grooms, 150 carts, 150 cart horses, and 150 drivers. The annual upkeep devolved upon the Board of Revenue. *Chia-ch'ing hui-tien* 39.32-33; *K'ang-hsi hui-tien* 100.1; *Yung-chêng hui-tien* 141.1.

[39] *Chia-ch'ing hui-tien* 39.32-33. It also took charge of communications between the

Among these agencies the Couriers Office played the chief part in the process of transmission. " Whenever the Grand Council sends [to the provinces] letters, or memorials which have received the imperial notation (p'i-chê 批摺), they are sealed up and handed over [to the Couriers Office] for despatch: the Grand Council hands [them] over [to the Couriers Office] carefully sealed ' We have received an imperial decree [ordering us] to send a communication ' 奉旨字寄. By this office they are sealed with nails [in the name of] the Board and covered with boards, and given to the official messengers of the Board of War to be distributed to the stations next in order, for express transmission. All provincial memorials presented by express, after they have received the vermilion notation, are sent back by the Grand Council; whether in despatch boxes or in boards, they also are sealed up by this office [the Couriers Office] and sent for transmission." [40]

In playing this part, the Couriers Office relied upon the cooperation of the central postal station (Huang Hua I), from which it requisitioned the necessary post horses. The central station " every day sends over horses to be ready for despatch by the Couriers Office of the Remount Department. According to the number of grooms and horses for which tallies have been filled in and issued, it meets the request of the officers and underlings of the express post. According to the number of li for which a notation has been made in the warrants it meets the request of the clerks and officers deputed to ride the express post." [41]

Emperor and the Grand Council when the latter was not in personal attendance, according to MAYERS.

[40] *Chia-ch'ing hui-tien* 39.32.

[41] *Ibid.* This text is over-concise. The relationship of these various agencies can be diagrammed as follows:

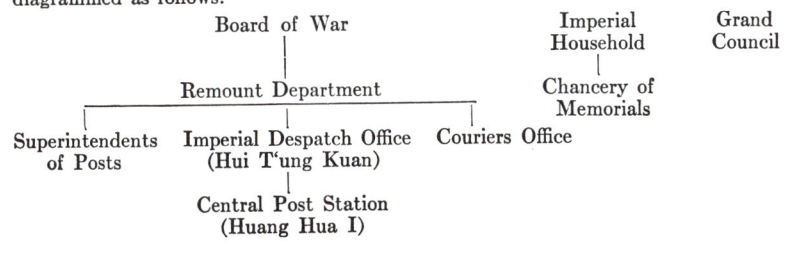

```
                        Board of War              Imperial        Grand
                             |                    Household       Council
                             |                        |
              ___Remount Department___         Chancery of
             |            |           |         Memorials
Superintendents  Imperial Despatch Office  Couriers Office
   of Posts       (Hui T'ung Kuan)
                         |
                  Central Post Station
                   (Huang Hua I)
```

27

From the résumé of the official regulations given above, we can now attempt to reconstruct the procedure normally followed in the conduct of foreign affairs. As research progresses, this picture will be subject to change without notice, but its main outlines seem certain. Decisions of policy were usually made by the Emperor and the Grand Council together. The resulting instructions were put in the form of an edict from the Emperor. This edict formed the content of a despatch sent by the Grand Council to the provincial officials concerned. This despatch was sent sealed from the Grand Council to the Couriers Office to be put between boards or otherwise prepared for transmission, and further sealed. At about this point an express tally (huo-p'ai) was issued, to be carried by the mounted courier who took the despatch, and an express warrant (huo-p'iao) was also issued, to be attached to the despatch specifying its route and rate of speed.[42] The central post station supplied the horses and other facilities named in these two documents; presumably the men sent as couriers came from the Couriers Office. It seems most unlikely that one courier could take an express despatch its entire distance; on this subject we lack information. Transmission of documents in the opposite direction, from the provinces to Peking, must have followed a procedure roughly similar to this, except that memorials went from the Couriers Office to the Chancery of Memorials (Tsou Shih Ch'u) for examination, before reaching the Grand Council and the Emperor.

2. The Actual Speed of Transmission in the Period 1842-1860

The data presented above has been drawn from the official regulations, and it remains to be seen whether actual practice corresponded to these rules. To what extent were documents relating to foreign affairs transmitted more rapidly than the regulations required? How fast could they be sent in time of crisis?

There is no indication that the Superintendents of Posts were concerned in the transmission of documents sent by express and dealt with by the Grand Council.

[42] Cf. *Chia-ch'ing hui-tien* 39. 23b: 凡差給驛者, 皆驗以郵符: 曰勘合, 曰火牌; *ibid.* 27a: 凡驛遞, 驗以火票.

28

To answer these questions, at least two bodies of material can be drawn upon. The first is the collection of documents published by the Palace Museum authorities in Peiping in 1930, cited above, and known as *Ch'ou-pan i-wu shih-mo*. Unfortunately, these published documents on barbarian affairs, having been compiled in the latter half of the last century for imperial use, omit the date of writing of each memorial. The entire series is dated and arranged according to the day on which the documents either were seen by the Emperor (in the case of memorials) or emanated from him (in the case of edicts). Consequently it is only possible to infer the date on which a given memorial was written from internal evidence, if such there be. From such evidence it is possible to calculate, in some cases, the time required for the transmission of a memorial to the capital, or of an edict to the provinces. Evidence so gleaned is presented in Table 4.

Another body of material exists in the archives, where, fortunately, the originals of the memorials received from the provinces bear upon them notations of the dates on which they were despatched and received. After the publication of the *I-wu shih-mo* documents, Prof. T. F. TSIANG 蔣廷黻 of the National Tsing Hua University, Peiping, had copies taken of unpublished documents on barbarian affairs supplementary to the *I-wu shih-mo* selection. The following table (3) has been constructed on the basis of these documents. It should be noted that relatively few of these unpublished documents were considered of an importance requiring the highest degree of express transmission, so that, as a class, the published documents appear to have been transmitted more rapidly.

Table 3 shows the time consumed in transmission of memorials to the Grand Council (Chün Chi Ch'u) 1842-1861 inclusive. It is abstracted from data given in *Documents Supplementary to the I-wu shih-mo, based on the Chün Chi Ch'u Archives* (Library of the National Tsing Hua University), used by kind permission of Dr. T. F. TSIANG, sometime head of the Department of History. These unpublished copies from the archives in most cases contain two dates, one written in the summary heading of the memorial, and also in the conclusion of it, indicating the day on which the

TABLE 3

Provinces Cities	Subject	Total no. of examples	Fastest time recorded	Slowest time recorded	Average time taken	Time most frequently taken
Kwangtung						
Canton	for. aff.	30	18	41	20.5	20 (9)
	for. tr.	40	19	81	43.3	37 (5)
Fukien						
Foochow	for. aff.	19	15	47	27.5	15 (3) 30 (2)
	for. tr.	40	29	128	58.1	30, 33, 34, 43, (2)
Chekiang						
Hangchow	for. aff.	15	6	22	9.5	7 (5)
	for. tr.	17	17	81	29.8	22 (3)
Kiangsu						
Nanking	for. aff.	20	10	25	12.4	10 (4)
	for. tr.	7	13	38	23.2	....
Shanghai	for. aff.	5	7	14	10	9 (2)
	for. tr.	3	18	38	25	....
Soochow	for. tr. only	17	13	25	17.7	15, 19 (3)
Chihli						
Tientsin	for. aff.	13	1	3	1.3	1 (10)
	for. tr.	32	2	10	3.2	3 (23)
Shanhaikuan	for. aff.	4	4	8	5.5	4 (2)
	for. tr.	2	10	29	....	....
Heilungkiang						
Aigun	for. aff. only	10	6	26	9.3	7 (6)
Sinkiang						
Ili	for. aff.	4	32	37	34.7	....
	for. tr.	2	40	47	....	....

Grand total 280

30

memorial was presented to the emperor, and a second date written in a separate column after the conclusion of the memorial, indicating the day on which it was despatched by the sender. In the case of published memorials, only the former of these dates is reproduced; these supplementary documents therefore provide data otherwise inaccessible outside the archives. Provinces for which this collection contains less than five examples are omitted. It will be obvious that the total number of examples analyzed in this table is too small to permit of exact statistical analysis. Figures under "Average time taken" and "Time most frequently taken" are therefore presented only to convey a rough impression; with that qualification, they are not without value. Under the latter category, figures in parentheses indicate the number of times that the preceding figure (for number of days consumed) appears in our list compiled from the documents. All other figures, except those in the last column, represent days. The distinction between "foreign trade" and "foreign affairs" represents a marked difference observed in the time taken for the transmission of documents relating to trade and to diplomacy, respectively; customs reports consistently took more time to reach the capital and receive consideration. Place names represent all the documents sent by officials who normally were stationed at those places; the documents themselves do not indicate the place from which they were despatched, and since some officials were driven from their official residences during the period of the Taiping Rebellion, it is obvious that the table contains an irremediable degree of error as a result of that fact. Such officials, however, were seldom driven far from their normal residences in the provinces here concerned; and our data in general do not indicate any appreciable lengthening of the time taken for transmission of documents during the years of the Rebellion.

Table 4 shows the time consumed in correspondence between Peking and provincial officials 1842-1860 inclusive. It is based upon the memorials and edicts published in *Ch'ou-pan i-wu shih-mo* and covers all documents in that collection between the dates indicated. Three types of data have been abstracted by comparing the dates on which memorials were presented to the Emperor

TABLE 4

Province	Type of data	Total no. of examples	Fastest time recorded	Slowest time recorded	Average time taken	Time most often recorded
Kwangtung	1)	7	15	49	24	15 (3)
	2)	9	26	77	45.2	37, 50 (2)
	3)	21	29	188	80.1	——
Fukien	1)	4	15	20	16.5	15 (2)
	2)	9	14	55	37	49 (2)
	3)	9	29	159	62.7	29, 36 (2)
Chekiang	1)	20	6	23	8.3	7 (11)
	2)	24	7	40	18	11 (3)
	3)	24	13	51	25.7	17 (3)
Kiangsu	1)	21	3	58	13.6	5, 6, 7 (3)
	2)	28	6	42	20.4	7 (4)
	3)	55	10	97	35.4	11 (4)
Anhwei	1)	3	6	11	8	——
	2)	5	7	26	12.4	——
	3)	6	12	26	16.6	——
Chihli	1)	32	1	15	2.6	2 (16), 1 (7)
	2)	39	2	20	6.7	3 (8)
	3)	42	3	95	10.5	3 (9), 4 (7)
Shantung	1)	2	5	4	4.5	——
	2)	5	6	14	8.4	7 (2)
	3)	8	8	158	14.7	11 (3)
Fengtien	1)	11	4	10	6.6	5 (4)
	2)	15	10	29	14.6	15 (3)
	3)	12	8	65	20.5	8, 15, 17 (2)
Kirin	3) only	5	11	42	26.4	——
Chahar	1)	5	2	3	2.4	2 (3)
	2)	5	3	12	7.2	——
	3)	5	4	14	8.6	8 (2)

Grand total 431

and edicts were issued by him, as published at the head of those documents, with other dates found in the body of some of the documents: (1) number of days elapsed between the issue of an edict to the Grand Council and the date of its receipt by the addressee in the provinces, i. e., time from Peking to the province; (2) number of days elapsed between the receipt of an edict in the provinces and the presentation to the Emperor of a memorial in reply to that edict, i. e., time for an answer from the province to Peking; (3) number of days elapsed between the issue of an edict at Peking and the presentation to the Emperor, again at Peking, of an answering memorial from the provinces, i. e., time for a round trip, Peking to Peking. As in the preceding table, the number of examples is too few to allow exact statistical analysis. It is obvious, also, that under 2 and 3 allowance must be made, to an indeterminate degree, for time consumed in the preparation of an answer to the imperial edict; the figures given undoubtedly are greater than the number of days consumed in transmission of the memorial in reply,—we do not know how much greater. Perhaps there is compensation in the fact that these figures do indicate the speed with which official business could sometimes be transacted. To students of the documents it seems unnecessary to explain the types of internal evidence, found in the body of some documents, which have here been used; to others it may be said in brief that one of the niceties of documentary style lies in the punctilious reference to the date of issue or receipt by the Emperor of all documents discussed. This alone makes possible the roundabout analysis summarized below. Names of provinces represent the high officials of those provinces, in nearly every case the Governor-General and/or Governor.

From these tables we may deduce that documents could regularly be transmitted between Canton and Peking in 15 days, and between Nanking and Peking in 5 days. The record time of 3 days between Nanking and Peking was made in 1842 and is an isolated example. It may be assumed that communication between other points and Peking could be established, when necessary, in periods of time proportionate to the different distances involved—except that transmission was slower over the difficult terrain of Kwangtung and Fukien and other regions noted in the regulations. Thus if we calculate the rates of speed achieved, without allowance for time required in handling at either end, we find the highest rate recorded is about 375 *li* a day from Canton, and from Nanking about 730 *li* a day (for the record time of 3 days) or about 440 *li* a day (for 5 days).[43]

References in the documents show that express rates above 300 *li* were used infrequently, their use being indicated by the insertion at the end of the document of such phrases as " memorialized by express post " 由驛馳奏, which apparently required merely the 300 *li* rate, " memorialized at the express rate of 400 *li*," or again " memorialized at the express rate of 500 *li*," or " memorialized secretly at the rate of 600 *li* " 由六百里密奏. Finally, orders were also given for the use of a rate of 800 *li* a day, although such a rate is nowhere mentioned in the official regulations. Examples are infrequent, but are scattered widely enough to indicate that the 800 *li* rate was an established mode of procedure.[44] In nearly every instance the express rates, including 800 *li*, are referred to in connection with a memorial rather than an edict; this reflects the fact that express rates were not to be used by the provincial authorities without authorization, and does not necessarily indi-

[43] The maximum observed rates of speed may be calculated as follows. In several cases, as between Tsinan and Peking, they show merely that no documents were sent with great urgency. We know that documents passed between Peking and Canton in 15 days, i.e. at a rate of *ca.* 375 *li* a day, by reference to Table 1. Between Peking and some other cities the rates were as follows:

    Foochow in 15 days at a rate of *ca.* 320 *li* a day
    Hangchow in 6 days " 510 "
    Shanghai in 7 days " 400 "
    Nanking in 3 days " 730 "
    Anking in 6 days " 430 "
    Tsinan in 5 days " 180 "
    Tientsin in 1 day " 250 "
    Mukden in 4 days " 375 "
    Aigun in 6 days " 550 "
    Ili in 32 days " 310 "

[44] For random examples see *I-wu shih-mo*, Tao-kuang period, 48.5a (" at 600 *li* or 800 *li* with extra urgency memorialize by express "), edict May 25, 1842; *ibid.* 55.3b (regarding an intra-provincial despatch sent at 800 *li*) memorial received July 23, 1843; *Wên-tsung-hsien huang-ti shêng-hsün* 文宗顯皇帝聖訓 (Sacred Instructions of the Emperor Wên-tsung-hsien) 16.1a (in 1853), 17.6a (1856).

cate that they were less used by the Grand Council in conveying edicts to the provinces.

We have found no reference to an express rate of 700 *li* per day, nor any indication when the 800 *li* rate may first have been used. Correlation between the various express rates and the number of days required for transmission by each has not been possible in any regular manner because of the paucity of data.[45]

By way of generalization it can only be remarked that the performance of the postal service in the period 1842-60 measures up, to a surprising degree, to the standards set in the regulations in force during the whole of the nineteenth century. Documents were transmitted faster than we might have supposed, in many cases, and faster than foreign observers at the time always realized. Since this data is offered primarily to assist students working upon specific problems presented in the documents, further comment seems unnecessary.

---

[45] Many references to the performance of the imperial post may, of course, be found among writings of contemporary western observers. In 1794 a memorial from Canton sent at 500 *li* a day secured an answer from Peking sent at 600 *li* a day within 30 days (J. J. L. DUYVENDAK, The Last Dutch Embassy to the Chinese Court 1794-95, TP 34.19). MACARTNEY was told in 1793 that despatches could go 1500 miles in 10 or 12 days (H. ROBBINS, *Our First Ambassador to China,* London 1908, 350). Although such references can be multiplied from western literature on the period 1842-60, their accuracy cannot often be controlled.

[Reprinted from *Harvard Journal of Asiatic Studies*, Vol. 5, No. 1, January, 1940.]

ON THE TYPES AND USES OF CH'ING DOCUMENTS

J. K. FAIRBANK and S. Y. TÊNG [1]

HARVARD UNIVERSITY

CONTENTS

1. Introduction, 1
2. Procedure in the Grand Secretariat (Nei Ko 內閣), 5
3. Procedure in the Grand Council (Chün Chi Ch'u 軍機處), 20
4. Select list of published collections of Ch'ing documents, 34
5. Catalogue of types of documents, 37

1. INTRODUCTION

This article, like its predecessor "On the Transmission of Ch'ing Documents,"[2] is designed to aid American students of modern Chinese history. As every such student realizes to his discomfort, the available Chinese documents[3] present several problems that are not presented to an equal degree by western documents. The problem of dating memorials has been attacked in the article mentioned above. Many more difficult questions await the coming generation. In general we lack knowledge of the administrative institutions of the Manchu dynasty which produced the documents now available. Like observers for centuries past, we are obliged to accept the utterances of the Emperor without clearly knowing who drafted them or how they were approved. It is obvious that our appraisal of imperial policy must wait upon our understanding of how it was made. As one step in this direction, the present study attacks the problem of the procedure followed by the central administration in dealing with the documents presented to it.

It need hardly be remarked that we are here concerned with

---

[1] We are indebted to Prof. K. N. BIGGERSTAFF of Cornell University for assistance in the preparation of section 5 of this paper.

[2] *HJAS* 4.12-46.

[3] The chief published collections of Ch'ing documents, which should be available in all Chinese libraries, are listed alphabetically by romanization in section 4 below, including abbreviated titles by which reference hereafter is made.

a very complex administrative system, the accumulation of centuries, parts of which were certainly in decay before 1900 but all of which continued formally in existence until after that time. The structure of this administrative system is on the whole faithfully portrayed in the *Institutes* or *Collected Statutes of the Ch'ing* (*Ta-ch'ing hui-tien* 大清會典),[4] from which we know the composition and duties of the central administrative organs,—the Grand Secretariat (Nei Ko) and Grand Council (Chün Chi Ch'u),[5]—and of the other offices at the capital. On the other hand, the actual functioning of these bodies, in close relation one to another, has been relatively little studied,[6] attention having been devoted thus far chiefly to the identification of the voluminous archives [7] which they left behind.

[4] Editions of the *Ta-ch'ing hui-tien* are cited below by the reigns in which they appeared, viz: *K'ang-hsi hui-tien* (pub. 1690), *Yung-chêng hui-tien* (preface 1732), *Ch'ien-lung hui-tien* and *Ch'ien-lung hui-tien tsê-li* (both completed 1764), *Chia-ch'ing hui-tien* and *Chia-ch'ing hui-tien shih-li* (both completed 1818), *Kuang-hsü hui-tien* and *Kuang-hsü hui-tien shih-li* (both pub. 1899).

These editions differ markedly in their treatment of some subjects. In general the K'ang-hsi and Yung-chêng editions are similar in content, the Ch'ien-lung edition differs greatly from its predecessors, and the Chia-ch'ing and Kuang-hsü editions are largely the same. Thus the various editions provide extensive material for the study of the evolution of the Ch'ing administration. We have taken the Chia-ch'ing edition (1818) as a basis; that of 1899 is modelled upon it.

[5] Translations of official titles follow H. S. BRUNNERT and V. V. HAGELSTROM, *Present Day Political Organization of China*, Shanghai 1912, cited as BRUNNERT. It is unfortunate that this comprehensive manual includes so many ephemeral titles created during the reforms that preceded the revolution of 1911-12. W. F. MAYERS, *The Chinese Government*, Shanghai 1897, revised by G. M. H. PLAYFAIR, cited as MAYERS, is briefer but often more accurate for the nineteenth century.

[6] HSIEH Pao-chao 謝寶樵, *The Government of China 1644-1911*, Balt. 1925, 68-87, summarizes parts of the *Kuang-hsü hui-tien* pertinent to this paper and contains much valuable data. Its usefulness as a reference work is seriously marred by the lack of an index; romanizations and footnote references are often imperfect in form. To Dr. HSIEH's credit it should be remembered that this was a pioneer work compiled before the publication of the *Ch'ing-shih kao* and most of the documentary collections.

[7] Much has been written during the last decade on Ch'ing archives, but often without reference to the subject of procedure. The more valuable articles include the following, cited below by author:

CHANG Tê-tsê 張德澤, *Chün-chi-ch'u chi ch'i tang-an* 軍機處及其檔案 (The Grand Council and its Documents), *Wên-hsien lun-ts'ung* 文獻論叢 (Collected Articles from the Historical Records Office), Palace Museum, Peiping, Oct. 1936, part 2, 57-84.

When taken together, the *Collected Statutes* and the archives give us an opportunity to study the progress of memorials and other documents as they passed through a succession of offices at the capital on their way to and from the imperial presence. On these routine journeys their progress was marked by the creation of other records in the form of duplicate copies, summaries, or entries in official registers, each of which was called by a special name. Moreover the various original and duplicate memorials, depending on their nature and on the Emperor's action in regard to them, became differentiated and deposited accordingly, under different classifications. When other types of correspondence and

CHAO Ch'üan-ch'êng 趙泉澄, *Pei-ching ta-hsüeh so-tsang tang-an ti fên-hsi* 北京大學所藏檔案的分析 (Archives in the National Peking University), *Chung-kuo chin-tai ching-chi-shih yen-chiu chi-k'an* 中國近代經濟史研究集刊 (Studies in Modern Economic History of China) 2 no. 2, May 1934 (Special Issue on Archives of Ming and Tsing Governments, cited below as *Ching-chi-shih yen-chiu*) 222-254.

FANG Su-shêng 方甦生, *Ch'ing-tai tang-an fên-lei wên-t'i* 清代檔案分類問題 (Problems in the Classification of Documents of the Ch'ing Dynasty), *Wên-hsien lun-ts'ung* 27-48.

HSÜ (1) Hsü Chung-shu 徐中舒, *Chung-yang yen-chiu-yüan li-shih yü-yen yen-chiu-so so-tsang tang-an ti fên-hsi* 中央研究院歷史語言研究所所藏檔案的分析 (Archives in the Institute of Philology and History, Academia Sinica), *Ching-chi-shih yen-chiu*, 169-221.

HSÜ (2): Hsü Chung-shu 徐中舒, *Nei-ko tang-an chih yu-lai chi ch'i chêng-li* 內閣檔案之由來及其整理 (The Origin and Reconditioning of the Archives of the Grand Secretariat), *Ming-ch'ing shih-liao* 1, 1-14.

HSÜ (3): Hsü Chung-shu, Tsai-shu nei-ko ta-k'u tang-an chih yu-lai chi ch'i chêng-li 再述 (Further Remarks on the Origin and Reconditioning of the Archives of the Great Storehouse of the Grand Secretariat), *CYYY* 3. 537-576, Peiping, 1934.

KOESTER, Hermann KÖSTER (sic), The Palace Museum of Peking, *Monumenta serica* 2. 167-190 (1936-7).

SHAN Shih-k'uei 單士魁, *Ch'ing-tai t'i-pên chih-tu k'ao* 清代題本制度攷 (The System of T'i-pên of the Ch'ing Dynasty), *Wên-hsien lun-ts'ung*, part 2, 177-189.

SHAN Shih-yüan (1) 單士元, *Ch'ing-tai tang-an shih-ming fa-fan* 清代檔案釋名發凡 (An Introduction to the Terminology of Documents of the Ch'ing Dynasty), *Wên-hsien lun-ts'ung*, part 2, 147-154.

SHAN Shih-yüan (2), *Ku-kung po-wu-yüan wên-hsien-kuan so-tsang tang-an ti fên-hsi* 故宮博物院文獻館所藏檔案的分析 (Archives in the Library of the Palace Museum), *Ching-chi-shih yen-chiu*, 270-280.

TÊNG Chih-ch'êng 鄧之誠, T'an chün-chi-ch'u 談軍機處 (A Lecture on the Chün Chi Ch'u), *SHNP* 2, no. 4, 193-198.

accounts are added, it is not surprising to find that the archives of an important body like the Grand Council are classified under one hundred and fifty-five different headings. A similar situation might be created if the British documents in the Public Record Office were sub-divided and classified according to whether they had been seen by the sovereign or not, whether they had been taken to a cabinet meeting or not, and so on, each category bearing a different name.

Thus the categories of classification in the archives mirror quite closely the steps in procedure followed in the actual conduct of administration. In short, to understand how decisions were taken one must understand the types of documents made in the process; the two problems cannot be divided. Therefore we present below in section 5 a catalogue of the chief types of documents; while in the pages that precede an attempt is made to summarize the administrative procedure in the Grand Secretariat and Grand Council. The activity of the Hanlin Academy (Han Lin Yüan 翰林院, also called the National Academy, or College of Literature), and of some other bodies which dealt with ceremonial rather than political matters, is touched upon only indirectly.

For the reader's guidance it may be noted that in form the administrative initiative usually rested with the Emperor's ministers rather than with the Emperor. Business of all kinds, great or small, was first brought up in a memorial to the Emperor; imperial action then followed. There were memorials of different types, and various forms that the imperial action might take regarding them. The most common of the latter were (1) a simple Endorsement (p'i 批), (2) a Rescript (chih 旨), usually somewhat more lengthy,—both of which were written on the original memorial,—and (3) an Edict (yü 諭), which was an independent document. (Our choice of English equivalents for these and other terms is explained in section 5 below, term by term.) These imperial declarations were considered important not only because they set in motion the wheels of state but also, and to a greater degree, because they partook of the sanctity of the imperial person. Just as all references to the Emperor or to things associated with him must be elevated (t'ai-t'ou 抬頭) from one to three characters above the ordinary text of a document, so all statements emanating from him received extraordinary and reverent attention. This attitude, combined with the fact that the Emperor usually ruled as well as reigned, provides a chief point of contrast with western administrative procedure. Thus a Chinese Edict often corresponds roughly to western Instructions, but it would hardly be correct to say that it was a mere equivalent.

2. Procedure in the Grand Secretariat (Nei Ko)

In brief, the Grand Secretariat was an institution inherited from the Ming and was the highest administrative body of the empire until the creation of the Grand Council in 1729.[8] After that date and throughout the nineteenth century the Grand Secretariat continued to function, but only as a body of secondary importance dealing with routine matters.[9] It became unimportant as a policy-

[8] For the date 1729, see note 39 below.

[9] YEH Fêng-mao 葉鳳毛, *Nei-ko hsiao-chih* 內閣小志 (A Brief Sketch of the Grand Secretariat), pub. 1765, describes the various sub-offices of the Secretariat, which were housed in a group of buildings inside the front gate of the Palace in the south-eastern section. His list omits two of the sub-offices listed in *Chia-ch'ing°* and *Kuang-hsü hui-tien* and includes six others not listed in the °*hui-tien*, among the latter being the Grand Council, a body that technically was an offshoot of the Secretariat in origin. The twelve sub-offices listed in the °*hui-tien* and in Hsü (1) 199 are as follows:

1. Archives Offices (Tien Chi T'ing 典籍廳), divided into a northern and a southern section, the northern section in general dealing with matters concerning the Emperor and the southern section in general dealing with matters concerning other offices of government and so having charge of the seals used in all correspondence of the Grand Secretariat.

2. Manchu Copying Office (Man Pên Fang 滿本房).

3. Chinese Copying Office (Han Pên Fang 漢本房).

4. Mongolian Copying Office (Mêng-ku Fang 蒙古房).

5. Manchu Registry (Man P'iao Ch'ien Ch'u 滿票籤處).

6. Chinese Registry (Han P'iao Ch'ien Ch'u 漢票籤處).

7. Honorary Titles Office (Kao Ch'ih Fang 誥敕房).

8. Inspectorate (Chi Ch'a Fang 稽察房).

9. Receiving and Forwarding Office (Shou Fa Hung-pên Ch'u 收發紅本處), i.e. for Hung-pên.

10. Mess Allowance Storehouse (Fan Yin K'u 飯銀庫).

11. Duplicate Memorial Storehouse (Fu-pên K'u 副本庫); BRUNNERT calls this Archives Office (no. 138) and contains no translation for Tien Chi T'ing.

12. Endorsement Copying Office (P'i-pên Ch'u 批本處).

The function of most of these offices will appear from the text and notes below.

making body but it still formed the apex of the routine administration. Details of its procedure are therefore recorded with some care in the various editions of the *Collected Statutes* and form a convenient starting point. For present purposes the multifarious ceremonial and ritualistic duties of the Grand Secretariat will be disregarded, except as they may be subsumed in the catalogue below, section 5, with reference to certain types of documents.

For the inauguration of administrative business there were two fundamental types of memorial, the T'i-pên 題本 and the Tsou-pên 奏本 (also called Tsou-chê 奏摺). As to the historical difference between them, which was not always very distinct, we quote below the evidence selected by a leading student of the subject.[10]

[10] SHAN Shih-k'uei's quotations and comments may be summarized as follows, beginning with the Ming period (quotations are from the next source indicated; we have inserted page references, in some cases to earlier editions):

Regulations for the Ch'i-pên 啓本, Tsou-pên, and T'i-pên were fixed in 1382, the system being that memorials from ministers or subjects to the Emperor were Tsou-pên, those to the heir apparent were Ch'i-pên. Later, because Tsou-pên from officers at the capital were inconvenient, T'i-pên were used for all public business. . . .

According to the Ming regulations, " all offices at the capital and in the provinces on all public matters use T'i-pên; but for all matters which, although of public concern, are routine reports or memorials of congratulation, such as requests for clemency, confessions of guilt, the return of imperial credentials, thanks for favors, petitions from soldiers and civilians, proposals and complaints,—they use Tsou-pên " (*Ming hui-tien* 212). Thus the Ming appear to have used Tsou-pên more than T'i-pên.

The Ch'ing followed the Ming tradition, but by 1725 began to make changes. " In 1725 imperial approval was given to systematize the usage of T'i-pên and Tsou-pên. The order was given to the various provincial Governors-General, Governors, Commanders-in-chief, and Brigade Generals that thereafter all matters concerning taxes and provisions, judicial cases, troops, (military) horses, and other matters large or small concerning local civil affairs, should all be presented in the form of T'i-pên, stamped with the seal (of the office of origin) and a subject-title written on the memorial (chü-t'i 具題). Private affairs concerning the official personally should all use the Tsou-pên form, and even though he were an official with a seal of office, he was not to be allowed to use the seal. If there were an offense against the fixed regulations for T'i-pên and Tsou-pên, it was to be referred to the Board (of Punishments) for discussion and sentence " (*Kuang-hsü hui-tien shih-li* 13. 4b line 6).

Further and more detailed regulations were established in 1729. " Hereafter for matters concerning the recommendation and impeachment of subordinate officials, taxes and provisions, troops and horses, law cases involving life or robbery, punishments, and all other public matters, according to the regulations T'i-pên should be used. Congratulatory expressions; reports of an official concerning his arrival at a new post,

From this it will be seen that T'i-pên concerned chiefly routine local civil affairs and bore the seal of the memorialist; Tsou-pên concerned chiefly important matters of state or the personal affairs of the memorialist and did not bear the seal of the memorialist.

taking over the seals of office, leaving his post, or handing over (to a successor); acknowledgments of the receipt of imperial commands (ch'ih) or edicts (yü) or of books distributed to all provincial offices, whether reporting dates of receipt or expressing gratitude; the sending of congratulations or statements of thanks on behalf of all the officials and people of a province; cases the reports of which are not originally clear and concerning which a rescript was received ordering a further memorial,—all these matters belong to the category of public affairs; T'i-pên ought to be used. As to (matters concerning) the arrival of any official at a new post, his promotion or transfer, his receipt of honorary distinctions, his being honorably recorded (for good service), or pardoned, or degraded and punished, or degraded and deprived of rank but left at his post; or matters concerning expressions of gratitude for special grants or rewards, or words of thanks on behalf of subordinate officials,—Tsou-pên ought to be used; none should be stamped with the seal of office" (*Kuang-hsü hui-tien shih-li* 1412. 4 line 9).

Thus the chief point of difference in the regulations is that Tsou-pên were not to be stamped with the memorialist's seal of office, while T'i-pên were to be stamped with the seal and were to have a subject-title written on them. Up to 1748 also, T'i-pên were used for public affairs and Tsou-pên for private affairs.

In 1748 a thorough-going change was attempted. An edict of that year declared that the forms of T'i-pên and Tsou-pên had been taken over from the Ming "because at that time the rules and regulations had been abandoned or relaxed and the Transmission Office and the Grand Secretariat utilized the names of public (affairs) and private (affairs) in order to facilitate the extension of its grasp (of government business). In reality all are statements presented to the throne. Why is it necessary to divide them into different kinds? Let T'i-pên be used in all cases where Tsou-pên have been used, with a view to showing administrative simplicity" (*Ch'ien-lung hui-tien tsê-li* 2. 3b line 7).

This reform did not succeed, however, and Tsou-pên continued to be used. In 1750 an edict specified that the action of provincial officials "in impeaching undutiful subordinate officers, whether requesting that they be deprived of rank, or requesting that they resign from office, or requesting that they be degraded pending reform,—all are local public affairs and are not at all matters which ought to be managed with secrecy, and it is right and proper to write a memorial and add a title to it,—which will then accord with the regulations. Recently there have been cases where the Governors-General and Governors have first prepared a memorial reporting to the Emperor in the form of a Tsou-pên and have expressed themselves separately in a T'i-pên impeaching (an official); this may still be considered permissable. But there are also cases constantly arising in which Chê-tsou (i. e. Tsou-pên) are used in place of T'i-pên; this really is not consistent with the regulations. Let circular instructions be issued to the Governors-General and Governors of the various provinces that whenever there arises an occasion for this sort of Tsou-pên of impeachment, they should

(The published memorials on foreign affairs in the nineteenth century are usually Tsou-pên.) In practice the memorials on routine administration which came to the Grand Secretariat were, ordinarily, T'i-pên; and the memorials on important matters which

use T'i-pên, in order to display great circumspection" (*Kuang-hsü hui-tien shih-li* 13. 7a line 9).

In 1795, because the usage regarding T'i-pên and Tsou-pên was still not uniform, it was decided that for ordinary routine matters Tsou-pên should be abolished and T'i-pên should be used instead. A memorial of Aug. 9, 1795, stated that "in the management of local affairs by the provincial Governors-General and Governors, all matters which concern the receipt of a rescript, or important cases involving life or robbery, heterodox religions, or changes in the old regulations, and all important matters which concern the sufferings or distress of the people, ought of course to be memorialized at the time in Tsou-pên. If there are ordinary routine affairs for all of which there are recorded decisions or archives which can be consulted, there is no need to present special Tsou-pên and stir up trouble. But the administration of the various provinces is not yet systematized. There are cases where T'i-pên are presented according to regulation but again a Tsou-pên is also presented to report (the same thing). There are cases where the various provinces memorialize the Emperor by the T'i-pên form, and yet one or two provinces alone use Tsou-pên. There are also instances where legal cases involving life or robbery have already been concluded and there are supplementary impeachments to be made in the case, which can be made uniformly through T'i-pên; and yet memorials of impeachment are nevertheless presented in Tsou-pên form. Again, in the case of T'i-pên (recommending) the promotion, transfer, or appointment of Sub-prefects and Magistrates to fill a vacancy,—if there are really important vacancies, it was originally permitted that a special memorial (Tsou-pên) be presented making the request; for other, ordinary vacancies of course one should follow the regulations and present T'i-pên. There are times when a certain man is required at a certain place, but the man's term of service is not yet complete; (in such cases) there is no bar to making a clear statement in a memorial. But Governors-General and Governors, because of the rule regarding special recommendations, abruptly go ahead and present a confusion of memorials and entreaties; this should also be ordered to stop" (*Kao-tsung shih-lu*, Aug. 9, 1795).

In this way Tsou-pên appear to have survived every attempt to abolish them. Meanwhile T'i-pên continued to be used, but, up to the later Ch'ien-lung period at least, no uniformity in their use had yet been achieved.

A second attempt at reform was made in 1901 when LIU K'un-i 劉坤一 and CHANG Chih-tung 張之洞 memorialized proposing the abolition of T'i-pên. "T'i-pên originally were the old system of the Ming. Since there were copies (Fu-pên) and summaries (T'ieh-huang) which had to be all copied in Sung characters, there were complications and delays. Our dynasty in the Yung-chêng period issued an edict ordering that the ministers and officials should make a change and put important affairs in Chê-tsou (i. e. Tsou-pên), which in simplicity, speed, and ease of reading far surpass T'i-pên. For fifty years past there have been many cases in which the various provinces have already changed to Tsou-pên. In the winter of the present year the ministers of state

ON THE TYPES AND USES OF CH'ING DOCUMENTS 9

came to the Grand Council were, ordinarily, Tsou-pên. We have found no statutory connection between the T'i-pên form of memorial and the Grand Secretariat, such that memorials of that type were required to go to that body. But since both came to be concerned chiefly with routine business, seasonal reports, accounts, and the like, the memorials coming to the Grand Secretariat were usually T'i-pên, and they are therefore the first thing to consider.

The chief key to what follows lies in the marked dichotomy [11] between the treatment of routine and of important affairs, which may be roughly diagrammed for the reader's future reference as follows:

	ROUTINE AFFAIRS	IMPORTANT AFFAIRS
Memorialized in the form of	T'i-pên	Tsou-pên
Submitted first to	Transmission Office or Grand Secretariat	Chancery of Memorials
First considered by	Grand Secretariat	the Emperor
Action proposed by	" "	Grand Council
Action taken in the form of	Rescript or Endorsement	Edict or Rescript or Endorsement

T'i-pên for eventual presentation to the Emperor came to the Grand Secretariat from two sources: (a) offices at the capital and (b) offices in the provinces. The offices at the capital included the

---

accompanying the Emperor have already memorialized requesting a temporary cessation of the use of T'i-pên. Hereafter it is proposed to request a careful investigation and discussion, that the T'i-pên may be forever dispensed with, and change made to Tsou-pên and despatches (tzŭ 咨), respectively" (*Tung-hua lu*, Oct. 2, 1901).

SHAN Shih-k'uei concludes, "the above-quoted memorial of CHANG Chih-tung and others requesting the abolition of the T'i-pên does not appear to have been carried out. Today the great storehouse of the Grand Secretariat still retains T'i-pên of the year 1903, which is sufficient proof of the fact." On the other hand, the *Ch'ing-shih kao* (*chih-kuan chih* 2.6b line 12) states that the Transmission Office was abolished in 1902 because the transformation of T'i-pên into Tsou-pên had deprived it of its special function.

The reader who has read thus far will perhaps agree that the subject of T'i-pên and Tsou-pên is a thorny one.

[11] Cf. KUNG Tzŭ-chên 龔自珍, *Shang ta-hsüeh-shih shu* 上大學士書 (A letter to the Grand Secretaries), in *Ting-an wên-chi pu-pien* 定盦文集補編 3.5 line 7, *Ssŭ-pu ts'ung-k'an* edition: "The Grand Council handles Edicts, the Grand Secretariat handles Rescripts; the Grand Council handles Tsou-pên memorials, the Grand Secretariat handles T'i-pên memorials. The difference between these two bodies was clearly distinguished."

44

Six Boards (Liu Pu 六部) and the various subordinate Courts, Departments, and Superintendencies; T'i-pên from these sources were called Pu-pên 部本. The offices in the provinces included those of Governors-General (Viceroys), Governors, Generals-in-chief (Tartar Generals), and the like; T'i-pên from these sources came through the postal service [12] and the Transmission Office (T'ung Chêng Ssŭ 通政司) and were called T'ung-pên 通本. An analysis of procedure must begin with the arrival of T'ung-pên from the provinces.

1. Routine memorials from the provinces (T'ung-pên) were delivered by the official post to the Transmission Office (T'ung Chêng Ssŭ), where they were first examined as to form and then, ordinarily, transmitted to the Grand Secretariat.

In form the memorial must comply with the regulations as to the number of lines and characters per page and as to the honorary elevation of certain characters; it must bear the writer's title and name at the beginning and the date of its despatch at the end; it should be stamped with the writer's seal of office, and a summary of its contents on a separate slip of paper (t'ieh-huang) should be attached at the end.[13] If such a summary were missing, it should be supplied by the Transmission Office.[14] If the memorial were in improper form, in any one of several respects, it might either be rejected and sent back to the sender or sent to the Grand Secretariat to secure an imperial decision regarding it.

Thus the power of the Transmission Office, although much less extensive than under the Ming,[15] was still considerable. As the

---

[12] Regarding the postal service for the transmission of documents to the capital, see our article cited in note 2 above.

[13] Summarized from *Chia-ch'ing hui-tien* 54.13a.

[14] Decreed in 1644; cf. *K'ang-hsi hui-tien* 148.1b last line; *Chia-ch'ing hui-tien shih-li* 781.2.

[15] The Transmission Office in the Ming period attained great power because all memorials intended for the Emperor had first to be opened and passed by it. Indeed, memorials on important matters had to be stamped and recorded by the Office before presentation to the throne, so that it became the chief means of communication (the " throat and tongue ") of the Emperor. This led to malpractices and eventual reform. Under the Ch'ing the power of the Transmission Office was cut down and it was arranged that secret memorials (fêng-shih 封事) presented at the palace gate should

first office at the capital to read Tʻi-pên from the provinces, it held a strategic position, with power to return a memorial unaccepted, to impeach the memorialist, and at times even to interpret the content of a memorial in making a summary of it. Only the secret memorials of officials in office were exempt from this scrutiny, and since the memorials here in question concerned routine business it is unlikely that many of them were secret. On the other hand, various measures were taken during the course of the Chʻing period further to restrict the power of the Transmission Office.[16] As will be noted below, the Grand Council was set up in 1729 partly for this purpose.

Here it should be noted that when a Tʻi-pên was first presented one or more duplicate copies were presented with it. Other copies might subsequently be made. Since these duplicates do not concern the main steps in procedure, they are discussed chiefly in section 5 below; see under Chieh-tʻieh, Fu-pên.

---

be transmitted to the throne directly by the Chancery of Memorials to the Emperor (Tsou Shih Chʻu 奏事處); Tʻi-pên from offices at the capital should be sent directly to the Grand Secretariat; and only Tʻi-pên from officials in the provinces should be sent first to the Transmission Office (*Li-tai chih-kuan piao* 歷代職官表 [Table of Offices and Officials of Successive Dynasties], *Ssŭ-pu pei-yao* 四部備要 edition 21. 17b; cf. also *Huang-chʻao wên-hsien tʻung-kʻao* 皇朝文獻通考 [Chekiang Press ed. 1882] 82. 11b-13). The regulations were of course by no means as simple as this summary would indicate. Thus an edict of 1645 provided that all Tsou-pên from offices at the capital should be presented through the Transmission Office (*Kuang-hsü hui-tien* 148. 1b; *Chʻien-lung hui-tien tsê-li* 151. 1a), an inconsistency explainable on the ground of its early date.

[16] The manifold regulations on this subject deserve summation in a separate article. Thus in 1682 an edict was issued that, "except for the secret memorials of officials in office, which should be sealed and presented to the Emperor as usual, the secret memorials of discarded and unemployed officials and of irresponsible shysters should first be examined by the Transmission Office; those that ought to be sealed, they will seal up for presentation to the Emperor, and those that ought not to be sealed they will strictly rebuke and return unaccepted" (*Yung-chêng hui-tien* 225. 3b line 4). But an edict of 1708 provided that, because the Transmission Office refused to accept so many memorials on account of improper form, thus delaying the conduct of business, it should therefore be ordered to report at the end of each month how many memorials had been rejected and their subjects (*op. cit.* 225. 2b line 6). In 1724 it was ordered that memorials should no longer be rejected and returned (*Chia-chʻing hui-tien shih-li* 781. 2). In 1738, however, there was a return to the system preceding 1724 (*ibid.*).

2. Routine memorials from offices at the capital (Pu-pên) were sent directly to the Grand Secretariat.

At first glance this statement might be challenged on the grounds of ancient tradition [17] and of various references in the literature, where it is sometimes declared that all memorials were presented for the Emperor's inspection before they were sent to the Grand Secretariat.[18] All memorials were of course presented

---

[17] The traditional practice had begun to decay in the late Ming period; cf. SUN Ch'êng-tsê 孫承澤, *Ch'un-ming mêng-yü lu* 春明夢餘錄, Ku-hsiang chai 古香齋 pocket edition, 23.28a: "The old regulation of our ancestors ... was that the eunuchs first set up the imperial table, then presented the official documents, and then retired outside the door; they waited until the imperial inspection was finished and then sent (the documents) to the Grand Secretariat for drafting (i-p'iao 擬票),—this was the usual practice. But in the early years of the Lung-ch'ing period (1567-72), I do not know why, the Emperor ... merely took the memorials in his hands and glanced over one or two lines in a cursory fashion, and there were some that he did not look at at all. ..."

[18] E. g. *Chia-ch'ing hui-tien shih-li* 10.3a last line; *Kuang-hsü hui-tien shih-li* 13.3a last line: " 1660 edict: as to the memorials (pên-chang) which are presented (tsou) by the various metropolitan offices, if they are sent down on the same day for the proposal (i. e. drafting) of a Rescript, since the memorials (pên-chang) are numerous and extremely important, it is to be feared that it will be difficult to deal with them carefully in a short time. Hereafter the memorials of the various offices and of the censors are all to be presented (tsou) to the Emperor every day at noon, to await the Emperor's opening and inspection. On the following day they are to be sent down for the drafting of rescripts, in order to facilitate careful examination, endorsement, and sending down. Memorials (pên-chang) of all sorts which are sealed up by the Transmission Office have first been sent to the Grand Secretariat to be read and presented. Hereafter let the said office itself proceed to seal them up and present them to the Emperor. After the Emperor has seen them, they will be sent down and read. If there are secret memorials (mi-pên), again let the said office seal them up and present them, no matter what the time may be. The various Boards should be informed in a transmitted edict, so that each may act accordingly."

It will be seen that the reference to types of memorials here are ambiguous and confusing, pên-chang being generally a generic term for memorials of all kinds. In the following passage, however, the all-important distinction between T'i-pên and Tsou-pên is more clearly brought out (*Chia-ch'ing hui-tien shih-li* 10.3a line 5): " 1656 edict: heretofore the memorials (tsou-chê) of the Censors and of the various Manchu and Chinese officials at the capital all have first been sent to the Grand Secretariat; hereafter all should follow the example of the Boards and go direct to the palace for presentation. The T'i-pên which are sent from the provinces to the Transmission Office and the memorials (pên-chang) of the various officials at the capital should still, as heretofore, be sent to the Transmission Office for it to send in turn to the Grand Secretariat." This was, of course, before the creation of the Grand Council.

ON THE TYPES AND USES OF CH'ING DOCUMENTS 13

to the Emperor at some point; the question here is whether T'i-pên from the capital (i. e. Pu-pên), as distinct from Tsou-pên, were presented to the Emperor first of all, rather than later in the procedure. The *Collected Statutes* seem to leave little doubt that Pu-pên were sent first to the Grand Secretariat instead of to the Emperor.[19] In view of the immense number of these documents and of the fact that they concerned routine business, this would seem to have been the only practical procedure. (As will be noted below in section 3, important memorials, i. e. Tsou-pên, went first to the Emperor.)

3. On arrival at the Grand Secretariat, routine memorials (T'i-pên) of both types (T'ung-pên and Pu-pên) were again examined for irregularities of form and were prepared for reading.

Thus if T'ung-pên arrived from the provinces written in Chinese only, as was no doubt usually the case, a copy of the summary was required to be prepared in Manchu.[20] A duplicate copy of the entire memorial (Fu-pên) was also made.[21]

4. At the Grand Secretariat the T'i-pên were read first by the minor officers of the Secretariat, who proposed what action should be taken upon them.

These minor officers of the Secretariat totalled in the nineteenth century nearly 250 men, of whom a good deal more than half were

---

[19] See, e. g., the passage just quoted, note 18.

[20] *Chia-ch'ing hui-tien* 2. 6a: "(Pu-pên and T'ung-pên) first arrive at the Grand Secretariat: when T'ung-pên arrive at the Secretariat, if they are not written in both Manchu and Chinese, the Chinese Copying Office translates the attached summary (T'ieh-huang) and the Manchu Copying Office copies it in Manchu characters and it is sent to the Registry (P'iao Ch'ien Ch'u)." Cf. *op. cit.* 2. 17b: in the Manchu Copying Office there were 39 Manchu Secretaries and 24 Manchu copyists (t'ieh-hsieh chung-shu 貼寫中書); *op. cit.* 2. 18b: the Chinese Copying Office had charge of the receiving and forwarding of T'ung-pên and its chief officers,—two Manchu and two Chinese Readers, with assistants,—decided whether the time limit for this operation should be long or short; thus for all matters concerning promotion, demotion, departure from a post, or dismissal, the Office set a time limit beyond which the work of translating and forwarding must not be delayed. The Secretaries of the Office,—31 Manchus, 8 Chinese bannermen, and 16 Manchu copyists,—had charge of the translation of memorials into Manchu.

[21] See section 5 below, Fu-pên.

Manchus, as may be seen by reference to the subjoined table.[22] It was one of their functions to suggest in the first instance what the imperial decision should eventually be. For each memorial they wrote on a slip of paper a draft [23] of an imperial Endorsement or Rescript. A draft Endorsement, for example, might order the matter in question to be referred to a Board for further deliberation, or it might be no more than the laconic and recurrent "noted" (chih-tao-liao 知道了). For all routine decisions there was of course an established phraseology.[24] In appropriate cases

[22] The personnel listed in the *Collected Statutes* may be summarized as follows:

	Manchus	Chinese	Chin. Bannermen	Mongols
K'ang-hsi hui-tien 2.1b	98	40	23	23
total 184				
Yung-chêng hui-tien 2.1b	id.			
Ch'ien-lung hui-tien 1.1	95	43	12	20
total 170				
Chia-ch'ing hui-tien 2 passim	164	46	14	28
total 252				
Kuang-hsü hui-tien 2 passim	id.			

The offices listed included Grand Secretaries (usually 4), Assistant Grand Secretaries (2 or 4), these two categories not being listed before the Ch'ien-lung period; Sub-Chancellors (usually 10), Readers (usually 8), Assistant Readers (usually 15), Archivists (usually 6), Secretaries (143, then 124, then 204). It will be seen that the personnel was increased in the nineteenth century chiefly by the addition of Manchu Secretaries. Secretaries, of course, merely assisted in drafting proposals.

[23] The phrases i-ch'ien 擬籤 and p'iao-i 票擬 may be translated "to write a proposal," in western parlance "to draft"; the regulations do not use the term kao 稿, the usual word for a rough draft or preliminary copy.

[24] *Chia-ch'ing hui-tien* 2.6b: "As to the form of the draft label, whenever the contents of T'ung-pên ought to be discussed and replied to, then they are given to the various Boards and departments at the capital, which are to 'deliberate and memorialize,' or 'investigate and deliberate,' or 'examine judicially and deliberate,' or 'deliberate and decide punishment,' or 'deliberate with great care,' or 'deliberate with haste.' When there is no need of deliberation and reply, then they are given to the various boards for their information." Cf. SHAN Shih-k'uei 185: "For the phraseology of the draft proposals there were established forms. Thus in the case of T'ung-pên it would be, 'Let the said Board be informed' (kai-pu chih-tao 該部知道), 'Let the Board of Civil Office be informed,' 'Let the Board of War be informed,' 'Let the Three High Courts of Judicature (San Fa Ssŭ) be informed,' and so on. If when a memorial was presented to the throne it was accompanied by a volume of documents or the like (ts'ê), then the draft proposal would be 'Let the said Board be informed and also send the volume,' or 'Let the volume be retained for inspection,' and so on.

two, three, or even four such phrases might be suggested, each one drafted on a separate slip according to certain regulations, and both or all presented at the same time as alternatives for the imperial choice.[25] In such cases, or even when a single draft was presented, a special note might be added to explain the basis on which the proposals had been made.[26] All drafts were written in both Chinese and Manchu and the two writers of the draft signed it on the back. The slip of paper bearing the draft, about four by seven inches in size, was then attached to the original memorial.[27] The readers also dealt with the maps, lists, accounts, bound volumes, and other enclosures that might accompany a memorial (see below, sec. 5: Huang-ts'ê), determining whether according to

If it were a Pu-pên, then it would be 'Let it be as recommended' (i-i 依議), 'Noted,' 'According to the proposal that he ought to be strangled, let him be held in prison until the autumn assizes are concluded and then be sentenced; for the rest, let it be as recommended,' and so on. Of the several hundred thousand T'i-pên with red endorsements preserved today from the Ch'ing period, the great part are of this sort." Other expressions commonly used by the Emperor in making endorsements included "Seen" (lan 覽), "Let the Nine Chief Ministries of State speedily deliberate and memorialize" (chiu-ch'ing su-i chü-tsou 九卿速議具奏), "The content of the memorial is thoroughly comprehended" (so-tsou chü-hsi 所奏俱悉). Any of these notations might of course be followed by remarks ad hoc.

[25] *Chia-ch'ing hui-tien* 2. 7a: "When there are two proposals, a pair of slips is written out: as to the form of a pair of slips, whenever the various Boards present T'i-pên requesting certain things, there are cases where (the officers of the Secretariat) do not dare to suit their own convenience as to whether permisssion ought to be given or refused; or where there is deliberation as to merit or guilt or rewards or honors, and the decision may be light or severe; or where punishments (of officials for administrative errors) ought to be deliberated upon or ought to be remitted; or where alternative requests are made in the memorial to await an imperial decision ... in all such cases a pair of slips is written out according to the draft." Cases of three slips or four slips were treated similarly.

[26] Cf. *Chia-ch'ing hui-tien* 2. 8a.

[27] SHAN Shih-k'uei describes a proposal slip as being smaller than the page of a T'i-pên, a bit over seven inches from top to bottom and a bit over four inches wide, the Manchu writing on the left and the Chinese on the right. The Assistant Readers and Secretaries who wrote the proposal slips signed their names on the reverse, the Manchu and the Chinese in the right and left corners, respectively. Slips of this kind are still preserved in the Palace, including some volumes of model forms to be used on T'ung-pên and Pu-pên, e. g. "For T'ung-pên with a single slip: We have read the minister's memorial of thanks; Seen; Let the said Board be informed; for Pu-pên with a single slip: Let the Palace examination be held on —— day; Let it be as recommended."

the regulations they should be submitted to the Emperor along with the memorial.[28]

It is evident that this drafting by the minor officers of the Secretariat was conventional in nature and involved questions of mere procedure rather than of policy. In any case the decisions of these men were reviewed by their superiors.

5. The drafts of Endorsements and Rescripts, together with the original memorials concerned, were then seen and passed upon by the Grand Secretaries (Ta Hsüeh Shih. 大學士)

There were usually four of these officials, two Manchus and two Chinese, plus two Assistant Grand Secretaries, one Manchu and one Chinese. We lack evidence as to whether, the institution of prime minister having been abolished, one of these half dozen high officials might make important decisions representing them all; no doubt the pressure of business would sometimes require it, in which case the ya-pan 押班 or head secretary on duty may perhaps have taken the decision.[29]

Every draft was approved, rejected, or changed by the Grand Secretaries.[30] It was then sent to the Manchu and Chinese Regis-

---

[28] *Chia-ch'ing hui-tien* 2. 6b: " If there are maps or volumes: reports on river works and all sorts of official construction regularly ought to be written up with both maps and bound volumes (of reports), to accompany the memorial when it is submitted to the Emperor. Reports on the taxes and crops of any place, and memorials from the court assize and the autumn assize, all are written in volumes [Similarly for the examination records]. If there is a list: if the memorial contains a list which regularly ought to be presented to the Emperor, such as lists of names, lists of vacancies, records of officials' careers, or lists of sacrifices,—having been examined as to whether they ought to be retained or ought to be sent on, all are differentiated and proposals made regarding them in the proposal slip. Those which are not covered in the regulations, as to whether they ought to be retained or sent, are not mentioned in the proposal slip."

[29] Cf. Wu Ao 吳鏊, *Nei-ko chih* 內閣志 (An account of the Grand Secretariat) 2b line 7, in *Chieh-yüeh-shan-fang hui-ch'ao* 借月山房彙鈔 3: " According to the state statutes there is a ya-pan, (the post) is assigned to a Manchu Grand Secretary; the order of precedence of the others (is decided by) asking the imperial will to settle it. . . ." A good deal of the office routine of the Secretariat is described in this work.

[30] This system had begun in the Ming period. According to *Li-tai chih-kuan piao* 4. 12b-13a, the Grand Secretaries were first commanded in the Hsüan-tê period (1426-35) to prepare drafts of rescripts and attach them to memorials that were to be presented. An edict of 1659 stated that the Secretariat had originally been established to save the Emperor's time and the Grand Secretaries had therefore been ordered to draft rescripts

tries (P'iao Ch'ien Ch'u 票簽 [or 處籤]) of the Grand Secretariat, where it was copied out in Manchu and Chinese on a formal double slip.³¹ It was then ready to be presented to the Emperor along with the memorial concerned.

6. On the following day at dawn the memorial (T'i-pên) was presented to the Emperor by the Grand Secretaries in audience, and the draft of the Endorsement or Rescript was subsequently approved, or changed, or if there were more than one, selected; or a separate Edict was issued to deal with the matter.³²

7. The imperial decision having thus been made, the memorial was endorsed (see below, sec. 5: P'i) accordingly.

In the case of T'i-pên this was seldom done by the Emperor's own hand. Rather, the memorial and the approved form of Endorsement were sent to the Office for Copying the Emperor's Endorsements (P'i Pên Ch'u 批本處), where a staff of Manchu

for the Emperor's final decision (*Chia-ch'ing hui-tien shih-li* 11. 7a line 6). For the Ch'ing regulations cf. *K'ang-hsi hui-tien* 2.7, *Ch'ien-lung hui-tien* 2.2b, *Ch'ien-lung hui-tien tsê-li* 2.8.

³¹ *Chia-ch'ing hui-tien* 2. 6b line 6: " Drafts are made and then copied on slips: every day the T'ung-pên and Pu-pên that ought to be submitted to the Emperor are carefully looked over and checked by the Assistant Readers and others, who write out draft proposal slips. After the Grand Secretaries have seen and decided upon these slips, they order the Secretaries of the Registries to copy them out in Manchu and Chinese on a formal double slip (ho-pi chêng-ch'ien 合璧正簽). On the following day at dawn they are respectfully transmitted to the Emperor " (We have taken ch'ien 簽 [in *Kuang-hsü hui-tien* 籤] in its most literal meaning as a slip of paper, which fits the context of the statutes). *Op. cit* 2. 19b line 7: " Every day, for the T'ung-pên and Pu-pên, slips are rough-drafted by the Chinese Assistant-Readers and their colleagues and sent to the Manchu Registry. The Assistant Readers and others (of the Registry) carefully compare the Manchu text and examine the slip to see whether it is in proper form. They rough-draft a slip in Manchu. They submit the duplicate copy (of the memorial) to the Grand Secretaries at the Grand Council 以副本呈軍機處大學士 and they submit the original copy to the Grand Secretaries at the Secretariat, who examine it and decide upon the draft. Thereupon the formal slip is copied out. . . . All memorials presented to the Emperor are differentiated as to whether they are urgent or not urgent, important or not important. They are reverently stored in a box," which is labelled accordingly. Cf. also *op. cit.* 2. 20a for the duties of the Chinese Registry.

³² Cf. *Chia-ch'ing hui-tien* 2. 8a. The Emperor might reserve some memorials (chê-pen, see under sec. 5) for further consideration; this step in procedure is discussed below, sec. 3.

secretaries copied the Endorsement in Manchu onto the memorial in red ink. The Endorsement in Chinese was copied on in red ink by the minor officers of the Grand Secretariat after the memorial had been returned to that body.[33] Both these Endorsements in red ink were called P'i-hung 批紅 (endorsed in red) to distinguish them from Chu-p'i 硃 (vermilion endorsements) or Yü-p'i 御 (imperial endorsements), which were sometimes written on documents by the Emperor's own hand. Memorials endorsed in red ink (P'i-hung) were given the name Hung-pên 紅本 (red memorials) and also called P'i-pên (endorsed memorials).[34] The imperial Endorsements were also copied onto the duplicates (Fu-pên) of the original memorials, already mentioned; but in this case the Endorsement was copied on in plain black ink. The duplicates were supposed to be stored in the Office of Imperial Historiography (Huang Shih Ch'êng 皇史宬).[35]

8. Within two days after its presentation, a memorial was required to be sent down from the imperial presence and action taken accordingly.[36]

---

[33] *Op. cit.* 2.23a line 7: "After memorials have been presented to the Emperor and sent back down again, the Office for Copying Imperial Endorsements, copying the slip of Manchu writing decided upon by the Emperor, and using red ink, writes the endorsement on the face of the memorial." *Op. cit.* 2.17b line 3: "After the memorials have been handed down and received, the Chinese Sub-Chancellors (of the Grand Secretariat), copying the slip of Chinese writing decided upon by the Emperor, and using red ink, write the endorsement on the face of the memorial."

[34] Cf. SHAN Shih-k'uei 185.

[35] Cf. *id.* 188. SHAN quotes several sources to show that the duplicates were required to be stored in the Huang Shih Ch'êng, including an eye-witness of the Ch'ien-lung period who saw them there piled as high as a mountain; SHAN adduces evidence that most of them must have been burned in 1899, to get rid of them,—at least very few have been found.

[36] *Chia-ch'ing hui-tien* 2. 8b line 9: "All memorials that have been presented (to the Emperor) are sent down at the end of two days; those that ought to be sent down immediately are not to take more than one day: after a memorial which has been submitted has received a rescript, it is sent down to the Office for Copying the Emperor's Endorsements. On the following day the Office writes on the endorsements, and on the day after that, (the memorial) is handed down to the Grand Secretariat. In case it is an important matter and the rescript is received that it is to be handed down with haste, it is immediately handed down to the Grand Secretariat on the same day that the memorial is (first) presented."

ON THE TYPES AND USES OF CH'ING DOCUMENTS 19

The original memorial (T'i-pên) was archived. Now endorsed in red, it was handed over to the Office for Receiving and Forwarding Red Memorials (Shou Fa Hung Pên Ch'u 收發紅本處), through which it was placed in the safekeeping of the Six Sections (Liu K'o 六科) of the Office for Scrutiny of Metropolitan Officials (Chi Shih Chung Ya Mên 給事中衙門), a part of the Censorate. At the end of every year all original memorials were required to be returned from this division of the Censorate and were stored by the Office for . . . Red Memorials.[37]

After notice had been given them by the Six Sections, copies of the original memorial were made by the offices of government concerned. Thus the imperial will was made known.[38]

9. If an Edict, instead of an Endorsement or a Rescript, were issued as a result of the presentation of a T'i-pên through the Grand Secretariat, then the Grand Council would usually be involved in the drafting. It is of course unlikely that many T'i-pên would call for an Edict in reply. In any case, since the activity of the Grand Secretariat in connection with the drafting of Edicts appears to have been in practice subordinate to that of the Grand Council, it will be considered below, section 3.

Under normal conditions, if we may trust the *Collected Statutes*, the procedure summarized above would have occupied about four days, from the time when the T'i-pên was first read until the time when the imperial Endorsement or Rescript had been formally copied onto it and further action could be taken accordingly. If necessary, the Emperor's decision could be returned to the Grand Secretariat on the same day that a memorial was presented.

By way of comment it may be pointed out that there was an ample arrangement in this procedure for checks and balances. Each draft Endorsement or Rescript was written out in both Manchu and Chinese, by secretaries who signed their names, and was then copied by another secretariat after the Grand Secretaries

---

[37] Cf. *op. cit.* 2. 21b line 8.

[38] *Op. cit.*, 2. 8a line 6: "After the endorsement has been written on in Manchu and Chinese, (a memorial) is a Hung-pên. Junior Metropolitan Censors from the Six Sections go to the Grand Secretariat and respectfully receive it, and subsequently give notice that it may be copied to the various yamen concerned."

had approved it. Similarly, following the imperial approval, the Manchu and Chinese versions of the Endorsement or Rescript were written onto the memorial in red ink by two separate offices. The likelihood of ill-considered drafting or of incorrect recording of decisions was thereby reduced. The announcement of the imperial will was hedged about with equal precautions. The imperial decision in each case could be copied by the other organs of government only after it had been received by the Censorate (the Six Sections, to be exact), although the decision had been originally suggested by the Grand Secretariat. The original document was then retained for the rest of the year by the officers of the Censorate while the Grand Secretariat itself retained only a copy. Certainly there was little opportunity for changes in the text of an imperial decision once it had been made. This ensured accuracy. But it must also have put a premium on the use of time-worn phraseology and the purely automatic treatment of official business. Minor secretaries were not likely to attempt innovations, and yet the initiative rested largely with them. From the point of view of an archivist, on the other hand, no more admirable system has ever been devised, and historians may well be grateful, even when they become lost in the profusion of records and copies.

3. Procedure in the Grand Council (Chün Chi Ch'u)

The Grand Council (lit. Military Plans Office, also called Privy Council or Council of State) was a smaller, more informal, and much more powerful body than the Grand Secretariat. In its first form the Council was established during the Yung-chêng reign in 1729 [39] to deal secretly with imperial military strategy, the most

---

[39] Various dates have been assigned for the creation of the Grand Council, probably because that body went through several reorganizations in its early years (e. g. Mayers 13,—1730; Ch'ing-shih kao, chih-kuan chih 1. 4a—1732; Kuang-hsü hui-tien shih-li 1051. 10, in memorial of 1783—1730; Hsieh Pao-chao 77—1730). However, the Shih-lu (cf. Chang Tê-tsê 57 quoting Shih-tsung shih-lu 世宗 82. 6a) and Ch'ing-shih kao (56, Chün-chi ta-ch'ên nien-piao 軍機大臣年表 [Chronological Table of Grand Councillors] 1) agree on the sixth month of 1729 as the date for the establishment of the Chün Chi Fang 軍機房. From this event the early evolution of the Grand Council may be traced as follows (op. cit. 1-8):

obvious cause of its creation being the contemporary campaigns in the Northwest. Further research is likely to show, however, that the Council filled a need long felt, for it is apparent that the early Ch'ing emperors had come to require the help of a compact, carefully selected, and rather unceremonious body to assist in their personal rule. The Grand Secretariat, having been the apex of the bureaucratic pyramid for generations past, could not serve this purpose. Accordingly the K'ang-hsi Emperor had made use of Fu Chêng Ta Ch'ên 輔政大臣 (assistant administrators) and later of the officials in the Nan Shu Fang 南書房 (south library) to assist him in dealing with important business. Similarly the Yung-chêng Emperor had set up an I Chêng Ch'u 議政處 (office for administrative deliberations) and drawn its personnel from the Grand Secretaries and Presidents of Boards. Later came the Grand Council, which thus appears to have been the final solution of a long-standing problem.[40]

We have already noted that the creation of the Council roughly coincided with the establishment of certain regulations concern-

1729 July 5—appointment of the Imperial Prince of I, Yün-hsiang 怡親王允祥, together with CHANG T'ing-yü 張廷玉 and CHIANG T'ing-hsi 蔣廷錫 as a board of three for the secret management of necessary military affairs.

1732 third month—the title of Chün Chi Fang was changed to Pan Li Chün Chi Ch'u 辦理.

1735—the duties of the latter office were taken over by the Tsung Li Shih Wu Ch'u 總理事務處.

1738 Jan. 17—the Pan Li Chün Chi Ch'u was restored.

1741—it began to be referred to simply as the Chün Chi Ch'u.

[40] The most informative modern studies of the Grand Council are those by TÊNG Chih-ch'êng and CHANG Tê-tsê (see note 7 above). The origin of the Council is also attributed to the fact that the offices of the Grant Secretariat were inconveniently located at some distance from the Emperor's apartments. The Secretariat was just inside the front gate of the Palace on the east; thus it was outside the first inner gate (T'ai-ho Mên 太和門) on the axis leading back through the main halls of the Palace complex. On the other hand, the Nan Shu-fang was just west of the Ch'ien-ch'ing Mên 乾清門, more than halfway along the main axis; and the Lung-tsung Mên 隆宗門 where the Grand Council had its offices, was on the western side of the same great court which led to the Ch'ien-ch'ing Mên on the north,—i. e. the Grand Council was located in the very heart of the Forbidden City, close to the Emperor. Cf. CHAO I 趙翼, Yen-pao tsa-chi 簷曝雜記 (Miscellaneous Notes) 1. 1a, in his Ou-pei ch'üan-chi 甌北全集 (Complete Works of Ou-pei [= CHAO I]), 1877.

ing the use of Tʻi-pên (memorials on routine public affairs bearing the memorialist's seal of office) and Tsou-pên (memorials on important or personal affairs and not bearing the memorialist's seal of office, see note 10 above). The latter form of memorial, as officials themselves testified, was simpler and more expeditious; it came to be used generally for communications to the Emperor passing through the Grand Council. It is evident that important political factors must have underlain these administrative changes, —both the Council and the Tsou-pên were tools making for greater efficiency, greater secrecy, and more freedom from bureaucratic impedimenta.

The power of the Council derived partly from its very informality. It was not given a separate section in the *Collected Statutes* until the Chia-chʻing edition of 1818. The number of Grand Councillors was never fixed. Usually there were five or six, but the number ranged between extremes of three and twelve.[41] They could be selected from among the Grand Secretaries and the Presidents and Vice-presidents of Boards, as well as from among the Secretaries of the Grand Council itself (Chün Chi Chang-ching 軍機章京, also called Hsiao Chün Chi 小). This arrangement was most important, for it made it possible to select carefully the really influential, or otherwise desirable, ministers, sidestepping the thorny problem of promotions from the bureaucratic hierarchy. Thus one or more of the Councillors (until after 1862) was always a Grand Secretary as well, and so formed a direct link between the two bodies. Statistics indicating the degree to which the Council and the Secretariat were merged together, through their common personnel, are given below.[42] In a similar

[41] Between 1729 and 1911 there were 47 years in which the number of Councillors was five, 48 years in which it was six, and 31 years in which it was 7; cf. *Chʻing-shih kao, Chün-chi ta-chʻên nien-piao.*

[42] The tables just mentioned and *Chʻing-shih kao, Ta-hsüeh-shih nien-piao* (Chronological Table of Grand Secretaries) give the names of the members of each body in each year. A simple addition of these lists of names, counting each name once each time it appears, gives a total of approximately 1140 names of Grand Councillors listed in the period 1729-1911, and approximately 1310 names of Grand Secretaries in the same period; a comparison of the two lists year by year gives the following results: years in which only one official was concurrently a Grand Councillor and a Grand Secretary—22,

ON THE TYPES AND USES OF CH'ING DOCUMENTS 23

manner, during the existence of the Tsung Li Ya-mên (for the management of foreign affairs) from 1860 to 1901 there were eighteen men who held office in both that body and the Council.[43]

A natural characteristic of this central organ of administration was the secrecy which surrounded its activities. Minor clerks were dispensed with and the clerical drudgery required for the handling of all important documents was borne by the Secretaries themselves, documents of less importance being sent to the Military Archives Office and elsewhere for routine treatment. At the beginning of the nineteenth century the number of Secretaries was fixed at 32, half Manchu and half Chinese, to be selected from the staffs of such bodies as the Grand Secretariat, the Six Boards, and the Court of Colonial Affairs; they had to be recommended by their superiors and were granted an audience with the Emperor. After 1860 four Manchu and four Chinese Secretaries were assigned to work in the Tsung Li Ya-mên. Thus the relatively small number of the Council's Secretaries, carefully selected and guaranteed as they were, made the Council staff a very compact body, quite closed to the uninitiated. Officials entering its service at first had to be instructed in the office routine.[44]

years in which 2 officials were in both bodies—78,
years in which 3 officials were in both bodies—41,
average number of officials in both bodies each year (1729-1911)—2.35.

In other words a little less than half of the personnel of the Council were, on the average, Grand Secretaries. It is noteworthy that during the T'ung-chih period (1862-74) there were only three years in which one official was in both bodies; in the other years of that period the two bodies had no personnel in common.

[43] CHANG Tê-tsê 61 lists them as follows: Prince Kung 恭 (I-hsin 奕訢), Wên-hsiang 文祥, Kuei-liang 桂良, Pao-yün 寶鋆, SHÊN Kuei-fên 沈桂芬, LI Hung-tsao 李鴻藻, Ching-lien 景廉, WANG Wên-shao 王文韶, Tso Tsung-t'ang 左宗棠 YEN Ching-ming 閻敬銘, Hsü Kêng-shên 許庚身, SUN Yü-wên 孫毓文, Hsü Yung-i 徐用儀, WÊNG T'ung-ho 翁同龢, LIAO Shou-hêng 廖壽恆, Yü-lu 裕祿 CHAO Shu-ch'iao 趙舒翹, Ch'i-hsiu 啟秀. It will be seen that these men represented loyalty as much as ability. The Manchu methods of preserving control in the central government are beyond the scope of this paper; HSIEH Pao-chao, op. cit. 81, gives some very interesting figures on the proportion of Manchus (a majority on the average) in the Grand Council.

[44] Cf. LIANG Chang-chü 梁章鉅, Shu-yüan chi-lüeh 樞垣記略 (Brief Notes on the Central Administration), author's preface dated 1823, revised by Prince Kung, I-hsin, who extended it to the Kuang-hsü period, adding 12 chüan to make a total of

58

This secrecy and compactness accorded with the fact that the volume of important business was relatively small, seldom amounting to more than fifty or sixty memorials a day.[45] In short, the Grand Council was in many respects a sort of imperial private secretariat, as exemplified in the fact that the Councillors followed the Emperor wherever he might go and had special apartments at Jehol or Yüan Ming Yüan.[46] As a result, the procedure of the Council is much less fully described in the statutes than is that of the Grand Secretariat, and can be summarized only approximately.

1. Tsou-pên (important memorials) from the provinces were

28; chüan 22. 4a line 9: "(the Council) for the purpose of secrecy has only (high) officials (kuan 官) and no minor officers (li 吏). Aside from the memorials which are issued for copying every day and handed over to the writers of the Military Archives Office to be transcribed,—all documents received or to be issued, archives to be registered, and items regarding which a rescript has been received and which are ordered to be sealed and deposited, are taken care of by the Secretaries (chang-ching) in person. The regulations and names (of documents) are handed down from the senior officials. Even for capable officials of other departments and bureaus, when they first enter the Council, there are things that they do not understand." *Id.* ch. 15-19 lists 109 Councillors and some 750 Secretaries up to 1875. For the regulations regarding the Secretaries, cf. *Chia-ch'ing hui-tien* 3. 11b.

[45] Cf. Têng Chih-ch'êng 197. Even this figure is probably high for the earlier part of the nineteenth century, if we consider that within the eighteen provinces there were only 18 Governors, 10 Governors-General, and 8 Generals-in-chief; two important memorials a week from each such official, not a low average perhaps, would produce only ten memorials a day for the consideration of the Emperor and the Council. The diary of the Grand Councillor Wêng T'ung-ho (*Wêng wên-chung kung jih-chi* 翁文忠公日記, 40 vols., Shanghai 1928, 21. 84b-101 et passim) in the busy years 1882-3 records some days on which the diarist drafted none or only one document, others on which he dealt with half a dozen edicts publicly issued (ming-fa 明發) and one or two court letters (tzŭ-chi 字寄, see under sec. 5 below), other days on which he (and his colleagues?) dealt with 15 documents in audience with the Emperor. A total of more than 50 endorsements to handle in one day is especially remarked upon, so also a total of 70 memorials received from the provinces (wai chê 外摺) in one day.

[46] Cf. *Chia-ch'ing hui-tien* 3. 1b. The sub-offices of the Council, listed in id. 3. 12a-16b, included: (1) the Military Archives Office (Fang Lüeh Kuan 方略館); (2) the Manchu-Chinese Translation Office (Nei Fan Shu Fang 內繙書房); (3) the Chancery for the Inspection of Imperial Edicts (Chi Ch'a Ch'in Fêng Shang Yü Shih Chien Ch'u, Brunnert 105a, "Publication" cannot be justified); (4) the Imperial Patent Office (Chung Shu K'o 中書科). Brunnert assigns all but the third of these to the Grand Secretariat; it is true that their staffs were partly derived from the Secretariat, but they are listed in the statutes under the Grand Council, with which their work was closely associated, as noted below.

delivered at the capital to an office at the Palace called the Chancery of Memorials to the Emperor (Tsou Shih Ch'u 奏事處).

This Chancery of Memorials thus occupied in relation to Tsou-pên a position comparable to that of the Transmission Office (T'ung Chêng Ssŭ) in relation to T'i-pên; but there is no evidence that it ever exercised comparable power. It had a small staff headed by an Imperial Bodyguard, a high official specially selected from the Guards within the Palace, who was assisted by six Secretaries (chang-ching) selected and guaranteed from other offices; there were also two Clerks.[47] Tsou-pên from the provinces, delivered by courier,[48] were marked on the outside "official despatch (kung-wên) to the Chancery of Memorials," and were received by the Clerks of the Chancery at whatever time they arrived. They were then handed to the Secretaries, who in turn handed them to the Chancery eunuchs for presentation, the latter being of course in a position to convey them to the Emperor's private apartments. Officials below a certain rank were not normally allowed to present Tsou-pên.[49] Other than this regulation, there is no indication in the statutes that the Chancery officials could emulate those of the Transmission Office in the manipulation of red tape for ulterior ends.

2. Tsou-pên from officials at the capital were likewise delivered to the Chancery of Memorials to the Emperor.

Every morning at dawn the Secretaries of the Chancery were required to receive memorials at the Palace gate. Memorialists who were presenting personal memorials were required to present them in person; this applied to Presidents of Boards and all others at the capital except princes and men over sixty (sui). The memorials so received were then handed to the Chancery eunuchs for presentation to the Emperor.[50]

[47] There were also Chancery eunuchs (Tsou-shih t'ai-chien 奏事太監) not described in detail in the statutes; and in addition to the staff which handled memorials (Tsou-pên) in Chinese and Manchu, there was another smaller one for Mongolian correspondence. There were of course detailed regulations regarding the handling of Tsou-pên from the capital, in yellow boxes; those that were secret were specially sealed between boards; cf. *Chia-ch'ing hui-tien* 65. 9b-12b.

[48] Cf. our article in *HJAS* 4. 37.   [49] Cf. regulations in *Chia-ch'ing hui-tien* 65. 10a, b.

[50] *Ibid.* The statutes do not support BRUNNERT 105 in the statement that "Metropolitan establishments present their memorials to the Grand Council direct."

3. Tsou-pên were presented from the Chancery of Memorials directly to the Emperor.

It need hardly be added that this would have significance only in proportion as the Emperor really desired to rule as well as reign; but the evidence indicates that the Manchu emperors invariably desired to do so.[51] Their early morning examination of memorials was no mere formality. On the contrary, the Chia-ch'ing Emperor forbade the practice of sending duplicates of Tsou-pên to the Grand Council.[52] There is a good deal of evidence to show that the Emperor usually saw important memorials before they were seen by his chief ministers.[53]

---

[51] Cf. CHAO I's account (op. cit. 1. 7a line 1) of the Ch'ien-lung Emperor's activity: "Ten or more of my comrades (in the Council) would take turns every five or six days on early morning duty and even so would feel fatigued. How did the Emperor do it day after day? Yet this was even in ordinary times when there was no (important) business. When there was fighting on the western border and military reports arrived, even at midnight he must still see them in person and would be inclined to summon the Grand Councillors and give instructions as to the proper strategy, using a hundred to a thousand words. I would draw up the draft at the time; from the first rough draft to the presentation of the formal version it might take one to two hours, and the Emperor, having thrown on some clothes, would still be waiting."

[52] One of the charges against Ho-shên, who usurped great power in the later years of the Ch'ien-lung period, was that he had improperly instructed the provincial authorities to make an extra copy of their memorials and send it to the Grand Council at the same time that the original was sent in for the Emperor. By the Chia-ch'ing Emperor the practice was vigorously denounced and prohibited for all time; an edict of Feb. 12, 1799, declared that all persons entitled to present Tsou-pên thereafter ought to present them "directly to the Throne, and it is not to be permitted that they send duplicates in addition to the Grand Council; the high civil and military officials of the various offices at the capital also shall not previously inform the Grand Councillors of the matters which they are presenting in Tsou-pên; after the various offices at the capital have transmitted their Tsou-pên, the Emperor can immediately see (the officials concerned) in audience so as to hold discussions and instruct the offices in question how to manage matters without the Grand Councillors' being involved in giving instructions" (LIANG Chang-chü, Shu-yüan chi-lüeh 1. 9b).

Pao-chao HSIEH, op. cit. 86, gives a very loose translation of this passage and interprets it without ascertainable justification as an imperial effort to break the power of the Grand Council; this interpretation appears to overlook the historical context, particularly the recent Ho-shên case. We have found no evidence to support HSIEH's implied statement, loc. cit., that before 1799 memorials were read by the Councillors before the Emperor saw them.

[53] Cf. CHÜ Hung-chi 瞿鴻禨, Pao-chih chi-lüeh 儤值紀略 (Brief notes of an official on duty), postface 1920, 8a-9b; we are indebted to Mr. Chaoying FANG of the

4. The Emperor inspected the memorials and made his decisions and comments regarding them.

At this first inspection he might make a simple Endorsement (P'i) settling the matter in question; in such case the imperial decision could be transmitted through the Council without further discussion or delay. On the other hand, matters which he wished to discuss with his Councillors, or regarding which he wished them to prepare the draft of an Edict or the like, would be so indicated. Thus his turning down one corner of a memorial would mark it for further consideration (see sec. 5, Chê-pên).

5. The memorials were then sent down to the Grand Council to be dealt with as indicated by the Emperor.

On their arrival at the Council, the Secretaries of that body classified and distributed them. Those on which an imperial decision had already been reached were dealt with in the routine manner described below. But usually some memorials were still a live issue,—those which bore no Endorsement or were endorsed "There is a separate Rescript" (ling yu chih 另有旨) or which were otherwise indicated for discussion, as by the turning down of a corner. Regarding these documents the Secretaries under the Councillors' direction, or perhaps the Councillors themselves, prepared drafts of an imperial decision, whether Edict, Rescript, or Endorsement, in preparation for the audience of the following morning. Such memorials were called "audience memorials" (chien-mien chê 見面摺). Usually there were only a few each day.[54]

Library of Congress for this reference and other assistance: "Memorials from the provinces are all transmitted (to the Emperor) a day ahead. When the Emperor and Empress Dowager have finished inspecting them, there are some which the Emperor has endorsed at the time, there are some which are set aside and not yet endorsed. Both types are sent down to the Councillors to be examined by them, which is called the "morning work" (tsao-shih 早事). (In the same way,) when they (the Councillors) have finished inspecting them, they first take the memorials which have Endorsements and hand them over to the Secretaries to be sorted out and recorded for the archives. For those which have been set aside and not yet endorsed, they may discuss the draft of an Endorsement or Rescript. They put the memorials in a box and insert a memorandum listing how many there are, and respectfully requesting that Vermilion Endorsements be sent down."

[54] Cf. Têng Chih-ch'êng 195; also under note 59 below.

6. On the following day at dawn the documents held over in this manner from the previous day were dealt with by the Emperor and the Grand Councillors in audience.[55]

Here again there are few regulations, except as to where the ministers should sit in the imperial presence. There was evidently no bar to thorough and informal discussion. The Councillors would present both the memorials in question and also their own drafts and memoranda or minutes (P'ien, see sec. 5).

7. When the imperial decision regarding a Tsou-pên had been made, either by the Emperor alone when he first saw the document or subsequently in concert with his Councillors, the documents concerned were then returned to the Grand Council and copies were made.[56]

---

[55] *Chia-ch'ing hui-tien* 3. 1a: "On ordinary days (the Grand Councillors) are on duty in the Forbidden City in order to await a summons to audience: the hall of the Grand Council is inside the Lung-tsung Gate. Every day in the period from three to five A. M. the Grand Councillors attend in this place. As soon as the management of affairs is finished, the eunuchs of the Chancery of Memorials to the Emperor transmit a rescript ordering them to disperse, whereupon they go off duty. They are summoned to audience at no fixed time, either once or several times (a day). When the Grand Councillors have come before the Emperor, mats are spread upon the floor and they are graciously allowed to sit down. All Tsou-pên which are sent down to various departments of government and which have received the vermilion endorsement "There is a separate rescript," or on which there is a rescript but not yet a vermilion endorsement,—all are offered up to await an imperial decision. When a rescript has been received, they go out."

[56] *Chia-ch'ing hui-tien* 3. 2a: "All Edicts and Rescripts which have been publicly issued, after they have been handed down, are sent down to the Grand Secretariat.

"Those which are handed down for a special purpose are called Edicts; those which are handed down in answer to a request presented in a memorial are called Rescripts; or if they are in answer to a request presented in a memorial and are to be proclaimed at the capital and in the provinces, they also are called Edicts. In form, an Edict reads 'the Grand Secretariat has received an imperial Edict'; a Rescript reads 'a Rescript has been received.' On each is recorded the year, month, and day on which it was received. After the drafts above mentioned have been presented to the Emperor and the imperial decision has been sent down, those handed down for a special purpose (i. e. Edicts) are immediately sent to be copied; those handed down in answer to a memorial (i. e. Rescripts) are sent to be copied together with the original memorial. Other memorials (tsou-chê 奏摺), such as those which have received the Vermilion Endorsements 'Let the Board in question deliberate and memorialize,' 'Let the Board in question be informed,' are also immediately sent to be copied. All those which have received the Vermilion Endorsement 'Seen' (lan 覽), or the Vermilion Endorsement 'Noted' (chih-tao-liao 知道了) or a Vermilion Endorsement approving or not

Ordinary Tsou-pên were sent to be copied by the Military Archives Office. But those which had been presented as secret, or bore Vermilion Endorsements which should be kept secret, or which were originals that were to be transmitted in Letters or Edicts, were all copied by the Secretaries of the Grand Council in person.[57]

8. The imperial will was then made known.

Copies might be sent to the Grand Secretariat or to the Board of War for transmission by horse post to the provinces or to various Boards at the capital for them to act upon. Edicts, which were drafted by the Grand Councillors as one of their chief functions, might be addressed to the Councillors themselves (see sec. 5, Yü) or to the Grand Secretariat. In any case, they would not

approving the matter memorialized, or a Vermilion Endorsement which teaches and admonishes, or which praises and encourages, all are examined to see whether they are matters which ought to be dealt with by the Boards and Departments at the capital (pu-yüan 部院), in which case they are sent to be copied; while those that do not concern the Boards and Departments are not sent to be copied.

"Those which are sent to be copied are given to the Secretaries of the Grand Secretariat, who receive and distribute them for copying (by clerks). Of Memorials which have not received a Vermilion Endorsement, a copy is made from the original memorial. Of Memorials which have received a Vermilion Endorsement, whether or not they are sent to be copied, a duplicate is made. An original memorial bearing a Vermilion Endorsement, if it was a memorial from an office at the capital, is deposited in the Grand Council; if it was a memorial from a province or city (government), then it is returned (to the memorialist).

"Memorials (tsou-chê 奏摺) which have been presented by a special messenger are given to the Chancery of Memorials to the Emperor in the palace to be sealed up and sent back. Memorials which have been sent in by horse post are sealed up by the Grand Council and given to the Couriers Office of the Board of War for transmission. If a memorial was originally sent in by horse post but there is no need of haste in returning it, it is sealed up and retained until a convenient opportunity for sending it.

"When the distribution and copying of the memorials at the Grand Secretariat is finished, then the memorials which have been received there are taken back, and together with the memorials which have not been sent to be copied, they are placed in the archives.

"Edicts ordering the Grand Councillors to take action, after they have been handed down, are then sealed up and sent off.

"Either an urgent Edict, or a secret Edict, which is not handed down publicly through the Grand Secretariat is called a Court Letter (t'ing-chi 廷寄). It is sealed up by the Grand Council and given to the Couriers Office of the Board of War for transmission."

[57] See under note 58 below.

be addressed to the high officials in the provinces; the latter would receive the imperial will in the form of a Court Letter (T'ing-chi, see sec. 5) sent to them by the Council and embodying in it the imperial Edict. On the other hand, Edicts of less importance or addressed to no particular officials would be publicly issued (ming-fa) by the Grand Secretariat, in which case they might subsequently reach the provinces through the medium of the Peking Gazette in one or another of its forms (see sec. 5, T'ang-pao). The fullest description of the procedure just described is that given by Prince Kung, which we quote in part below.[58]

[58] Cf. LIANG Chang-chü, op. cit. 22. 4b-6: "Every day between four and eight A. M. memorials (tsou-pên) must be sent down from the Emperor to the Grand Council; the Secretaries divide them up and send them to the various Grand Councillors in succession to read and examine. This is called Receiving the Memorials (chieh-chê 接摺). All Memorials which have received a Vermilion Endorsement 'There is a separate Rescript,' or for which there is a Rescript but no Vermilion Endorsement as yet received, are collected separately in a yellow box and given to the Grand Councillors, who offer them up respectfully in audience and ask for a Rescript. This is called Having an Interview (chien-mien 見面).

"The Secretaries on duty for a certain day take the Tsou-pên which have been received on that day, the Memoranda (p'ien-tan 片單) which have been transmitted, and the Edicts and Rescripts which have been received from the Emperor and carefully classify and record them. Vermilion Endorsements are respectfully recorded in toto, while the particulars of Edicts, Rescripts, and Memorials are epitomized. On those which should be sent to the Grand Secretariat they mark the character 'Transfer' (chiao 交); on those which should be sent to the Board of War they mark 'For Transmission by Horse' (ma-ti 馬遞) and the number of li to be covered per day. (All these documents) are bound up in thick volumes, one for the spring and summer seasons, one for the autumn and winter seasons. This is called Keeping up with the Work on Hand (sui-shou 隨手; cf. remarks of SHAN Shih-yüan 149 on Sui-shou teng-chi tang 隨手登記檔).

"In copying Edicts and Rescripts that are publicly issued and all types of Memoranda, paper with six ruled lines is used; in copying Letters (chi-hsin 寄信) and Edicts to be transmitted (ch'üan-yü 傳諭), paper with five ruled lines is used, each line having twenty characters. This is called Having on hand for Transmission (hsien-ti 現遞).

"If there are some that have too great a number of characters and must be copied and transmitted in haste, then one man is ordered to cut the draft up into sections, which are divided and quickly copied. This is called Marking off Sections (tien-k'ou 點扣). When the parts have been copied out, they are pasted together again. This is called Joining up Sections (chieh-k'ou 接扣).

"After the documents have been handed to the Ta-la-mi (head of a section of eight secretaries) to be proof-read, they are collected in a yellow box and sent to the Grand Councillors who carefully examine them to see that there are no errors and then give

It is an interesting question how long this process usually required. From the statutes we know that memorials from the capital were to be handed in at dawn, those from the provinces might arrive at any time. The Emperor read memorials at dawn. He also saw the Grand Councillors at that time, and they remained

them to the palace eunuchs for presentation to the Emperor. This is called Reporting of Rescripts (shu-chih 述旨).

"Documents which have been revised by the Vermilion Pen (chu-pi 硃筆) are said to have Passed the Vermilion (kuo-chu 過硃). (KUAN Shih-ming 管世銘, *Yün-shan-t'ang shih-chi* 韞山堂詩集 [Collected Poems of Yün-shan-t'ang] ed. 1894, 15.2 line 2 explains this as To Transfer the Vermilion, i.e. onto a copy of the original document.)

"When a proposed Edict or Rescript has been prepared ahead of time, and after copying has been kept in a box with a view to its being submitted at the proper time, it is called a Document Prostrate on the Ground (fu-ti k'ou 伏地扣).

"When the Emperor happens to go on a journey and a document is submitted at the first post station, it is called Transmitted at Dismounting (hsia-ma ti 下馬遞).

"Whenever an Edict or Rescript accompanying a Memorial is given to the Chinese Registry of the Grand Secretariat, or whenever an Edict or Rescript not called for by a Memorial but handed down specially is given to the Manchu Registry of the Grand Secretariat, or whenever Letters and Edicts to be transmitted by horse post are given to the Board of War, or if they are to be given to the various Boards to be discussed in haste or dealt with in haste and so are given specially to the Boards,—in all these cases the recipient is made to sign his name and mark in a notebook. This is called to Transfer for Issue (chiao-fa 交發).

"All copying of Memorials is the business of the Military Archives Office; in the case of Memorials which have been secretly presented or which are the originals used in Letters or in Edicts to be transmitted with care, or which have Vermilion Endorsements and ought to be kept secret,—in all such cases the Secretaries of the Grand Council themselves make the copies. As each copy of a Memorial is finished, the Secretary in question takes the original and the copy and compares them, and then records on the face of the copy what was memorialized by a certain man on a certain subject, the month and day, and whether or not it is to be transferred (chiao 交). This is called Filling in the Face (k'ai-mien 開面).

"The Secretaries on duty for the day take the original Memorials from the provinces which have been received on that day, putting each in its original envelope, and deliver them to the Chancery of Memorials to the Emperor. This is called Transferring the Memorials (chiao-chê 交摺).

"The Edicts and Rescripts received on that day and the Memoranda transmitted are copied and bound into a volume; day by day this is added to, and it is changed for a new volume every month. This is called Cleaning the Archives (ch'ing-tang 清檔).

"Memorials and Memoranda despatched from the Grand Council, or returned from the Grand Secretariat or elsewhere, and preserved in this office form one bundle every day and a package every half-month. This is called the Monthly Memorials (yüeh-chê 月摺)."

on call to be seen at any other time it might be necessary. Memorials seen by the Emperor were sent down to the Council in the morning, providing their "morning work" (tsao-shih 早事). Finally, it is stated that memorials were usually seen by the Emperor one day before they were considered by the Council. From this and similar evidence we may conclude that, ordinarily, a memorial might be presented at dawn or during the course of one day and be seen by the Emperor on that day or at dawn of the following day; in either case it would ordinarily be sent down to the Council on the second day; if it was to be discussed further, it would then be brought back by the Councillors on the morning of the third day for a final decision. This may have been the routine with business which was not pressing. On the other hand, there was every opportunity to speed up the process ad libitum, and an urgent memorial might be received, presented, and discussed by the Emperor and his Councillors all within the space of a few hours.[59]

9. Finally, the memorials (chê) were returned through the Chancery of Memorials to the original memorialist, whether in the provinces or at the capital. This afforded a form of direct contact between the Emperor and his officials, at least in the case of memorials bearing an imperial notation.[60]

[59] Prof. Têng Chih-ch'êng 197 states that it was a rule that the issuing of all imperial Edicts must be completed by the Council officers on the same day that the decisions concerned were handed down from the Emperor.

[60] Cf. *Chia-ch'ing hui-tien* 3.2a, espec. last line; also 65. 11b and *Kuang-hsü hui-tien* 82. 12a: "Every day the various memorials (chê) which are transmitted (excepting those memorials transmitted by express post, all of which are handed by the Chancery eunuchs directly to the Grand Council for sealing and returning [fa 發], and which are not returned [fa-hsia 下] by the Chancery),—all other memorials from the provinces, no matter whether they have received a Rescript or not, are securely sealed by the Chancery eunuchs; on the following day they are handed to the Chancery to be returned (in each case) to the man originally transmitting the memorial, to be reverently received by him. As to the various memorials transmitted at the capital (excepting those which are retained by the Emperor and are returned by the Grand Council, or which are ordered to be handed to the ministers of state having audience on that day, to be returned by them),—regarding all other memorials which are returned by the Chancery, whether they have received the Rescript 'Let it be as recommended' or have received the Rescript 'Noted,' straightway the Chancery transmits the imperial will that (the memorial) may be received (by the memorialist)." The

A brief conclusion may be suggested. First, it is plain that this paper is no more than a preliminary survey. We have touched upon a score or more of institutions and steps in procedure, on each of which a monograph should be written. For such work the various editions of the Cases Supplementary to the *Collected Statutes* (°*hui-tien tsê-li*, or *shih-li*), cited above, provide an inexhaustible storehouse of material, which may be supplemented by the documentary collections and writings of Chinese officials. American students of government and political science have so far left it untouched.

Secondly, this survey confirms the view that the Grand Council was all-important and the Grand Secretariat almost negligible in the making of important decisions of policy during the nineteenth century, particularly before 1860. In the investigation of the origins of Manchu policy, either in internal or in foreign affairs, the Grand Councillors and the Secretaries to the Grand Council must be the foci of attention; the latter had more influence in the drafting of Edicts and such documents than did the high dignitaries of the Grand Secretariat who were not in the Council, yet we have at present few studies regarding them.

Finally, for an understanding of Manchu policy attention must be centered upon the personality of the Emperor and the influences affecting him. Our survey indicates that the Emperor was required to play a part, passive though it might be, in the making of every important decision. This fact of personal rule has been commented upon for generations past, yet its implications, from an administrative point of view, have seldom been explored. From the summary of procedure given above, it is patent that the Emperor was obliged to act as a sort of clearing-house for all important matters. We may well inquire whether this did not produce a bottle-neck in the flow of administrative business. Under an Emperor of only ordinary vigor it is a pertinent question whether the press of routine work did not stifle both his initiative and his adaptability.

later fate of returned memorials is a puzzling question. Hsü (1) 186 describes the vast number of Tsou-pên, over 100,000 for the Ch'ien-lung period, preserved in the Palace archives. The question whether and in what manner returned memorials would have found their way into the archives demands further attention.

In other words, the central administration of the Ch'ing, and indeed the whole Chinese tradition of the personal rule of the Son of Heaven, demanded a superman at the head of affairs. The lack of a superman, and the rapid multiplication of state affairs, must be an important factor in the collapse of the Manchu administration during the nineteenth century. Considerations such as the above challenge the attention of the political scientist, while for the diplomatic historian they are all-important.

4. SELECT LIST OF PUBLISHED COLLECTIONS OF CH'ING DOCUMENTS

This list is presented partly to facilitate references in section 5 below and partly to call this material to the attention of students who have not been specializing in bibliography. The list is in no sense exhaustive, and new collections of documents are continually appearing. It is meant to include the chief examples of the material now available, which would not be out of place in every Chinese library. Several collections of documents obviously based on collections here noticed have been omitted. There is a large and rapidly growing critical bibliography relating to these various collections, the description of which is beyond the scope of this paper; but attention should be called to an early comprehensive study of Ch'ing historical literature in general by Erich HAENISCH (Das Ts'ing-shi-kao und die sonstige chinesische Literatur zur Geschichte der letzten 300 Jahre, *AM* 6.403-44 [1930]) and to the recent study by K. N. BIGGERSTAFF, Some Notes on the Tung-hua lu and the Shih-lu (*HJAS* 4.101-15), in which further references may be found. There is an obvious need for further studies similar to Prof. BIGGERSTAFF's and dealing with single collections. For a more complete list of Palace Museum publications of documents than that here presented, cf. KOESTER.

Chang-ku ts'ung-pien 掌故叢編 (Collected Historical Documents) pub. monthly by the Department of Historical Records (Wên Hsien Kuan 文獻館), Palace Museum, Peiping; first issue Jan. 1928, beginning with the eleventh issue the title was changed to *Wên-hsien ts'ung-pien* 文獻叢編, see below.

ON THE TYPES AND USES OF CH'ING DOCUMENTS

Chin-tai Chung-kuo wai-chiao shih tzu-liao chi-yao 近代中國外交史資料輯要 (A Source Book of Important Documents Relating to the Modern Diplomatic History of China), compiled with prefaces by CHIANG T'ing-fu 蔣廷黻 (T. F. TSIANG), 2 vols. Shanghai 1931-4.

Ch'ing-chi wai-chiao shih-liao 清季外交史料 (Historical Materials Concerning Foreign Relations in the Late Ch'ing Period 1875-1911), 218 chüan, 卷首 1 chüan, and for the Hsüan-t'ung Period (1908-11) 24 chüan, compiled by WANG Yen-wei 王彥威 and WANG Liang 王亮 Peiping 1932-5.

Ch'ing Hsüan-t'ung ch'ao Chung-Jih chiao-shê shih-liao 清宣統朝中日交涉史料 (Historical Materials Concerning Sino-Japanese Relations in the Hsüan-t'ung Period 1908-11), 6 chüan, Palace Museum, Peiping 1932.

Ch'ing Kuang-hsü ch'ao Chung-Fa chiao-shê shih-liao 清光緒朝中法交涉史料 (Historical Materials Relating to Sino-French Relations in the Kuang-hsü Period 1875-1908), 22 chüan, Palace Museum, Peiping 1933.

Ch'ing Kuang-hsü ch'ao Chung-Jih chiao-shê shih-liao 清光緒朝中日交涉史料 (Historical Materials Concerning Sino-Japanese Relations in the Kuang-hsü Period 1875-1908), 88 chüan, Palace Museum, Peiping 1932.

Ch'ing san-fan shih liao 清三藩史料 (Historical Materials Concerning the Three Feudatories of the Early Ch'ing Period, i. e. WU San-kuei et al.), 5 vols., Palace Museum, Peiping 1932.

Ch'ing-tai wai-chiao shih-liao 清代外交史料 (Historical Materials Concerning Foreign Relations in the Ch'ing Period), 6 vols. for the Chia-ch'ing period 1796-1820 and 4 vols. for the Tao-kuang period 1821-50, Palace Museum, Peiping 1932-3.

Ch'ing-tai wên-tzu-yü tang 清代文字獄檔 (Archives on the Ch'ing Literary Inquisition), 12 vols., Palace Museum, Peiping 1931 et seq.

Ch'ou-pan i-wu shih-mo 籌辦夷務始末 (The Complete Account of Our Management of Barbarian Affairs), photolithograph of the original compilation, 80 chüan for the later Tao-kuang period 1836-50, presented to the Emperor 1856; 80 chüan for the Hsien-fêng period 1851-61, presented 1867; 100 chüan for the T'ung-chih period 1862-74, presented 1880; Palace Museum, Peiping 1930.

Chu-p'i shang-yü 硃批上諭, same as *Chu-p'i yü-chih*, q. v.

70

Chu-p'i yü-chih 硃批諭旨 (Vermilion Endorsements and Edicts [of the Yung-chêng Period 1723-35, Including the Memorials Concerned]), preface of the Ch'ien-lung Emperor dated 1738, 112 vols.

I-wu shih-mo, see Ch'ou-pan i-wu shih-mo.

Ku-kung o-wên shih-liao 故宮俄文史料 ("Documents in Russian Preserved in the National Palace of Peiping," K'ang-hsi and Ch'ien-lung periods, 1662-1722 and 1736-95), compiled by LIU Tsê-jung 劉澤榮, with Chinese translation by WANG Chih-hsiang 王之相, pp. 312, Peiping 1936.

Liu-shih-nien-lai Chung-kuo yü Jih-pên 六十年來中國與日本 (China and Japan in the Last Sixty Years), 7 vols., compiled by WANG Yün-shêng 王芸生, Tientsin 1932-4.

Ming-ch'ing shih-liao 明清史料 (Historical Materials of the Ming and Ch'ing Periods), 4 vols., edited by the Institute of History and Philology, Academia Sinica, 1930-1.

Ming-ch'ing shih-liao i-pien 乙編 (second series), 10 vols., Commercial Press, Shanghai 1936.

Shêng-hsün, see Shih-ch'ao shêng-hsün.

Shih-ch'ao shêng-hsün 十朝聖訓 (Sacred Instructions or Exhortations of Ten Reigns, 1616-1874), 922 chüan, 286 vols., last preface Jan. 6, 1880.

Shih-liao hsün-k'an 史料旬刊 (Historical Materials Published Every Ten Days), 40 vols., Palace Museum, Peiping 1930-1.

Shih-liao ts'ung-k'an ch'u-pien 史料叢刊初編 (Miscellaneous Historical Materials, First Series), 10 vols., compiled by Lo Chên-yü 羅振玉, Tung-fang hsüeh-hui, 1924.

Shih-liao ts'ung-pien 史料叢編 (Miscellaneous Historical Materials), 12 vols., compiled by Lo Chên-yü 羅振玉, 1933.

Shih-lu, see Ta-ch'ing li-ch'ao shih-lu.

Ta-ch'ing li-ch'ao shih-lu 大清歷朝實錄 (Veritable Records of Successive Reigns of the Ch'ing Dynasty), 4485 chüan, Ōkura Shuppan Kabushiki Kaisha 大藏出版株式會社, Tōkyō 1937-8; cf. W. FUCHS, Beiträge zur mandjurischen Bibliographie und Literatur, Tōkyō 1936, 58-71.

T'ai-p'ing t'ien-kuo chao-yü 太平天國詔諭 (Proclamations and Edicts of the T'ai-p'ing t'ien-kuo Era), compiled by HSIAO I-shan, 1 vol.,

National Academy of Peiping 1935. Also *T'ai-p'ing t'ien-kuo ts'ung-shu* 太平天國叢書 (Collected Writings of the T'ai-p'ing t'ien-kuo) compiled by the same, 10 vols., Shanghai 1936.

T'ai-p'ing t'ien-kuo wên-shu 太平天國文書 (Documents on the T'ai-p'ing t'ien-kuo), 1 vol., Palace Museum, Peiping 1933.

Tung-hua lu 東華錄, various editions; cf. K. N. BIGGERSTAFF in *HJAS* 4. 101-15.

Wên-hsien ts'ung-pien 文獻叢編 (Collectanea from the Historical Records Office), 19 vols., Palace Museum, Peiping 1930-7.

Yung-chêng shang-yü 雍正上諭 (Edicts of the Yung-chêng Emperor, 1723-35), 24 vols., compiled by CHANG T'ing-yü 張廷玉 and others, 1741.

5. CATALOGUE OF TYPES OF DOCUMENTS

One type of document is distinguished from another chiefly by the character or characters that introduce the main body of the text. Thus an Edict normally begins simply with the character *yü*, meaning in effect that the Emperor issued the Edict which then follows. Memorials usually begin with the memorialist's official title and name, followed by a character which indicates the type of the memorial. But in the case of less important documents, such as correspondence between minor local officials, classification by this method becomes less trenchant, and the highly technical documentary phraseology gradually evaporates into the dull words of every day. We have tried to draw the line at the point where this unhappy process becomes noticeable (cf. e.g. GILES 9816).

This catalogue is arranged alphabetically by WADE-GILES romanization and is meant to serve two purposes. In the first place, we wish to suggest English designations for the commoner types of documents in order to facilitate the establishment of a generally accepted usage among western translators. An accepted usage is particularly desirable because much research on modern China will probably be published without benefit of Chinese characters. The old custom, each translator his own terminology, is likely to produce a confusion of edicts, decrees, mandates, commands, and other referents that will tax our mental agility. Fortunately, western research on the Ch'ing period is so little advanced that the opportunity still exists to agree upon a common vocabulary, with the efficiency and economy which it would provide, providing a miraculous coöperation to that end can be achieved. We hope therefore that the suggestions of other workers, which will be offered in modification of our own, will be given publicity. It is not the object of the present compilation to put forward a revised terminology; we have tried, like the sage, merely to codify that which is already established. As with a system of romanization, English translations of Chinese terms are often mere conventions. It is important first that the translation should be reasonably accurate in meaning, and then that it should follow the tradition to be found in the literature of the field.

All translators of Ch'ing documents will be familiar with three text-books, in which the traditional usage is chiefly recorded:

1. T. F. WADE, 文件自邇集 *Wên-chien tzŭ-erh chi*, A series of papers selected as specimens of Documentary Chinese, designed to assist students of the language as written by the officials of China; in sixteen parts with key, London 1867, 2 vols;

2. F. HIRTH, 新關文件錄 *Hsin-kuan wên-chien lu*, Text Book of Documentary Chinese, with a vocabulary, for the special use of the Chinese Customs Service, Shanghai 1885, 2 vols, cited as HIRTH;

3. The second edition of No. 2, rearranged, enlarged, and edited by C. H. BREWITT-TAYLOR, Shanghai 1909-10, 2 vols., is cited as BREWITT-TAYLOR.

To these volumes should be added W. F. MAYERS, *The Chinese Government*[3], Shanghai 1896, revised by G. M. H. PLAYFAIR, Appendix sec. 3, " Forms of Official Correspondence "; and H. A. GILES, *A Chinese-English Dictionary*[2], Shanghai 1912. All these works were compiled by men who had spent long years in official service in China, often in daily correspondence with the authorities. The translations of Chinese terms which they adopted, especially those in GILES' dictionary, which we cite frequently below, represent the considered usage of a generation or more of consular and customs officials. They have entered so largely into the literature on nineteenth century China that little can be gained by a wanton revision of terms, except where clarity makes it necessary. On the other hand, it must be remembered that these observers were not versed in the inner workings of the metropolitan administration, knew little of its procedure, and were not personally acquainted with many types of documents which have been published from the archives in the last decade. What follows is intended to supplement rather than to include the notes and suggestions available in BREWITT-TAYLOR.

In the second place, this catalogue is intended to indicate how a given type of document was used, again for the convenience of western students. To this end, references have been given where possible to published examples of each type. We omit from the list minor variations of a given type and also a multitude of names of various kinds of archives and records which are referred to by modern Chinese archivists (see note 7 above) but the exact nature of which is not always clear, and which are in any case not available to students outside the archives. It has not seemed worth while to record the formal phraseology with which each type of document normally begins and ends; many follow the form exemplified in the Chao-hui, beginning . . . wei chao-hui shih 爲照會事 (in the matter of a communication) and ending . . . hsü-chih chao-hui chê 須至照會者 (a necessary communication), cf. BREWITT-TAYLOR 2. 10 " Col. 12."

A division of the catalogue into sub-categories would not be easy, for there is no sharp and useful dividing line between documents exchanged between government offices and documents submitted to the Emperor, nor between the latter and documents issued by the Emperor. To facilitate the study of related types we offer the following incomplete analytical summary.

1. DOCUMENTS EXCHANGED BETWEEN GOVERNMENT OFFICES

In the Chinese scheme of things the typological names of these documents often serve to indicate the relative rank of the correspondents. This relationship can be indicated in translation only by a convention, since documents of this sort in the west would nearly all be called despatches. To indicate the three general forms of relationship between the correspondents, we suggest Order or Orders (from a superior), Communication (from an equal), and Report (from a subordinate or inferior); these might also be rendered " a despatch ordering," or " a despatch communicating," and so on. A despatch from an inferior in rank who is not a direct subordinate presents a nice problem, which we have not tried to solve.

Communications: Chao-hui, Chao-fu, Chih-hui, I-hui, I-tzŭ, I-wên, Kung-han, Tzŭ, Tzŭ-ch'êng, Tzŭ-hsing, Tzŭ-hui, Tzŭ-pao, Tzŭ-wên.

Despatches from ministers of state, in most cases the Grand Council, conveying imperial Edicts or the like: Chi-hsin, Chiao-chih, Chiao-p'ien, Ch'üan-yü, Han, T'ing-chi, Tzŭ-chi.

Orders: Cha, Cha-fu, Ku-tieh, Kuan-wên, Ling, P'ai, P'ai-p'iao, Tieh.

Petitions: several of the entries below under Reports are translated as Petition in certain contexts, e. g. when presented to an official by a commoner.

Reports: Ch'êng, Ch'êng-wên, Hsiang-wên, Ping, Shên, Shên-wên, Tieh-ch'êng, Tzŭ-ch'êng.

2. DOCUMENTS SUBMITTED TO THE EMPEROR

Copies of memorials: Chieh-t'ieh, Fu-pên, Shih-shu, Lu-shu.
Endorsed memorials: Hung-pên, see also P'i-hung.
Memorials: Chê-tsou, Ch'i-pên, Liu-ts'ao chang-tsou, Pên-chang, Piao-chang, Piao-pên, Po-pên, Pu-pên, T'i-pên, T'i-tsou, Tsou-chê, Tsou-pên, T'ung-pên.
Summaries of memorials: Lu-shu, Shih-shu, T'ieh-huang.
Supplementary memorials: Chia-p'ien, Fu-p'ien, Fu-tsou, P'ien, P'ien-tsou, Tsou-p'ien.
Tributary memorials: Kung-piao, Wai-fan piao-chang.

3. DOCUMENTS ISSUED FROM THE EMPEROR

Commands: Ch'ih, Ch'ih-yü, Ch'üan-ch'ih, Tso-ming-ch'ih.
Decrees: Chih, Chih-shu, Chih-tz'ŭ, Ling-chih.

Edicts: Chu-yü, Shang-yü, Yü, Yü-chih.
Endorsements: Chu-pi, Chu-p'i, P'i-hung, Yü-p'i.
Instructions: Hsün-yü, Shêng-hsün.
Ordinance: Kao.
Patents: Ch'ih-ming, Kao-ming, Ts'ê.
Proclamations: Chao, Chao-huang, Chao-kao.
Rescript: Chih.
Utterances in general: Ssŭ-lun, copies: T'a-huang and T'êng-huang.

4. DOCUMENTS ENCLOSED IN OTHER DOCUMENTS
Chia-p'ien, Ch'ing-tan, Ch'ing-ts'ê, Huang-ts'ê, Pao-hsiao-ts'ê, P'ien, Tsou-hsiao-ts'ê.

CHA 扎 or 劄 ORDER
A document sent from a superior to a subordinate, GILES 127, 142; an order from a superior to a subordinate under his jurisdiction, *Tz'ŭ-hai* 辭海 (no better authority found).
Ex.: *Shih-liao hsün-k'an* 7.221, from the Grand Council to provincial officials. For 劄 cf. *Chang-ku ts'ung-pien* 2. section 2.15a, from the Grand Council to the Ch'ang Lu salt administrator.

CHA-FU 劄付 ORDER
Used from provincial treasurers to prefects and magistrates, MAYERS 139; from provincial commanders-in-chief to Prefects and lower local officials, and from provincial Governors to Colonels and lower military officials, *Tz'ŭ-hai* citing *Ch'ing-hui-tien* (exact reference not found).
Ex.: photographs of originals issued by WU San-kuei, *Ch'ing san-fan shih-liao* 2 and 3.

CHA-HSING 劄行 DECLARATION
By the treaty of Nanking 1842 art. xi, Chinese high officers in the provinces were to address subordinate British officers under the term "Declaration" (Cha-hsing), but the term did not become well established and was superseded by Chao-hui; cf. also French treaty of Whampoa 1844 art. xxxiii.
Ex.: HIRTH no. 48, Tsungli Yamên to Inspector General of Customs 1870; no. 66, same to same 1882.

CHAO 詔 Imperial PROCLAMATION, MANDATE
One of the Ssŭ-lun, q. v., uttered by the Emperor; see also under Kao; to announce to the people as has been the custom for Emperors since the time of the Han dynasty, GILES 470.
Ex.: *Ho-pei ti-i po-wu-yüan pan-yüeh-k'an* 河北第一博物院半月刊 (Semi-monthly Publication of the First Museum of Hopei) no. 17, May 25, 1932, a circular order of the Shun-chih period for the seizure of CHÊNG Ch'êng-kung (Koxinga); *Yung-chêng shang-yü*, K'ang-hsi 61st year, eleventh month.

CHAO-FU 照覆 [or 復] COMMUNICATION IN REPLY
A reply to a Chao-hui, q. v.
Ex.: *Wên-hsien ts'ung-pien* 23. section 2. 1b, from Lord Elgin to Prince Kung 1860.

CHAO-HUANG 詔黃 Yellow bill bearing a PROCLAMATION
A copy of an imperial utterance (Sssŭ-lun) written in black on yellow paper; another name for T'êng-huang, q. v.

CHAO-HUI 照會 COMMUNICATION
Addressed to an official slightly inferior in rank; MAYERS 139 gives eight situations in which it was used; the treaty of Nanking 1842 art. xi declares that " Her Britannic Majesty's Chief High Officer in China shall correspond with the Chinese High Officers, both at the Capital and in the Provinces, under the term ' Communication ' 照會 " (Chao-hui). By degrees the term became accepted for correspondence between Chinese and foreign officials generally, irrespective of rank. The American treaty of Wanghsia 1844 art. xxx provided that Chao-hui should be used by the superior authorities, the consuls, and the local officers, civil and military, of both countries. The French treaty of Whampoa 1844 art. xxxiii followed the British definition. Cf. *Ch'ing-chi ko-kuo chao-hui mu-lu* 清季各國照會目錄 (Index of Communications with the Various Countries in the Late Ch'ing Period), Palace Museum, Peiping 1935.
Ex.: *Shih-liao hsün-k'an* 4. 108b, reference to a Chao-hui to the ruler of Annam in the Yung-chêng period; *Wên-hsien ts'ung-pien* 17, photograph of a Chao-hui of 1884.

CHAO-KAO 詔誥 Imperial PROCLAMATIONS AND ORDI-NANCES

Used as a general term for imperial pronouncements of several kinds, equivalents to the Ssŭ-lun, q. v. Cf. P'ÊNG Wên-chang 彭蘊章, preface to the *Nei-ko han-p'iao-ch'ien chung-shu shê-jên t'i-ming* 內閣漢票簽中書舍人題名 (Names of the Secretaries of the Chinese Registry of the Grand Secretariat), edition 1861, 2. 4-5: "Proclamations and ordinances are the chief writings of the Grand Secretariat" (also quoted by Hsü [1] 183).

CHÊ-PÊN 折本 MEMORIAL

Lit. folded memorial, i.e. with the corner of one sheet turned down; done by the Emperor when reading it, to mark it for further treatment. Cf. *Nei-ko hsiao-chih* (A Brief Sketch of the Grand Secretariat) 3 line 9; "When the Emperor looked at the memorials, if there were some on which he wished to change the draft proposal (ch'ien 簽), then he would turn down one corner and send it out . . . ." The memorials so marked were then brought in for discussion when the ministers had audience with the Emperor, cf. *Chia-ch'ing hui-tien* 2. 17a line 10; 8a line 8: "After Pu-pên have been submitted, those which have not yet received an Edict or Rescript in reply and have been folded (chê pên) and sent down are collected and stored according to the day."

CHÊ-TSOU 摺奏 MEMORIAL

Same as Tsou-pên, q. v.; the terms Chê-tsou and Tsou-chê occur more often than Tsou-pên; the latter has been used in the text above for convenience, to contrast with T'i-pên.

Ex.: *Shih-liao hsün-k'an* 1 gives examples beginning with title, date, and chin-tsou 謹奏 (reverently memorializes), and ending with chin-tsou and date; *Wên-hsien ts'ung-pien* 6. third section. 1.

CH'ÊNG 呈 REPORT, Petition

Addressed by subordinate to superior officials; used by minor district officials to Prefects, MAYERS 140; when addressed to an official by a commoner, Petition, cf. *Fa-lü ta-tz'ŭ-shu* 法律大辭書 (Dictionary of Legal Terms), Shanghai 1936, 534; also used of presentation of documents to the Emperor.

Ex.: *Ch'ing san-fan shih-liao* 2. 111 et passim; *Shih-liao hsün-k'an* 13. 445a.

CH'ÊNG-WÊN 呈文 REPORT, Petition

Addressed by subordinates to superiors, same as Ch'êng; cf. MAYERS 140.

Ex.: *Chang-ku ts'ung-pien* 10. 3.

CH'I-CHÜ-CHU 起居注 CHRONICLES

Lit. Notes of the Emperor's activity,—a brief day-by-day record of the Emperor's actions, chiefly those of a ceremonial and routine administrative nature, nominally including both his statements and his movements, recorded by a staff of officials in a separate department (Ch'i Chü Chu Kuan 館, BRUNNERT 204: Office for Keeping a Diary of the Emperor's Movements; we prefer to follow the translation suggested by Dr. FERGUSON, *Wên-hsien lun-ts'ung* 33). These notes were sent to the Grand Secretariat at the end of each year and kept in the storehouse. They were based partly on the duplicate copies of memorials which were sent to the Grand Secretariat; see under Chieh-t'ieh. For the regulations regarding types of material to be included in the Chronicles cf. *Chia-ch'ing hui-tien shih-li* 792. 8b.

Ex.: *Shih-liao ts'ung-k'an ch'u-pien* 4 et passim; *Shih-liao hsün-k'an* 1. 16a; *Shih-liao ts'ung-pien* passim.

CH'I-PÊN 啓本 MEMORIAL

Practically the same as T'i-pên: memorials presented to the regent of the Shun-chih period in 1644-6, after which the form was no longer used; cf. HSÜ (1) 187-8; *Tung-hua lu* June 5, 1646 (Shun-chih 6. 5b, 1911 edition).

Ex.: *Ming-ch'ing shih-liao* 2. 102 et passim; *Ch'ing san-fan shih-liao* 1. 2.

CHIA-P'IEN 夾片 SUPPLEMENTARY MEMORIAL

Lit. inserted slip; submitted with a memorial for the purpose of adding to it after it had been formally concluded; but see under P'ien.

Ex.: *Shih-liao hsün-k'an* 10. 350b.

CHIAO-CHIH 交旨 DESPATCH

Lit. to transfer a Rescript: from ministers of state to subordinate departments, ordering that certain action be taken in accordance with an imperial decision; cf. *Kuo-hsüeh lun-wên so-yin* 國學論文索引 (Index to sinological articles) 3. 113: "... after the ministers have received the imperial will, they transmit it to their subordinates to be carried out accordingly,—this is called Chiao-chih."

Ex.: *Tung-fang tsa-chih* 東方雜誌 (*The Eastern Miscellany*), sixth year (1909) nos. 3, 13.

CHIAO-P'IEN 交片 SHORT DESPATCH

From ministers of state (Grand Councillors) to other departments; see also under P'ien; cf. TÊNG Chih-ch'êng 196.
Ex.: *Wên-hsien ts'ung-pien* 14. section 2. 2.

CHIEH-T'IEH 揭帖 1. placard, 2. duplicate COPY

1. In common parlance, a placard,—usually of a libellous or seditious character; also an accusation, a plaint (GILES 1455).
Ex.: *Shih-liao hsün-k'an* 5. 143b, copy of a seditious placard. This meaning appears to have been used also technically in the procedure, cf. *Chia-ch'ing hui-tien* 2. 6: " To T'ung-pên . . . on which there is writing in improper form or a seal which is not clear or a date which is erased and rewritten, the Transmission Office should attach a placard 加揭帖."

2. Duplicate copy of a memorial of any kind; according to the statutes three such copies were to be made, at least of T'ung-pên; cf. *Chia-ch'ing hui-tien* 54. 13b: " Three copies accompany a memorial 隨本之揭帖三; one is kept at the (Transmission) Office, one is sent to the Board (in question), one is sent to the Section (of the Office of Scrutiny of the Censorate, i. e. the particular Section concerned with the Board in question). Five days after a T'i-pên has been sealed and sent to the Grand Secretariat (from the Transmission Office), the duplicate copies for the Board and the Section are handed to the Superintendents of Military Posts for distribution." The existence of these duplicate copies necessitated repeated efforts at secrecy; and it was ordered that the

copies should on no account be distributed until five days after the original T'i-pên had been sent to the Grand Secretariat; cf. *Chia-ch'ing hui-tien shih-li* 781. 7b, memorial sanctioned in 1734. In addition to the copies already mentioned, in 1729 it was decided that "for all T'i-pên and Tsou-pên of the various provinces one additional copy (chieh-t'ieh) shall be written and sent to the Chronicles Office (Ch'i Chü Chu Kuan, BRUNNERT 204: Office for Keeping a Diary of the Emperor's Movements). After it has been used in compiling the records, the copy shall then be sent to the Grand Secretariat for preservation"; cf. *Kuang-hsü hui-tien shih-li* 14. 35b (by count; next to last page of the chüan); Hsü (1) 188.

Ex.: *Wên-hsien ts'ung-pien* 13 passim; *Ming-ch'ing shih-liao* 1, 2 passim. Chieh-t'ieh end with the formula "In addition to preparing a T'i-pên (Tsou-pên, Ch'i-pên), there is dutifully prepared a copy; a required copy" 除具題外 (or 除具奏外, or 啟外), 理合具揭, 須至揭帖者. Apparently as a development of the above, we find that reports of legal cases were called Hsing-pu 刑部 chieh-t'ieh; cf. *Fa-lü ta-tz'ŭ-shu* 1426. There were also Ping-pu 兵部 chieh-t'ieh; cf. *Wên-hsien ts'ung-pien* 13. 3.

CHIEN 柬 LETTER

Lit. a slip of paper; chien-shu 柬書 a note, a letter,—written on a card, GILES 1668.
Ex.: *Shih-liao hsün-k'an* 2. 61b, 63b, from the ruler of Annam to Chinese Governors-General regarding a boundary settlement.

CHIH 旨 Imperial RESCRIPT, imperial DECREE

Fundamentally, the imperial will; hence, the imperial decision on a memorial, recorded in red ink on the original. In practice it appears usually to be translated Rescript when found attached to the memorial, Decree when there is no reference to the original memorial. Differs from an Edict (yü) in that the latter is throughout a separate document; differs from an Endorsement (p'i) usually by giving specific rather than routine orders regarding the subject matter of the memorial. In length a Rescript is usually shorter than an Edict, longer than an Endorsement. Rescripts were drafted by the Grand Secretariat, Edicts by the Grand Council; cf. *Shu-yüan chi-lüeh* 22. 2b.

Ex.: Decrees (chih) published separately: *Ch'ing-tai wên-tzu-yü tang* 2. section 4. 3, section 5. 4; 4. section 3. 4, section 7. 4.

CHIH 制 Imperial DECREE

One of the imperial utterances (Ssŭ-lun), q.v.; examination lists, patents, and the like began with the phrase "Having received from Heaven the imperial succession, the Emperor decrees as follows . . ." 奉天承運皇帝制曰.

Ex.: *Wên-hsien ts'ung-pien* 14. photographic reproduction.

CHIH–HUI 知會 COMMUNICATION

Lit. to notify, to inform; used in correspondence between government offices; similar to I-hui, q.v., except that the latter appears usually to send documents as well as to inform about a subject, whereas Chih-hui merely informs.

Ex.: *Ming-ch'ing shih-liao* 7. 699, from the Board of Ceremony to the Inspectorate of the Grand Secretariat (Chi Ch'a Fang); *Wên-hsien ts'ung-pien* 21. section 2. 1 from the Imperial Household to the Board of Ceremony.

CHIH–SHU 制書 Imperial DECREE

An imperial command, GILES 1910; lettre du souverain, COUVREUR 859; Ta-ch'ing lü-li an-yü 大清律例按語 (Commentary on the *Ta-ch'ing lü-li*) 1847 edition, preface by HUANG Ên-t'ung 黃恩彤 3. 4 chih-shu section: "The words of the Son of Heaven are called Chih; Shu is then the recording of his words, as in Chao 詔, Ch'ih 敕, Yü 諭, Cha; matters which have been memorialized, sanctioned, and put into practice are not in this category."

CHIH–TZ'U 制辭 Imperial DECREE

Appears to be practically the same as Chih alone, q.v.

CH'IH 敕, 勅, or 勑 IMPERIAL COMMAND

One of the imperial utterances, see Ssŭ-lun.

CH'IH–MING 敕命 PATENT BY COMMAND

Used to confer titles of honor on officials below the fifth rank, and others; cf. *Chia-ch'ing hui-tien* 2. 4b: "The conferring of titles by imperial command on the dependencies of the empire (wai-fan, i.e. in Mongolia, Tibet, etc.), the extending of favor and conferring of titles of honor on officials of the sixth rank and below, and hereditary nobility not in perpetuity (i.e. gradually diminished), is (done by) a patent by command." It must follow a fixed form, according to the rank involved.

Ex.: *Wên-hsien ts'ung-pien* 14, photographic reproduction.

CH'IH–SHU 敕書 Letters PATENT

Similar to Kao-ch'ih, q.v.

CH'IH–YÜ 敕諭 COMMAND–EDICT (?)

Used to depute officials and to issue special edicts; there are many different forms, among which are two sub-types: (1) a Nominative Command (Tso-ming ch'ih), and (2) a Transmitted Command (Ch'üan-ch'ih); cf. *Chia-ch'ing hui-tien* 2. 4b: "Instructions and announcements to the dependencies of the empire (wai-fan) and officials in the provinces by means of Nominative Commands and Transmitted Commands are called Command Edicts"; *Ch'ien-lung hui-tien* 2. 5: "(In appointing) officials to posts outside the capital,—to Governors-General, Governors, Literary Chancellors, Salt Controllers, Superintendents of the Imperial Manufactories, provincial Commanders-in-chief, Brigade-Generals, et al., a Nominative Command is composed and issued; to provincial Financial Commissioners, Judicial Commissioners, Intendants, Grain Intendants, and Colonels, Lieut. Colonels, and Majors, a Transmitted Command only is given."

Ex.: *Shih-liao ts'ung-k'an ch'u-pien* 9. 1.

CHING–PAO 京報 PEKING GAZETTE

See under T'ang-pao.

CH'ING–TAN 清單 LIST, INVENTORY, etc.

A list of items; a general term,—the list may deal with any subject and may be used in any way, sometimes appended to other documents and submitted to the Emperor.

83

ON THE TYPES AND USES OF CH'ING DOCUMENTS 49

Ex.: *Wên-hsien ts'ung-pien* 14. last section; *Shih-liao hsün-k'an* 5. 159b, introduced by the phrase chi-k'ai 計開 (as follows).

CH'ING–TS'Ê 清册 or 青册 GREEN BOOK

Accounts, lists, reports, and such documents appended to memorials and submitted in yellow binding to the Emperor (i. e. Huang-ts'ê, q.v.) were copied and submitted to the metropolitan office concerned in a blue-green binding, whence the name Ch'ing-ts'ê. Thus Green Books were usually copies of Yellow Books, cf. Hsü (1). 190. Their origin (?) is explained as follows: in 1651 a Metropolitan Censor memorialized that "the ministers of the central government control the expenditure of the national revenue, the ministers of the provinces control its income. When the amount of income is not clear, then the amount of expenditure is obscure. It is requested that beginning in 1651 the office of the Financial Commissioner of each province should calculate the revenue of the entire province, dividing it into various items, and make a bound volume for submission to the Governor-General, Governor, and Judicial Commissioner of the province for their examination and comparison; this should respectfully be copied into a Yellow Book and the Governor should join (with the Governor-General) in memorializing the total amount submitting (the Yellow Book) along with the memorial for the Emperor's inspection. There should also be made a Green Book, which should be sent in a despatch to the various offices concerned at the capital, for examination and checking. Then it may be possible to put a stop to the provincial authorities' deceitful concealment, and it may also be possible to examine into the incongruities of the metropolitan authorities' (accounts)." Cf. *Tung-hua lu*, 1911 edition shun-chih 16. 17 line 4 (August 1, 1651).

Ex.: *Shih-liao ts'ung-k'an ch'u-pien* 7. sec. 2, sec. 3.

CHU–PI 硃筆 THE VERMILION PEN, or ENDORSEMENT

Same as Chu-p'i, q.v.

CHU–P'I 硃批 VERMILION ENDORSEMENT

A conventional term for an endorsement or comment (see under P'i) written on a memorial by the Emperor's own hand, as distinct

from P'i-hung (q.v.) made by the officials of the Grand Secretariat,—both being in red ink.
Ex.: *Shih-liao hsün-k'an* 1. 20b (in text), 21a (at end).

CHU-YÜ 硃諭 VERMILION EDICTS
Copies of imperial utterances, written in red on yellow paper, see under T'êng-huang.

CH'ÜAN-CH'IH 傳敕 TRANSMITTED COMMAND
From the Emperor to lower provincial officials and the dependencies of the empire, see under Ch'ih-yü.

CH'ÜAN-YÜ 傳諭 TRANSMITTED EDICT
Sent from the Grand Council to lower provincial officials and embodying in its text important imperial commands, a form of T'ing-chi, q.v.
Ex.: *Chang-ku ts'ung-pien* 7. 43b; *Shih-liao hsün-k'an* 6. 192.

FU 覆 interchangeable with 復 IN REPLY
Combined with the names of various kinds of documents to indicate a reply to the document received, as Chao-fu, q.v., Tzŭ-fu (cf. *Shih-liao hsün-k'an* 2. 64a), etc.

FU-PÊN 副本 COPY, duplicate of a T'i-pên
A copy made at the Grand Secretariat for preservation at the Office of Imperial Historiography (Huang Shih Ch'êng) after the imperial endorsement (copied onto the original T'i-pên in red ink) had been copied onto it in black ink; cf. Hsü (1) 188; *Chia-ch'ing hui-tien* 2. 6a: " For all memorials a duplicate is prepared: in addition to the original copy (chêng-pên 正本) of T'ung-pên and Pu-pên, a duplicate (fu-pên) is copied out. After the original memorial has obtained a Rescript, it is sent to the Section (k'o, i.e. one of the Six Sections of the Censorate). The duplicate is stored for reference."

FU-P'IEN 附片 SUPPLEMENTARY MEMORIAL
A memorial (Tsou-pên) sent under the same cover with another, usually on a different although related subject; but see under P'ien.

Ex.: those printed in *Shih-liao hsün-k'an* 4.130 et passim, are often headed p'ien, begin with the character tsai 再 (further), and are referred to in the conclusion as fu-p'ien; *op. cit.* 10.363b is headed fu-p'ien and concluded 謹附片具奏.

FU-TSOU 附奏 SUPPLEMENTARY MEMORIAL
Same as Fu-p'ien, q.v.

HAN 函 LETTER
An example of the breakdown of the traditional terminology; in general, a letter of any kind; GILES 3809 gives a dozen uses. In the later nineteenth century used by the Tsung-li ya-mên in its correspondence with other offices, often combined as mi-han 密函 (secret letter), hsin-han 信函 (letter), or tzŭ-han 咨函 (despatch-letter).

Ex.: *I-wu shih-mo*, T'ung-chih section 50.28b line 7, mi-han from the Ya-mên to high provincial authorities; id. line 10, the text of the letter referred to is headed hsin-han; id. 52.24a, tzŭ-han; *Chang-ku ts'ung-pien* 7, sec. 1.42a gives a document sent from the Grand Council in 1793 and designated han by the compiler.

HSIANG-WÊN 詳文 Detailed REPORT
Addressed by a subordinate to a superior, MAYERS 141 gives situations for its use.

Ex.: *Wên-hsien ts'ung-pien* 22, sec. 5.32b, a report of the British consul at Tientsin to LI Hung-chang; FAN Tsêng-hsiang 樊增祥, *Fan-shan chêng-shu* 樊山政書 (My Writings on Administration), Nanking 1910, 2.24.

HSÜN-YÜ 訓諭 INSTRUCTIONS AND EDICTS
Not a type of document; used to refer to edicts in general.
Ex.: *Chang-ku ts'ung-pien* 1, sec. 4.1; *Shih-liao hsün-k'an* 39.408a line 4.

HUANG-TS'Ê 黃册 YELLOW BOOK
Also called Pao-hsiao-ts'ê and sometimes Tsou-hsiao-ts'ê, q.v. Tax accounts, construction reports, examination results, and such documents submitted to the Emperor along with memorials, i.e.

in a manner similar to western " enclosures," were normally bound in yellow paper or silk, whence the name; see under Ch'ing-ts'ê. Yellow Books were thus key documents in routine administration; they dealt with a wide variety of subject and were of several different kinds; SHAN Shih-yüan (2) 272-5 lists some 60 different categories, classified by content, among those preserved in the Palace archives. WANG Chêng-kung 王正功, *Chung-shu tien-ku hui-chi* 中書典故彙紀 (Collected Notes on the History and Regulations of the Grand Secretariat) 1916 edition, 3.36b line 8, states that " the Yellow Books which are submitted along with the memorials of the various metropolitan officials and provincial Governors-General and Governors are given to the Records Office to be preserved in the Great Storehouse (of the Grand Secretariat) ." Most of them were submitted annually, some monthly and others triennially, and it has been estimated that the offices at the capital must have received every year well over 2000 volumes. Unfortunately these volumes appear to have been less valuable than memorials, from the point of view of the official historian, and only some 13,000 are now said to survive in the Palace archives; see Hsü (1) 190-4.

Ex.: *Shih-liao ts'ung-pien*, 二集, 3.

HUNG-PÊN 紅本 ENDORSED MEMORIAL

Lit. red memorial, so called because it bore an imperial Endorsement written on it in red ink by the officials of the Grand Secretariat after imperial approval of the form of Endorsement; see text, section 2. Two kinds of Hung-pên are distinguished, those submitted through the Grand Secretariat and those submitted through the Imperial Household Department (Nei Wu Fu). SHAN Shih-yüan (1) 150-1 quotes the passage in the *Collected Statutes* cited above in section 2 note 33, which defines Hung-pên as T'i-pên endorsed in red, and then adds his own observation that Hung-pên is another name for T'i-pên because they bear the memorialist's seal, which would be in red, while Po-pên, q. v., is another name for Tsou-pên because the latter do not bear the memorialist's seal. This explanation seems possible but improbable because it gives the term Hung-pên two meanings one of which includes the other (i. e. T'i-pên as a class include all T'i-pên endorsed in red). SHAN himself adheres in a previous article (2) 271 to the definition we prefer, given in the *Collected Statutes*. The subject deserves clarification.

I–HUI 移會 COMMUNICATION

Used in correspondence between government offices; similar to Chih-hui, except that it appears to imply the sending of documents as well as information.
Ex.: *Ming-ch'ing shih-liao* 7. 685-98, from the Board of War to the Archives Office, and also to the Inspectorate, of the Grand Secretariat.

I–TZU 移咨 COMMUNICATION

Between officials of equal or approximately equal rank; cf. GILES 12, 342.
Ex.: *Shih-liao hsün-k'an* 1. 19a line 4; *Chia-ch'ing hui-tien shih-li* 12. 22a, from Hanlin Academy to Grand Secretariat.

I–WÊN 移文 COMMUNICATION

Between officials of equal or approximately equal rank, cf. MAYERS 138.

KAO 稿 ROUGH DRAFT

Not a technical term but used to designate some published items.
Ex.: *Chang-ku ts'ung-pien* 1. sec. 1, drafts of edicts of the K'ang-hsi period; *Shih-liao hsün-k'an* 4. 108b, draft of a communication to Annam.

KAO 誥 ORDINANCE

One of the imperial utterances, see Ssŭ-lun; not greatly different from Chao (Proclamation); cf. *Ch'ien-lung hui-tien* 2. 2: " to announce to the empire is called Chao, to make manifest instructions is called Kao." Judging by the documents remaining in the archives, however, Hsü (1) 184 concludes that, in general, proclamations emanating from the Emperor were called Chao, while those from the father of the Emperor, the Great Empress Dowager, and the Empress Dowager, of which there are very few remaining, were called Kao. Three of the twenty-five imperial seals were used for issuing ordinances: to ministers and officials, for foreign countries, and the whole empire, respectively; cf. *Chiao-t'ai-tien pao-p'u* 交泰殿寶譜 (Imperial seals in the Chiao-t'ai Hall), Peiping 1929.

KAO–CH'IH 誥敕 PATENT

A collective term for Kao and Ch'ih considered together; credentials, letters patent (entitles the holder to use ch'in-ming, by imperial command), GILES 1943; see under Ch'ih-shu; cf. *Chia-ch'ing hui-tien* 2.21b: "the Patent Office (Kao Ch'ih Fang 房) has charge of the receiving and issuing of Patents; it investigates into their selection and drafting and the form in which it would be best to write them out." An imperial seal for conferring patents by command was used to seal Kao-ch'ih; cf. *Chiao-t'ai-tien pao-p'u*, cited above under Kao.

KAO–MING 誥命 PATENT BY ORDINANCE

Used to confer titles of honor on officials of the fifth rank and above, and others; cf. *Chia-ch'ing hui-tien* 2.4b: "to extend favor and confer titles of honor on officials of the fifth rank and above, and hereditary nobility which may be handed down in perpetuity (i.e. without diminution) is (done by) a patent by ordinance." It must follow a fixed form, according to the rank involved. See Ch'ih-ming.

K'OU–KUNG 口供 VERBAL DEPOSITION

Not a technical term, but used to designate material of the type indicated; viva voce evidence, GILES 6572.
Ex.: *Shih-liao hsün-k'an* 8.281.

KU–TIEH 故牒 ORDER

From superior to subordinate officials; cf. MAYERS 139 for typical situations.

KUAN–WÊN 關文 ORDER

From superiors to subordinates; cf. MAYERS 140 for typical situations; GILES 6368, a passport; no published examples found.

KUNG–HAN 公函 COMMUNICATION

Lit. official letters; a very general term, for despatches between independent departments of government; see Han; cf. *Fa-lü ta-tz'ŭ-shu* 法律大辭書 158: "Public documents used in communication between administrative organs which are not subordinate one to another, are called Kung-han."

KUNG–PIAO 貢表 TRIBUTARY MEMORIAL

The memorials submitted to the Emperor together with tribute objects from the rulers of the seven tributary states adjoining China, viz. Korea, Liu Ch'iu, Annam, Nan-chang 南掌 (or Lao-huo 老撾 on the southern border of Yünnan), Siam, Sulu, Burma, as listed in *Kuang-hsü hui-tien* 39.2.

Ex.: *Ku-kung yüeh-k'an* 故宮月刊 (The Palace Monthly) no. 5, Jan. 1930, photograph of a list of tribute from Annam.

KUNG–TAN 供單 DEPOSITION

Same as Kung-tz'ŭ, q.v.
Ex.: *Shih-liao hsün-k'an* 34.246, 250.

KUNG–TZ'U 供詞 DEPOSITION

Not a type of document; similar to K'ou-kung; the evidence in a case; GILES 6572.

Ex.: *Shih-liao hsün-k'an* 34.232b, recording both questions and answers in evidence; *I-wu shih-lo*, Tao-kuang section 68.37a, deposition of an official.

KUO–SHU 國書 National letter, CREDENTIALS

A document given to (the ruler of) a foreign country; in the nineteenth century and later, diplomatic credentials.

Ex.: *Shih-liao ts'ung-k'an*, ch'u-pien 1. sec. 2 a letter from the Emperor T'ai-tsung (1627-43) to the king of Korea; *Wên-hsien ts'ung-pien* 8.12b; *Chung-ying-fa wai-chiao tz'ŭ-tien* 中英法外交辭典 (Dictionary of Words and Phrases of International Law and Diplomacy in English and French with Chinese Translations), Ministry of Foreign Affairs 1925, 152-159.

LING 令 ORDER

A general term, not important as a type of Ch'ing document; a modern name for official documents used in proclaiming laws, appointing and dismissing officials, and generally for commands to subordinates, cf. *Fa-lü ta-tz'ŭ-shu* 253.

LING-CHIH 令旨 DECREE

Issued from the Emperor during the early years of the dynasty, apparently similar to ordinary Chih 旨.
Ex.: *Shih-liao ts'ung-pien* 4, of date 1644 and later.

LIU-TS'AO CHANG-TSOU 六曹章奏 MEMORIALS

Lit. memorials of the six (i. e. Boards) officials; another name for the Shih-shu, q. v.
Ex.: *Shih-liao ts'ung-pien* 4; *Shih-liao ts'ung-k'an*, ch'u-pien 6, summaries of the memorials of various of the Six Boards.

LU-SHU 錄書 COPIED MATERIALS

Summaries of Hung-pên kept at the Six Sections of the Censorate; see under Shih-shu.

LUN-YIN 綸音 IMPERIAL UTTERANCES

Lit. silken sounds, i.e. the Emperor's words, see under Ssŭ-lun.

P'AI 牌 ORDER

From superior to subordinate officials; MAYERS 140.
Ex.: *Ch'ing san-fan shih-liao* 5, photograph of a ling-p'ai 令.

P'AI-P'IAO 牌票 ORDER

From superior to subordinate officials, same as P'ai; cf. MAYERS 140.

PAO-HSIAO-TS'Ê 報銷册 REPORT, etc.

A common type of Huang-ts'ê, q. v.

PÊN-CHANG 本章 MEMORIAL

General term for T'i-pên and Tsou-chang 奏章 considered together.

91

P'I 批 ENDORSEMENT, COMMENT

A word of broad meaning used technically with reference to the notations made by an official on a memorial presented to him. In general such notations might be either comment or instructions, the latter probably couched in administrative jargon. Notations of the latter type, when made by or on behalf of the Emperor, correspond in a general way to the notations made by western rulers, cabinet ministers, and others, on the back or on the docket of a diplomatic document. In China the term was also used of the reply made by an official to a subordinate; GILES 9048 gives half a dozen such compounds. But the typical imperial notations, such as the set phrase chih-tao-liao (Noted) or kai-pu chih-tao (Let the Board in question be informed), are mere signals for administrative action, not comments or replies, and we have therefore suggested the translation Endorsement.

P'I–HUNG 批紅 RED ENDORSEMENT (lit. endorsed in red)

The act of writing onto a memorial in red ink the Endorsement which has been approved by the Emperor; unlike Vermilion Endorsements (Chu-p'i), a Red Endorsement was not added by the Emperor's own hand; see text section 2.

PIAO–CHANG 表章 Tributary MEMORIAL

A memorial to the Emperor; under the Ch'ing often a memorial from the ruler of a tributary state; see Kung-piao.
Ex.: *Ming-ch'ing shih-liao* 7. 641-64, from the king of Korea to the Emperor on a variety of subjects; *Ho-pei ti-i po-wu-yüan pan-yüeh-k'an* (Semi-monthly Publication of the First Museum of Hopei) 2. 1 (Oct. 10, 1931), photograph of Korean Piao-chang of the Ch'ien-lung period.

P'IEN 片 SHORT, SUPPLEMENTARY

Lit. a single sheet or slip of paper, which may be contrasted with chê 摺 as in Tsou-chê meaning a folded paper, i. e. a longer document. We are in doubt as to the exact implication of this term. In the phrases Chia-p'ien, Fu-p'ien, and Tsou-p'ien (q. v.) it sometimes appears to indicate an additional statement submitted to the Emperor along with a memorial; but it also denotes a brief memorial, or "minute," in answer to a Rescript or on a simple topic (so also with Ch'êng-p'ien, a supplementary or brief report). The problem is complicated by the fact that items headed P'ien are published without any indication as to whether they did or did not originally accompany another document.

Ex.: P'ien submitted in response to a Rescript, *Chang-ku ts'ung-pien* 1.12b, 2.17a, 7.28b, 8.49a-b, et passim. P'ien which appear as short informal memorials, *op. cit.* 7.42b, 44a, 8.58b, 59b, 62a, et passim; *Shih-liao hsün-k'an* 8.277a et passim prints P'ien of the Grand Council (Chün-chi-ch'u p'ien) which seem similar to western minutes; id. 13.471 gives both a memorial and the P'ien which accompanied it. The problem deserves further attention.

PING 稟 REPORT, PETITION

A general term, used technically of a document to a superior from a minor official or a common citizen.

Ex.: *Ch'ing san-fan shih-liao* 3.272 et passim; *Shih-liao hsün-k'an* 39.424b.

PING-CH'ÊNG 稟呈 REPRESENTATION

The French treaty of Whampoa 1844 art. xxxiii provided that French and Chinese merchants or other non-official persons should use the form Representation in addressing officials of the other country. We have found no examples of its use.

PING-MING 稟明 REPRESENTATION

By the treaty of Nanking 1842 art. xi, merchants and others not in official positions, either Chinese or British, were to address the British and Chinese officials, respectively, under the term Representation. The American treaty of Wanghsia 1844 art. xxx made a similar provision.

PO-PÊN 白本 UNENDORSED MEMORIAL

Lit. white memorial, as distinct from Hung-pên (red memorial) on which an imperial endorsement had been written in red ink; hence Po-pên are memorials (T'i-pên) which have not been seen by the Emperor, cf. Hsü (1) 186, SHAN Shih-yüan (1) 150-1. For further discussion, see under Hung-pên.

PU-PÊN 部本 MEMORIAL

Memorials of the T'i-pên type from the offices of government at the capital (pu-yüan); see text sec. 2; cf. *Chia-ch'ing hui-tien* 2.6a: " Memorials from the Six Boards and memorials from the offices of the various departments, palaces, courts, and superintendencies (in Peking), after they have been submitted to the Six Boards, are in general called Pu-pên." According to Hsü (1) 186, they were submitted in both Chinese and Manchu versions.

SHANG-YÜ 上諭 IMPERIAL EDICT

A rather general term, used to refer to Edicts (yü), and sometimes also to Rescripts (chih).
Ex.: *Shih-liao hsün-k'an* 6.178b-85. six examples beginning with date and " the Grand Secretariat has received an Imperial Edict " (nei-ko fêng shang-yü); *op. cit.* 7.237, two examples headed Shang-yü and beginning with date and " a Rescript has been received " (fêng chih).

SHÊN 申 REPORT

Addressed by subordinates to superior officials; GILES 9816 gives half a dozen compounds, the more important of which are given below.
Ex.: *Ch'ing san-fan shih-liao* 3.253 et passim.

SHÊN-CH'ÊNG 申呈 STATEMENT

By the treaty of Nanking 1842 art. xi, subordinate British officers were to address Chinese high officers in the provinces under the term Statement (Shên-ch'ên); but the term did not become firmly established, and was superseded by Chao-hui. The American treaty of Wanghsia 1844 art. xxx provided that Shên-ch'ên should be used by inferior officers of either government in addressing superior officers of the other. The French treaty of Whampoa 1844 art. xxxiii followed the British definition and called it " exposé."

SHÊN-CH'ÊNG 申稱 TO REPORT

See under Shên.

Ex.: HIRTH no. 48, Inspector General of Customs to Tsungli Yamên 1870.

SHÊN-WÊN 申文 REPORT

See under Shên; cf. MAYERS 140 for uses.

SHIH-SHU 史書 HISTORICAL MATERIALS

Copies of the summaries (T'ieh-huang) of endorsed memorials. Cf. *Kuang-hsü hui-tien* 69.3b: " All memorials that are received back (by the Six Sections of the Censorate) are added to the Shih-shu and Lu-shu (q.v.) . . . After Hung-pên have been sent for copying, two other copies are taken by the Section (k'o). Those presented to the official historians to be recorded are called Shih-shu; those stored at the Section for compilation are called Lu-shu. Both are proof-read and stamped with a seal; the Shih-shu are sent to the Grand Secretariat, and the Lu-shu are kept at the Section." According to SHAN Shih-yüan (1) 151, the Shih-shu now preserved in the storehouse of the Grand Secretariat are all copies of the T'ieh-huang (Summaries) of Hung-pên, not of the Hung-pên themselves in full. HSÜ (1) 188 agrees that Shih-shu are summaries of Hung-pên and so form a detailed index to the latter; in the Ming period, he adds, Shih-shu were called Liu-ts'ao chang-tsou (q.v.) and Lu-shu were called Lu-su 錄疏.

SSǓ-LUN 絲綸 IMPERIAL UTTERANCES

Lit. silken cords; cf. the *Li-chi* 禮記 (Book of Rites) 30, Tzǔ-i 緇衣 (COUVREUR 2.517): " the prince's words are like silk threads, they issue forth like cords " (GILES, s. v). A general term for Decrees, Proclamations, Ordinances, and Commands emanating from the Emperor; cf. *Chia-ch'ing hui-tien* 2.4a: " The Emperor's words (lun-yin) which are transmitted to the people are called Decree (Chih), Proclamation or Mandate (Chao), Ordinance (Kao), or Command (Ch'ih); all are drafted in proper form and submitted to the Emperor. Whenever there is a great ceremonial observance to be promulgated to all the officials, then the form Decree (chih-tz'ŭ) is used; whenever there is a great political matter to be announced to the ministers and the people and to be handed down as a rule of law, then the Proclamation or Ordinance is used. . . . All are drafted ahead of time and submitted to the Emperor, to reverently await the imperial decision. . . ."

T'A–HUANG 搨黃 YELLOW PRINTS

Printed copies of imperial utterances (Ssŭ-lun), see also under T'êng-huang; according to Hsü (1) 185, imperial utterances " which were printed on yellow paper from wood-cut blocks were called Yellow Prints, such as the Command-Edicts (ch'ih-yü) which were issued to the officials who had audience with the Emperor in the early Ch'ing period."

TANG 檔 ARCHIVE

Also Tang-an 檔案 and Tang-tzŭ 子, used extensively in compounds designating various archival collections. The ramifications of the Ch'ing archives are indicated in the literature cited above, note 7; no attempt is made to comprehend the subject in this paper.

T'ANG–PAO 塘報 PEKING GAZETTE

Lit. courier news, also called Ching-pao, Ti-ch'ao, Ti-pao, etc. Not a type of document but one of the chief means of dissemination of important documents into the provinces, consisting of copies of documents sent from the capital to the high provincial officials for their information; sometimes printed, and sometimes reprinted in the provinces for further circulation; also made up and distributed by private firms. The term Peking Gazette thus is a generic term, including many forms, both official and non-official. On T'ang-pao see our article " On the Transmission of Ch'ing Documents," *HJAS* 4, 35-6. The most thorough account of the subject in general is R. S. BRITTON, *The Chinese Periodical Press 1800-1912*, Shanghai 1933, 7-17, which also reproduces facsimiles. The Peking Gazette is an ideal subject for an extensive monograph. Ex.: BRITTON, *op. cit.*; *Ch'ing san-fan shih-liao* 3. 259 et passim; *Ming-ch'ing shih-liao* 2. 116 et passim. We take this occasion to present a document not otherwise available:

A memorial of August 5, 1842, presented by the Governor of Chekiang, LIU Yün-k'o 劉韻珂, and the acting Governor, PIEN Shih-yün 卞士雲, describes the private distribution of the Peking Gazette. It had been complained that copies were obtained and examined regularly by the British, who consequently knew the plans of the empire. " We would humbly observe that the Capital News (ching-pao 京報) respectfully copies the Edicts and Rescripts which are publicly issued from the Emperor every day, and it also inserts memorials (tsou-chê) from the ministers at the capital and in the provinces. Its original purpose was to acquaint the provincial authorities in detail with the affairs of the empire. All matters with which it is concerned can be dealt with forthwith; for this reason it has not been forbidden. But all councils of state are uniformly inserted in it in detail; it is essential that it be kept secret . . . (Measures would therefore be taken to apprehend the traitors who conveyed it to the English). . . . As to the Capital News which your servants read every day, it is copied and sent out by the Superintendent of Courier Posts stationed at the capital, and relayed by the Superintendent stationed at the provincial capital. But we have heard that aside from this there are also a Liang-hsiang News (良鄉報 i. e. from Liang-hsiang Hsien in Shun-t'ien Fu, Chihli) and a Cho-chou News 涿州報 i. e. from Cho-chou, also in Shun-t'ien Fu, Chihli). The matters which they publish are comparatively more detailed than the Superintendent of the Posts' News; and their transmission is also relatively faster. We hear that at Liang-hsiang and Cho-chou there are men who manage this business; and many of the officials and gentry at great expense buy and read these Gazettes. Consequently in the affairs of each province there are things of which the officials have not yet been informed and which others know ahead of them, and there are also things which the officials do not know and others do know. We would humbly observe that the transmission of the Capital News to the rebellious barbarians surely is the deed of traitorous natives in the other provinces, and it is to be feared that the men who copy and send it for them also are not limited to one place . . . (Measures should therefore be taken first at the capital itself)." *Documents Supplementary to the I-wu shih-mo, Based on the Chün Chi Ch'u Archives*, Tsing Hua University Library, no. 1504-5 [a ms.], courtesy of Dr. T. F. TSIANG.

T'ÊNG–HUANG 謄黃 YELLOW COPIES

Copies of imperial utterances (Ssŭ-lun); GILES 10, 884 gives the colloquial definition " yellow notices, in Chinese and Manchu, placarded in the street to announce some joyful event such as a general pardon, remission of the land-tax, etc."; Hsŭ (1) 185 gives the technical explanation,—" Proclamations and Ordinances, Command-Edicts (ch'ih-yü), and Palace examination lists [and other types of imperial utterances] were all written in black characters on yellow paper and were called Yellow Copies or Yellow Proclamations (chao-huang). Those which used yellow paper and vermilion characters were called Vermilion Edicts (chu-yü)." See T'a-huang.

TI–CH'AO 邸抄 PEKING GAZETTE
See under T'ang-pao.

TI–PAO 邸報 PEKING GAZETTE
See under T'ang-pao.

T'I–PÊN 題本 MEMORIAL
Memorials to the Emperor usually on routine public business and submitted through the Grand Secretariat, as contrasted with Tsou-pên, and Ch'i-pên, q. v. T'i-pên as a general type were further differentiated, according to their origin or the treatment they received, as T'ung-pên or Pu-pên, Hung-pên or Po-pên, and the like. The evolution of the T'i-pên is summarized in the text above, section 2 note 10. We summarize below SHAN Shih-k'uei's description of the regulations regarding the size and format of the T'i-pên (page references to his sources are inserted where possible):

The T'i-pên of the Ming and Ch'ing periods were not the same size. The Ming T'i-pên was generally smaller than the Tsou-pên, but in the Ch'ing period it was generally larger.

Since the Ming Tsou-pên was said to be one foot three inches from top to bottom (Chinese measurement), and the T'i-pên was said to be smaller, the latter must have measured about one foot (i. e. 14 English inches). T'i-pên of the Ch'ing period measured 7.9 in. (Chinese) vertically and 3.6 in. horizontally. Tsou-pên of the Ch'ing period measured 7 in. vertically and 3.4 in. horizontally. Thus both types of documents appear to have been smaller in the Ch'ing than in the Ming period. On the Ch'ing T'i-pên, the t'ang-k'ou (i. e. the space available for writing, exclusive of margins at top and bottom) was 5.3 inches. An edict of Aug. 17, 1652 (printed in *Tung-hua lu*), ordered that all memorials conform to the proper size.

The regulations for writing T'i-pên were on the whole the same in the Ming and Ch'ing periods. " In both cases, each page had six columns, and each column twenty characters. But in the Ming form there were twenty spaces (in each column); the ordinary text was written in (the lower) eighteen spaces, with the upper two spaces for honorary elevation of characters. The Ch'ing form also had twenty spaces, with ordinary text in (the lower) eighteen spaces and three spaces for honorary elevation (i.e. one space above the column),—this was a point of difference." It was settled in 1651 (*Ta-ch'ing hui-tien shih-li* 1042. 1) that references within a memorial to the imperial palaces should be elevated one space; to his majesty the Emperor, an imperial Edict, a Rescript, or anything imperial,—two spaces; to heaven and earth, the ancestral temples, the imperial tombs, temple names of Emperors, and Edicts and Rescripts of imperial ancestors,—three spaces, hence protruding one space into the upper margin.

In 1528 it had been settled that the chief offices, brevet titles, surnames and given names of officials should all be written in one column, with no limit as to the number of characters; and the Ch'ing followed this rule. In both cases the official title and personal name of the memorialist was followed by the phrase "reverently presents a T'i-pên regarding" a certain subject 謹題爲某事.

At the end came the phrase "reverently presented, requesting the imperial will" 謹題請旨.

The number of characters which might be written in a T'i-pên was not limited in the Ming period, although the total was required to be noted. In 1645, however, the Ch'ing established the regulation that no T'i-pên should exceed three hundred characters in length (*Chia-ch'ing hui-tien shih-li* 10. 2b line 7). "Although for memorials on criminal cases and on revenue matters it will be difficult to adhere to that number of characters, yet it is not permitted that they be repetitious and prolix. Take the main ideas of the memorial and gather them together in a summary (T'ieh-huang) in order to facilitate its being looked over; it should not exceed one hundred characters. If the number of characters surpasses the limit, and a great many clauses are inserted, or if the summary in comparison with the original memorial is confused and different in meaning, the office in question must not seal it up for presentation but take it to be an offense against the regulations and conduct an examination and impeachment."

However, this regulation of 1645 was not meticulously followed in practice, and by 1724 it had become a dead letter. (Although

Mr. SHAN does not suggest it, one cannot help wondering if the Transmission Office was not taking advantage of the technicality; see note 15 above). *Chia-ch'ing hui-tien shih-li* 10. 4a quotes an imperial decision of 1724 which states, " T'i-pên and Tsou-pên according to the old regulations, except for criminal cases and revenue matters, were not to exceed three hundred characters and the summaries were not to exceed one hundred characters; and if the number of characters overflowed the limit, the Transmission Office was authorized to refuse the memorial and send it back. But important memorials, such as those dealing with how to promote prosperity, do away with abuses, encourage the doing of good, or punish evil,—properly ought to be quite detailed, which will be of advantage to government; if there is a fixed limit to the number of characters and it is not allowed to raise many topics, the result must be to omit too much or be too brief. Hereafter, as regards T'i-pên and Tsou-pên, except those in which there are mistakes regarding the proper form or honorary elevation (of certain characters), the Transmission Office should not act on its own authority and refuse and return them because the number of characters or of items dealt with is excessive and offends against the regulations."

Ex.: *Wên-hsien ts'ung-pien* 24 passim; *Ming-ch'ing shih-liao* 2. 119, 138, 171; 4. 311; 7. 671; *Ho-pei ti-i vo-wu-yüan pan-yüeh-k'an* (Semi-monthly Publication of the First Museum of Hopei) no. 23 (Aug. 25, 1932) gives a photograph of a T'i-pên of 1655.

T'I–TSOU 題奏 MEMORIALS

T'i-pên and Tsou-pên considered together as a class.

TIEH 牒 ORDER

Addressed by superior to subordinate officials, MAYERS 140; no examples found.

TIEH–CH'ÊNG 牒呈 REPORT

Addressed by subordinate to superior officials, MAYERS 140; no examples found.

T'IEH-HUANG 貼黃 SUMMARY

Lit. yellow sticker, a slip of paper attached to a memorial (T'i-pên) at the end, bearing a summary of the contents to facilitate reference; not allowed to exceed one hundred characters, cf. SHAN Shih-k'uei (1) 185 quoted under T'i-pên above. Cf. *Kuang-hsü hui-tien* 69. 13: " On a separate sheet of paper there is copied a selection of the important statements in the memorial, which is pasted on at the end of the memorial and is called a T'ieh-huang "; also *Ch'ien-lung hui-tien* 81. 14. SHAN Shih-yüan (1) 151 states that the term was not confined to summaries made for T'i-pên but applied to all ordinary public documents written on yellow silk or paper and presented for imperial inspection. A form of T'ieh-huang was also used by the Board of War; and by usage the term was applied to summaries not written on yellow paper. T'ieh-huang were eventually bound up to form the Shih-shu, q. v.

T'ING-CHI 廷寄 COURT LETTER

In general, a secret document sent from the Grand Council to provincial officials embodying in its text imperial commands; used only on important business. Included two sub-types: (1) Tzŭ-chi, sent to provincial officials of higher rank, and (2) Ch'üan-yü, sent to provincial officials of lower rank, s. v.

Cf. *Chia-ch'ing hui-tien* 3. 2b: " Either an urgent Edict or a secret Edict, which is not handed down publicly through the Grand Secretariat, is called a Court Letter. [It is sealed by the Grand Council and given to the Courier's Office for transmission at a certain rate of speed]. As to its form, if it goes to a Generalissimo, an Imperial Commissioner, a General-in-chief, an Amban, a Lieut.-General, a Deputy Lieut.-General, an Imperial Agent and Commandant of the Forces, a Governor-General, a Governor, or a Literary Chancellor,—it is called a ' Despatch (Tzŭ-chi) sent by the Grand Council.' If it goes to a Salt-Controller, a Superintendent of Customs, or a provincial Judicial or Financial Commissioner,— it is called a ' Transmitted Edict (Ch'üan-yŭ) from the Grand Council.' Both bear the year, month, and day on which the imperial will was received." Cf. also *Shu-yüan chi-lüeh* 27. 3a-b. The statement in GILES 11, 284 defining T'ing-chi as " a confidential letter sent directly from the palace to the highest provincial officials, with instructions for their guidance in important matters," thus refers really to the sub-form Tzŭ-chi.

Ex.: *Wên-hsien ts'ung-pien* 14, sec. 2. 9b; *Shih-liao hsün-k'an* 3. 101a, 102a, headed T'ing-chi and reading chün-chi ta-ch'ên tzŭ-chi 軍機大臣字寄. All those printed in id. appear to be Tzŭ-chi rather than Ch'üan-yü; they conclude with the phrase tsün-chih chi-hsin ch'ien-lai 遵旨寄信前來 (in obedience to the imperial will a letter is sent forward), cf. id. 5. 153b. Thus it is apparent that the form of T'ing-chi addressed to the higher provincial officials (i. e. Tzŭ-chi) came to stand for T'ing-chi as a whole.

TS'Ê 冊 PATENT

Used for establishing the titles of an Empress, imperial concubine, and the like, of various types; cf. *Chia-ch'ing hui-tien* 2. 2a.

Ex.: Boston Museum of Fine Arts, loaned from coll. of M. KAROLIK, 230. 38: " Jade book " of 1723.

TSO-MING-CH'IH 坐名敕 NOMINATIVE COMMAND

From the Emperor to higher provincial officials and the dependencies of the empire; see under Ch'ih-yü.

TSOU-CHÊ 奏摺 MEMORIAL

Same as Tsou-pên, q. v.

TSOU-HSIAO-TS'Ê 奏銷冊 ACCOUNTS, REPORTS

See under Huang-ts'ê.

TSOU-PÊN 奏本 MEMORIAL

Also called Tsou-chê and Chê-tsou; memorials submitted to the Emperor usually through the Chancery of Memorials to the Emperor (Tsou Shih Ch'u) on important public business or the private business of the memorialist and not bearing his seal of office,—as contrasted with T'i-pên, q. v. For the long battle between the two chief forms of memorial, see text section 2 note 10. In general the Tsou-pên was a more direct, simple, and expeditious type of memorial, usually more valuable historically but unfortunately less highly differentiated than T'i-pên into sub-categories susceptible of study. For the procedure followed in presenting Tsou-pên, see text section 3.

Ex.: the memorials printed in *I-wu shih-mo* throughout consist almost entirely of Tsou-pên; *Shih-liao ts'ung-k'an ch'u-pien* 2 publishes Tsou-pên dated from 1632 on; *Shih-liao hsün-k'an* passim prints several Tsou-pên originating from the Grand Council (chün-chi-ch'u tsou).

TSOU-P'IEN 奏片 SHORT MEMORIAL, MINUTE?

P'ien-tsou also appears; see under P'ien. Evidently a short memorial or "minute," usually in response to a Rescript; cf. TÊNG Chih-ch'êng 195.

Ex.: *Shih-liao hsün-k'an* 3. 99a et seq.; *Chank-ku ts'ung-pien* 7. sec. 1. 42b.

T'UNG-PÊN 通本 MEMORIAL

Memorials of the T'i-pên type from the higher provincial authorities submitted through the Transmission Office (T'ung Chêng Ssŭ) and the Grand Secretariat. Usually submitted only in Chinese, a Manchu translation being made at the Grand Secretariat; cf. Hsŭ (1) 186. Cf. *Chia-ch'ing hui-tien* 2. 6a: " Memorials from the Generals-in-Chief, Governors-General, Governors, provincial Commanders-in-chief, Brigade Generals, Literary Chancellors, and Salt Controllers of the various provinces, from the Prefects of the Metropolitan Prefecture and of Mukden, and from the Five Boards at Mukden, all of which are sent to the Transmission Office and from the Transmission Office to the Grand Secretariat,—are Tung-pên."

TZŬ 咨 COMMUNICATION

Used between officials of equal or approximately equal rank: MAYERS 138, GILES 12, 344; sent to the Grand Council in particular from other offices at the capital and in the provinces. Used in many compounds, see below.

Ex.: *I-wu shih-mo*, Tao-kuang section 67. 48b, from General-in-Chief to Governor-General; id. 68. 34a, from Board of Revenue to Governor-General.

TZŬ-CH'ÊNG 咨呈 COMMUNICATION

Addressed from one official or office to another slightly superior in rank, MAYERS 139; from an official or office not directly subordinate, *Fa-lü ta-tz'ŭ-shu* 875; GILES 12,344 states, "to submit to the consideration of,—used (e. g.) by an officer while temporarily holding a higher appointment than his own, to a high official, provided that his personal rank allows of the use of a Tzŭ in correspondence."

Ex.: *Shih-liao hsün-k'an* 13. 472a, from the substantive Shantung Governor to the Grand Council in 1832; *Ming-ch'ing shih-liao* 7. 679, from the Board of Ceremony to the Grand Secretariat.

TZŬ-CHI 字寄 DESPATCH

Sent from the Grand Council to higher provincial authorities and embodying important imperial commands, a form of T'ing-chi, q. v.

Ex.: *Chang-ku ts'ung-pien* 2, sec. 2, an example sent under the name of a Grand Secretary (i. e. concurrently a Grand Councillor); *Shih-liao hsün-k'an* 5. 153.

TZŬ-HUI 咨會 COMMUNICATION

An official despatch between equals, GILES 12, 344.

Ex.: *Shih-liao hsün-k'an* 4. 110a, draft copy of a communication to Annam, Yung-chêng period (this seems inconsistent with GILES); *I-wu shih-mo*, Tao-kuang section 67. 46b, from one Governor-General to another; id., Hsien-feng period 42. 24a line 7, from an Imperial Commissioner to the American chieftain.

TZŬ-HSING 咨行 COMMUNICATION

An official despatch between equals, GILES 12, 344.

Ex.: *I-wu shih-mo*, Tao-kuang section 67. 7b, from Governor-General to Superintendent of Customs.

TZŬ-PAO 咨報 COMMUNICATION

A report, as from a Minister to the Foreign Office, GILES 12, 344.

Ex.: *Shih-liao hsün-k'an* 13. 474b, reference to a Tzü-pao to the Shantung Governor from the Têngchow Brigade General.

TZŬ-WÊN 咨文 COMMUNICATION

An official despatch between equals, GILES 12, 344.
Ex.: *Ming-ch'ing shih-liao* 8.701, from the Board of War to the Board of Revenue.

TZŬ-YÜ 字諭 ORDER

To inferiors, especially from officials to commoners, a general term for letters.
Ex.: *Shih-liao hsün-k'an* 5. 168-9, three examples from the Chinese authorities to British merchants in 1822, *Wên-hsien ts'ung-pien* 1, photograph of a Tzŭ-yü from the Yung-chêng Emperor.

YU-TSOU 又奏 ADDITIONAL MEMORIAL

Not a separate type of document; when one memorialist submits more than one memorial at a time, those after the first bear this heading, sometimes followed by tsai 再 (further) as in the case of Fu-p'ien, q. v. Edicts are similarly treated (yu-yü).
Ex.: *I-wu shih-mo* passim.

YÜ 諭 Imperial EDICT

A strong case could be made for translating this term as Instruction, by analogy to western procedure; but since it is the best known and most important of all documents issuing from the Emperor, it seems particularly desirable to follow the traditional usage. The early British officials like T. F. WADE usually translated it Decree; but Dr. H. B. MORSE and others since then have generally used Edict. Being a separate document, an Edict usually opens with a summary of a memorial or of previous business; it may be addressed to the Grand Council, or the Grand Secretariat, or others, or to no one at all. Discussed in text above, section 3.

YÜ-CHIH 諭旨 Imperial EDICT

A general term used to refer to Edicts (yü) or Rescripts (chih) which have been received.
Ex.: *Shih-liao hsün-k'an* 3. 99b, headed Yü-chih, the text reading nei-ko fêng shang-yü (the Grand Secretariat has received an im-

perial Edict); id. 103b, headed Yü-chih, the text reading fêng chih (a Rescript has been received).

YÜ-PAO 御寶 IMPERIAL SEAL
Twenty-five imperial seals are listed in the *Collected Statutes*, each with a different name and form; cf. *Chia-ch'ing hui-tien* 2. 9a-10b: "Whenever the Emperor's words (lun-yin) are made known, an imperial seal is requested and used." The officers of the Grand Secretariat have charge of their use, together with the palace eunuchs, who have charge of their safe-keeping. For each occasion when a seal is to be used a memorial must be presented, except for the conferring of patents (Kao-ming, Ch'ih-ming, and Ch'ih-shu). *Ch'ien-lung hui-tien* 2. 5b states that requests for a seal are merely presented to the Imperial Household Department. The subject merits further study; cf. W. FUCHS, Beiträge zur mandjurischen Bibliographie und Literatur, Tōkyō 1936, 108-11.
Ex.: *Chiao-t'ai-tien pao-p'u* (Imperial seals in the Chiao-t'ai hall), gives photographic reproductions of the twenty-five seals.

YÜ-P'I 御批 IMPERIAL ENDORSEMENT
Same as Chu-p'i, q. v.
Ex.: *Shih-liao hsün-k'an* 7. 236b.

YÜ-TIEH 玉牒 IMPERIAL GENEALOGY
Lit. jade record; the genealogical record of the imperial family, GILES 11,122; cf. *Ch'ien-lung hui-tien* 1 (the Imperial Clan Court) 1b.
Ex.: *Wên-hsien ts'ung-pien* 20. 22 gives a photographic illustration.

WAI-FAN PIAO-CHANG 外藩 TRIBUTARY MEMORIAL
See under Kung-piao and Piao-chang: memorials submitted to the Emperor by the political or religious dignitaries of Mongolia, Sinkiang, Tibet, etc. (wai-fan) and of tribes and feudatories such as Turfan, etc.; cf. Hsü (1) 194-5.

ON THE CH'ING TRIBUTARY SYSTEM

J. K. FAIRBANK AND S. Y. TÊNG
HARVARD UNIVERSITY

CONTENTS	PAGE
1. The traditional role of tribute	135
2. Tributaries of the late Ming	144
Table 1: Ming tributaries c. 1587	151
3. The Li Fan Yüan (Court of Colonial Affairs) under the Ch'ing	158
4. Ch'ing tributaries from the south and east,—general regulations	163
Table 2: Regular Ch'ing tributaries	174
Table 3: Frequency and routes of tribute	176
5. European countries in the tributary system	178
Table 4: European embassies to the Court of Peking	188
6. Ch'ing tribute embassies and foreign trade	190
Table 5: Tribute embassies 1662-1911	193
Table 6: Non-tributary trading countries 1818	202
7. A selected list of Ch'ing works 1644-1860 on maritime relations	206
8. Index of tributaries listed in six editions of the *Collected Statutes*	219
Appendix 1: Bibliographical note	238
Appendix 2: Additional lists of Ch'ing tributaries	243
Appendix 3: Author and title index to section 7	245

1. THE TRADITIONAL ROLE OF TRIBUTE

Chinese foreign policy in the nineteenth century can be understood only against its traditional Chinese background, the tributary system. This system for the conduct of foreign relations had been directly inherited from the Ming dynasty (1368-1644) and modified to suit the needs of the Manchus. As a Confucian world-order in the Far East, it continued formally in existence until the very end of the nineteenth century, and was superseded in practice only gradually, after 1842, by the British treaty system which has until recently governed the foreign relations of Siam, Japan, and other states, as well as China. The Chinese diplomatic documents of a century ago are therefore really unintelligible unless they are studied in the light of the imperial tributary system which produced them.[1]

---

[1] We are indebted to Prof. C. S. GARDNER for assistance on several points, particularly regarding the table of western embassies in part 5. This article, like its predecessors, is intended to deal with administrative problems of importance for the study of Chinese foreign relations in the nineteenth century. Cf. J. K. FAIRBANK and S. Y. TÊNG, On the Transmission of Ch'ing Documents, *HJAS* 4.12-46; On the Types and Uses of Ch'ing Documents, *ibid.*, 5.1-71 (Corrigendum p. 59, Shên-ch'êng: for ch'êng 呈 read ch'ên 陳).

The ramifications of this vast subject, in political theory, in international trade, and in diplomacy, have been explored by a few pioneer scholars,[2] some of whom have traced the development of the administration of foreign trade from the Sung up to the late Ming, while others have painstakingly established translations of texts concerning the seven great Ming expeditions of the early fifteenth century. These expeditions under the eunuch CHÊNG Ho and others in the period 1403-1433 took Chinese fleets of as many as 60 vessels and 27,000 men into the Indian Ocean and in some cases as far as Arabia and Africa, and the period has rightly attracted attention as the high point of Chinese tributary relations. Studies of the tributary system in the Ch'ing period, however, are less numerous; relatively little effort has been made to link the sorry Chinese foreign policy of the nineteenth century with the great tradition which lay behind it. To do so will require the efforts of many workers over a long period.

The present article attempts a preliminary survey of the tributary system as it developed under the Ch'ing dynasty of the Manchus (1644-1912). In order to reach useful conclusions on a subject of such magnitude, we have based this study chiefly upon the various editions of the *Collected Statutes* (*Hui-tien*),[3] which not only are the fundamental official source for the general structure of the system, but also reflect its history, as mirrored in successive changes and revised editions, over a period of more than two hundred years. The *Collected Statutes*, moreover, were issued both as a record of administrative practice and as a guide to the bureaucracy in its day by day activities. In this they excel for our purposes the official compilations of a later date, such as the *Draft History of the Ch'ing Dynasty* (*Ch'ing-shih kao*), which are at one remove from the scene and compiled by, if not for, posterity. Before proceeding to the presentation and analysis of this material, we offer below a brief ex-

---

[2] [For this long bibliographical note, including the abbreviations used in footnotes, see appendix 1 at end of this article.]

[3] *Ta-ming hui-tien* 大明會典 or *Ch'in-ting ta-ch'ing hui-tien* 欽定清; the various editions are cited hereafter by the reigns in which they were issued, chronologically as follows:

Wan-li hui-tien (*Ta-ming hui-tien*, preface dated 1587),
K'ang-hsi hui-tien (*Ta-ch'ing hui-tien*, pub. 1690),
Yung-chêng hui-tien (pref. 1732),
Ch'ien-lung hui-tien, and *Ch'ien-lung hui-tien tsê-li* (both completed 1764),
Chia-ch'ing hui-tien, and *Chia-ch'ing hui-tien shih-li* (both completed 1818),
Kuang-hsü hui-tien, and *Kuang-hsü hui-tien shih-li* (both pub. 1899).

planatory discussion of the function of tribute in the Chinese state, which may serve to pose further problems for research.

For purpose of analysis it may be pointed out (1) that the tributary system was a natural outgrowth of the cultural preeminence of the early Chinese, (2) that it came to be used by the rulers of China for political ends of self-defense, (3) that in practice it had a very fundamental and important commercial basis, and (4) that it served as the medium for Chinese international relations and diplomacy. It was, in short, a scheme of things entire, and deserves attention as one historical solution to problems of world-organization.

Behind the tributary system as it became institutionalized in the Ming and Ch'ing periods lay the age-old tradition of Chinese cultural superiority over the barbarians.[4] Continuously from the bronze age, when Shang civilization first appears as a culture-island in North China, this has been a striking element in Chinese thought, perpetuated by the eternal conflict between the settled agrarian society of the Yellow River basin and the pastoral nomads of the steppe beyond the Wall, as well as by the persistent expansion of the Chinese to the south among the tribes whose remnants are now being absorbed in Yunnan and Kweichow. From this contact with the nomads of the north and west and with the aborigines of the south, the Chinese appear to have derived certain basic assumptions which may be stated as follows: first, that Chinese superiority over the barbarians had a cultural rather than a mere political basis; it rested

---

[4] Satisfactory equivalents of certain key terms are not easily established. Fan 藩 (fence, boundary, frontier) as used with reference to countries outside China has a connotation somewhere in between " foreign " and " barbarian "; we have usually used the gentler term.

Man, I, Jung, and Ti 蠻夷戎狄 in conjunction refer to the barbarians of the south, east, west, and north, respectively; but I serves also as a generic term for all barbarians together (Cf. Wên-hsien t'ung-k'ao 324. 4). The term Ssŭ-i 四夷 (lit. " Four barbarians ") is a collective term for the various barbarians dwelling in the four quarters of the compass on the periphery of the civilized world of which China was the center. It therefore indicates the barbarians in general,—all the barbarians, not those of any particular places. BRUNNERT 392 is in error in translating Hui T'ung Ssŭ I Kuan 會同四譯 (for 夷)館 as " Residence for Envoys of the Four Tributary States; here were domiciled Envoys from Korea, Siam, Tonkin, and Burma. . . ."

Under the Ming the Ssŭ I Kuan had had charge of relations both with the barbarians of the north and west and with those of the east and south, there being no Li Fan Yüan (see sec. 3 below). Thus the Ssŭ-i-kuan k'ao 四夷館考 (Lo Chên-yü ed., 1924) records relations with the Mongols, Samarkand, Turfan, Tibet, Hami, etc., and also with Champa, Japan, Java, Burma, and the like.

less upon force than upon the Chinese way of life embodied in such things as the Confucian code of conduct and the use of the Chinese written language; the sign of the barbarian was not race or origin so much as non-adherence to this way of life. From this it followed, secondly, that those barbarians who wished to "come and be transformed" (lai-hua), and so participate in the benefits of (Chinese) civilization, must recognize the supreme position of the Emperor; for the Son of Heaven represented all mankind, both Chinese and barbarian, in his ritual sacrifices before the forces of nature. Adherence to the Chinese way of life automatically entailed the recognition of the Emperor's mandate to rule all men. This supremacy of the Emperor as mediator between Heaven and Earth was most obviously acknowledged in the performance of the kotow, the three kneelings and nine prostrations to which European envoys later objected.[5] It was also acknowledged by the bringing of a tribute

[5] YANO (2) 151-180 summarizes numerous Chinese and western references to the subject.

It should be emphasized that the relationship to the Son of Heaven expressed by the kotow was shared by all mankind, Chinese and barbarian alike. The highest dignitaries of the empire performed this ceremony on appropriate occasion,—as did the Emperor himself when paying reverence to Heaven (pai-t'ien 拜天). The kotow performed unilaterally, on the other hand, expressed an inferiority of status in the universal order, without which there could be no order. It was therefore appropriate, honorable, and indeed good manners when performed in the right context. Other contexts might require less elaborate ceremonies, such as one kneeling and three prostrations. Strictly speaking, this was also a "knocking of the head," k'o-t'ou 磕頭. For clarity we suggest the term "full kotow" for three kneelings and nine prostrations, (theoretically) knocking the head upon the ground, san-kuei chiu-k'ou li 三跪九叩禮; "modified kotow" for three kneelings and nine reverences bowing the head over the hands upon the ground, san-kuei chiu-pai li; and "single kotow" or "double kotow" for one-third or two-thirds, respectively, of the full kotow,— i-kuei san-k'ou li, êrh-kuei liu-k'ou li.

This universal order of ceremony which expressed the order of all mankind may be illustrated by the following random references to the Ta-Ch'ing t'ung-li (chüan 42 chün-li, military ceremonial): in the ceremony of announcing the sacrifices, the Emperor performed the modified kotow (4b). On receiving a seal indirectly from the Emperor, a generalissimo (Ta Chiang Chün; cf. B 658: Field Marshal) and his staff performed the full kotow (12b). In another ceremony, they and the princes and high ministers of state followed the Emperor in the modified kotow (21). The princes and ministers later performed one kneeling and one prostration (i-kuei i-k'ou li), and again one head-knocking from their seats 各於坐次行一叩禮 (21b). When a Mongolian prince met a prince of the imperial Manchu clan, they both performed a double kotow (Ch. 46 pin-li, ceremonial for guests. 1). Officials at the capital and in the provinces saluted each other with three formal bows (5, 11, 15 san-i 三揖;

of local produce, by the formal bestowal of a seal, comparable to the investiture of a vassal in medieval Europe, and in other ways. Thus the tributary system, as the sum total of these formalities, was the mechanism by which barbarous non-Chinese regions were given their place in the all-embracing Chinese political, and therefore ethical, scheme of things.[6]

This general theory is of course familiar to the most casual student of Chinese history, and yet the realities of the situation are still a matter of dispute. In the intercourse between the Chinese state and the barbarians, commercial relations became inseparably bound up with tributary. Trade was conducted by barbarian merchants who accompanied the tributary envoy to the frontier or even to the capital; sometimes it was conducted by the members of the mission itself. That tribute was a cloak for trade has been a commonplace ever since merchants from the Roman orient arrived in China in 166 A. D. claiming to be envoys of Marcus Aurelius. Thus Benedict DE GOEZ, crossing Central Asia in the year 1604, describes the "sham embassies" of merchants from the western kingdoms who "forge public letters in the names of the kings whom they profess to represent" and "under pretence of being ambassadors go and offer tribute to the Emperor."[7] Innumerable other examples could be cited where-

---

cf. GILES 5394 tso-i 作 ("to make a salute by bending the body until the hands touch a little below the knees, and then rising and raising the hands to the level of the eyebrows"). To a superior official, a single kotow might also be used, perhaps followed by three bows (14b, 16b, 17). Bows and similar formalities were also prescribed for apprentices, friends, and relatives (20-21). In all this, the prescriptions regarding precedence in entering doors and directions faced in sitting were equally detailed.

It should be noted (1) that all ceremonies between individuals were reciprocal in the sense that both parties took part; (2) that the ceremonial for barbarian visitors (chüan 45, pin-li) was an integral part of the whole body of ceremonial just referred to. Egalitarian westerners were ill-prepared to maintain their proper status, or any other, in this system of rites.

[6] Various aspects of the rationale of tribute have been eloquently set forth by T. C. LIN (2), and its general background by Owen LATTIMORE, *Inner Asian Frontiers of China*, New York, 1940.

[7] Sir Henry YULE, revised by H. CORDIER, *Cathay and the Way Thither* . . . , (4 vols. London 1913-16) 4.235, 242, 243 n. For other examples cf. GROENEVELDT 4-5, DUYVENDAK (1) 74 n., (2) 378-9. CHANG Hsing-lang 張星烺 [*Chung-hsi chiao-t'ung shih-liao hui-p'ien* 中西交通史料滙篇 (Miscellaneous historical materials on Sino-western relations), vol. 5, p. 534] states that the Kansu Governor reported in 1502 that there were more than 150 self-styled rulers (wang) trading from the Western Regions; cf. *Ming-shih* 332.6 (T'ung-wên shu-chü ed. 1894).

in tribute, in the minds of the tribute bearers, was merely a formality connected with trade; at Macao and Canton, indeed, the Europeans in their concentration upon the substance of commerce eventually forgot all about the formality which theoretically still went with it.

This economic interpretation, however, is made from the point of view of the barbarians. The motivation of the Court is a different matter.

The argument that the tributary system was developed by the Court chiefly for political defense has been succinctly stated by Dr. T. F. TSIANG: " Out of this period of intense struggle and bitter humiliation [the eleventh and twelfth centuries], the neo-Confucian philosophy, which began then to dominate China, worked out a dogma in regard to international relations, to hold sway in China right to the middle of the nineteenth century. . . . That dogma asserts that national security could only be found in isolation and stipulates that whoever wished to enter into relations with China must do so as China's vassal, acknowledging the supremacy of the Chinese emperor and obeying his commands, thus ruling out all possibility of international intercourse on terms of equality. It must not be construed to be a dogma of conquest or univeral dominion, for it imposed nothing on foreign peoples who chose to remain outside the Chinese world. It sought peace and security, with both of which international relations were held incompatible. If relations there had to be, they must be of the suzerain-vassal type, acceptance of which meant to the Chinese acceptance of the Chinese ethic on the part of the barbarian. . . .

" It must not be assumed that the Chinese Court made a profit out of . . . tribute. The imperial gifts bestowed in return were usually more valuable than the tribute . . . Chinese statesmen before the latter part of the nineteenth century would have ridiculed the notion that national finance and wealth should be or could be promoted by means of international trade. On China's part the permission to trade was intended to be a mark of imperial bounty and a means of keeping the barbarians in the proper state of submissiveness. . . ."[8]

Thus we might conclude that trade and tribute were cognate aspects of a single system of foreign relations, the moral value of tribute being the more important in the minds of the rulers of China, and the

[8] T. F. TSIANG (CHIANG T'ing-fu 蔣廷黻), "China and European Expansion" (*Politica* 2 no. 5, Mar. 1936, pp. 1-18), pp. 3-4. A lecture delivered at the London School of Economics.

material value of trade in the minds of the barbarians; this balance of interests would allow mutual satisfaction and the system would continue to function. From this it might be concluded further that the tributary system really worked in reverse, the submission of the barbarians being actually bought and paid for by the trade conceded to them by China. But this last is an over-simplification which runs counter to the whole set of ideas behind the system, and it also overlooks the interesting possibility, which deserves exploration, of an imperial economic interest,—for instance, in the silk export trade. In short it seems impossible at present to make more than one generalization: that the tributary system was a framework within which all sorts of intersts, personal and imperial, economic and social, found their expression. Further study should reveal an interplay between greed and statecraft, dynastic policy and vested interest, similar to that in other great political institutions.

One untouched aspect of the system is its functioning as a diplomatic medium. Since all foreign relations in the Chinese view were ipso facto tributary relations, it followed that all types of international intercourse, if they occurred at all in the experience of China, had to be fitted into the tributary system. Thus Chinese envoys were sometimes sent abroad to spy out the enemy or to seek allies, and foreign envoys came and conducted negotiations at the capital, all within this framework. As an introduction to this aspect of the subject, we quote below from the prefaces to the sections on tributary ritual in the *Ta-Ming chi-li* 大明集禮 (Collected Ceremonies of the Ming Dynasty), an official work of the Ming period.[9] Naturally, these prefaces recount what the Court hoped everyone would believe had generally occurred during the course of Chinese history, but this merely enhances their value for our purpose. (We omit passages recounting details concerning various tribes and rulers.)

" CEREMONIAL FOR VISITORS: 1. FOREIGN KINGS PRESENTING TRIBUTE AT COURT (Fan-wang ch'ao-kung 蕃王朝貢).

" The kings of former times cultivated their own refinement and virtue in order to subdue persons at a distance, whereupon the barbarians (of the east and north) came to Court to have audience. This comes down as a long tradition 其來尙矣.

---

[9] *Ta-Ming chi-li* (Palace edition, 1530). We quote from the first two or three pages, respectively, forming general introductions (tsung-hsü 總序) to ch. 30-32 (pin-li 賓禮 Ceremonial for Visitors 1-3).

"In the time of King T'ang of Yin (trad. dates B.C. 1766-1754), the Ti-ch'iang [an ancient Tibetan tribe in E. Kansu and Kokonor], distant barbarians, came to offer gifts and to visit the king. In the time of (King) T'ai Mou (trad. dates B.C. 1637-1563) the remote tribes [ch'ung-i 重譯 i.e. those so far off as to require repeated interpretations] which came to Court (consisted of) 76 countries.

"When King Wu of the Chou (trad. dates 1122-1116) overcame the Shang, (there was) a great meeting of the feudal lords and the barbarians on the four quarters (ssŭ-i), and there was written (the chapter on) the meeting of the princes.[10] In the autumn officials (section) of the *Chou li*,[11] (it is stated that) the interpreting officer had charge of the envoys of the countries of the wild tribes of the south and east (man-i), of Min (Fukien?), of the north (mai), and of the west (jung-ti), and gave them instructions and explanations.

"The Han dynasty established (an officer) in charge of guests and official interpreters, a chief and assistants, to guide the barbarians (ssŭ-i) who came to Court to present tribute. Also they established (an office) in charge of dependent states, and a chief interpreter of the nine [languages; i.e. one capable of speaking the tongues of foreign nations]. Under the Emperor Wu in 111 B.C. the Yeh-lang [chieftain, from the Yunnan-Szechwan frontier] came to Court. Thereafter the outer barbarians sent tribute to Court without interruption. In 53 B.C. the chieftain of the Hsiung-nu came to the Court. In 51 B.C. the Hsiung-nu chieftain, Chi-chü-shan [12] 稽居狦 came to Court. Both had audience at the Sweet Spring Palace.[13] In 28 B.C. the barbarians from all sides (ssŭ-i) came to the Court and received direction from the grand master of ceremonial for ambassadors.[14] Under the Emperor Shun in 136 A.D. the king of the Wo-nu (Japan?) came to Court. For all of these there were regulations for entertainment at banquets and the bestowal of gifts.

[10] Wang-hui 王會, forming chüan 7 in the *I chou shu* 逸周書; cf. Kuang han-wei ts'ung-shu 廣漢魏叢書, 1592 edition, ts'ê 34-36.

[11] Cf. *Chou Li* 周禮, Hsiang-hsi 象胥 38.14b (in Shih-san-ching chu-su 十三經注疏, Kiangsi edition, 1815) (BIOT 2. Kiu 34. fol. 26-27).

[12] Cf. *Ch'ien Han shu* (Palace edition, 1739) 94 sec. B. 3b. Established as chieftain 58 B.C., *ibid.* sec. A. 37. The name is given here as Chi-hou-shan 㺃; likewise in *K'ang-hsi tzŭ-tien* 康熙字典 under 狦.

[13] Kan-ch'üan kung 甘泉宮, a summer palace in Shensi, N.W. of Ch'ang-an, dating from the time of the First Emperor, cf. GILES (*A Chinese-English Dictionary*, 1912) 5823.

[14] Ta hung lu 大鴻臚, cf. Hung Lu Ssŭ 寺, Court of State Ceremonial in T'ang and Ch'ing, B 935; KUWABARA 7.14 refers to it as "the office of foreign affairs."

"Under the T'ang there was established the Chu K'o Lang Chung 主客郎中 (Secretary in Charge of Guests), in charge of all the barbarians (fan) who came to Court. His activities in receiving and entertaining (them) were four in number: Going out to meet and greet them (lao 勞); preparing them for audience (i. e. warning them); foreign kings receiving an audience; banqueting the rulers of foreign states. The ceremonies for these (activities) were detailed....

"In the Sung period there were more than forty states which presented tribute at Court, all of them merely sending envoys to present the tribute. Although foreign kings did not regularly themselves come to the Court for audience, still the ceremonies for reception and audience which appear in the books of ceremony are about the same as for the T'ang.

"Yüan dynasty: in 1210 the king of the Uigurs, I-tu-hu 奕都護, came to Court. Under Shih-tsu (Kublai Khan) in 1264, an imperial command was given to the King of Korea (Kao-li), Chih 植, ordering him to cultivate the ceremony of shih-chien.[15] In the sixth month Chih came to the Court at Shang-tu ["Xanadu," near modern Dolonor]. Thereafter when the (rulers of) foreign countries came to Court, they waited for the day of a great Court assembly on the first day of the first month or on an imperial birthday, and then performed the ceremony.

"Now it is proposed, as to the reigning dynasty, that when foreign kings come to Court, there shall first be despatched an official of the city of Nanking (Ying-t'ien fu) to go out to meet them and greet them. When they have arrived at the Residence [16] there shall be sent

---

[15] 世見 Cf. *Chou li* 大行人 Ta hsing jên 37.20: 世壹見 (BIOT 2.406: En un siècle ou dans un age d'homme, ils doivent une visite a l'empéreur).

[16] Kuan 館, standing for Hui T'ung Kuan 會同. This refers of course to the Hui T'ung Ssŭ I Kuan 四譯 (or 夷) under the Board of Ceremonies, rather than to the Hui T'ung Kuan (Imperial Despatch Office, MAYERS 182 xiv) under the Board of War; but it presents a typical problem of translation,—the reference being known to all, what English words shall be generally used for it? BRUNNERT 392 gives Residence for Envoys of the Four Tributary States, an erroneous interpretation as noted above (note 4). CHANG Tê-ch'ang 273 uses the romanization Hui-tung-kwan, without attempting a translation, but this otherwise sound procedure involves in this case ambiguity with the office above mentioned under the Board of War. T. C. LIN (2) 879 offers Cosmopolitan Palaces, which is sound in meaning but perhaps a bit flamboyant. CHANG T'ien-tsê 50 sidesteps the problem of translating Hui T'ung Kuan by using Ssŭ-i-kuan; this is no solution for the non-sinological reader. In order to conform as

further (an official of) the Board (of Ceremony) at the capital to prepare a feast. Thereupon they shall practice the ceremonies. They are to have imperial audience in the Fêng-t'ien Hall 奉天殿 and to have audience with the Heir-apparent in the Eastern Palace. When the imperial audiences are finished, a banquet is offered to them. The officers and departments (of government) at the capital all are to prepare banquets to entertain them. When they return, officers are to be sent to escort them out of the boundaries. Now all their ceremonial is drawn up to form the section on " Foreign kings presenting tribute at court. . . ." [17]

" 2. FOREIGN ENVOYS PRESENTING TRIBUTE AT COURT (Fan-shih ch'ao-kung 蕃使朝貢).

" According to the *Chou li,* ' when the envoys from the four quarters arrive, if they are great guests then they are received ceremoniously; if they are small guests then their presents are accepted and their statements are listened to.' [18] By small guests is meant the official envoys sent by foreign countries. The envoys of foreign countries all are barbarians, and do not practice these ceremonies. Therefore one only listens to their statements, and that is all. When King Wu overcame the Shang, he opened communications with the nine I (eastern barbarians) and the eight Man (southern barbarians).... States at a great distance came to offer up presents; in all cases their offerings were accepted and their statements were listened to.

" Under the Han . . . (a total of) thirty-six states were all dependents of the Middle (Kingdom) and offered tribute . . . (when) they came to present offerings, they all received rewards so as to send them away with gifts.

" In the T'ang when foreign envoys offered tribute, the ceremonies for their banqueting and audience had four parts: going out to meet and greet them; preparing them for audience; receiving the foreign envoys' congratulatory memorials and presents; and the Emperor's banquet for the envoys of foreign countries. . . .

closely as possible to the chief manual now available (BRUNNERT) we suggest Residence for Tributary Envoys.

DUYVENDAK (3) 45-49 uses " lodginghouse " but not as an official title, and agrees that LIN has " rather overtranslated." Prof. DUYVENDAK also describes (from the *Chia-ch'ing hui-tien shih-li*) some seven locations of establishments used to house embassies at various dates, all nominally under or part of the Hui T'ung Kuan, a title which therefore cannot easily be associated with one particular place.

[17] *Ta-Ming chi-li* 30. 1-2b.

[18] Cf. *Chou Li,* Hsiao hsing jên 37. 24 (BIOT 2. 411).

"Under the Sung when the envoys of foreign countries arrived, they were feasted and given audience in the hall of the palace (tzǔ-ch'ên tien 紫宸殿) and in the Ch'ung-chêng Hall 崇政殿. The ceremonies for going out to meet and greet (the envoys), preparing them for audience, and entertaining them at banquets, all were the same as for the T'ang. . . .

"In the Yüan period from the time of the Emperor T'ai-tsu (Jenghis Khan, 1206-1227) the Uigurs (wei-wu-êrh 畏吾兒), the Moslems (hui-hu 囘鶻), the Tanguts (Hsi Hsia), the Western Regions, and Koryŏ all sent envoys to present tribute. After the time of the Emperor Shih-tsu (Kublai Khan 1260-1294), Annam, Champa, Yunnan, Laos,[19] Northern Burma (Mien kuo 緬國), Tali (in Yunnan), and Fu-lang,[20] all sent envoys to offer up tribute.

"Under the reigning dynasty in 1369, the country of Champa sent a minister (named) Hu-tu-man 虎都蠻 to come with tribute; Koryŏ sent a minister, the President of the Board of Ceremonies, HUNG Shang-tsai 洪尚載; Annam sent a minister, T'UNG Shih-min 同時敏, and others. All presented tribute of local produce. When they had arrived (at the borders of China), an officer memorialized for the Emperor's information and went out of the capital (ch'u kuo mên 出國門) to meet and greet them. On an appointed day after they had presented a tributary memorial and presents of local produce at the Fêng-t'ien Hall, they presented their memorials and local produce at the central palace (i. e. to the Empress) and at the eastern palace (to the Heir-apparent). After the Emperor sent officials to the Residence (hui-t'ung-kuan) to give them banquets, the Heir-apparent again sent officials to treat them ceremoniously. The departments and offices at the capital all held banquets. When they were about to return, a legate was sent to console them and escort them out of the boundaries. If it was an ordinary Court, then the clerks in the Grand Secretariat (chung-shu) took receipt of the tributary memorials and the local produce. On the following day the envoys followed the ushers into an imperial audience, and their banquet was conferred upon them. The Emperor and the Heir-apparent composed rescripts (to the tributary memorials) and treated (the envoys) ceremoniously. We now arrange these ceremonies to form the section on 'Foreign envoys presenting tribute at court. . . .'"[21]

[19] 金齒 chin-ch'ih, lit. gold teeth, Laos or Shan tribes who gilded their teeth.

[20] 拂郎 GILES 3659 identifies this with Fu-lin 菻, now recognized as the Eastern Roman Empire or Syria.

[21] *Ta-Ming chi-li* 31. 1-3.

"3. SENDING (CHINESE) ENVOYS (ABROAD) (Ch'ien-shih 遣使).

"In ancient times the Son of Heaven, toward the feudal princes who had submitted to him, occasionally would observe the ceremony of inquiring about charities, congratulations, or mourning sacrifices. Envoys were not yet sent to pay visits outside the Nine Chou (i.e. the empire).

"In the Han period the Emperor Kao (B.C. 206-195) sent LU CHIA 陸賈 on a mission to Nan-yüeh (Kwangtung-Kwangsi), conferring upon him a seal of office. In the time of the filial (Emperor) Wên (179-157) LU CHIA again was sent, receiving an imperial mandate (chao) to go to Nan-yüeh. When the filial (Emperor) Wu (140-87) had dealings with the barbarians (ssŭ-i) he sent CHANG Ch'ien 張騫 on a mission to the Western Regions (in the capacity of) an imperial guard (lang 郎), and SU WU 蘇武 on a mission to the Hsiung-nu as a lieutenant-general (chung lang chiang 中郎將). Thereafter whenever a foreign kingdom had a bereavement, condoling inquiries were made; when they came with inquiries and presents, they were answered and rewarded; when they tendered their allegiance, an imperial seal was bestowed upon them. The Emperor Kuang-wu in A.D. 50 sent the lieutenant-general TUAN Ch'ên 段郴 and the assistant governor WANG Yü 王郁, on a mission to the southern Chieftain (of the Hsiung-nu). The Chieftain prostrated himself to receive the imperial mandate. In 55 A.D. the Chieftain died and (the Emperor) sent the lieutenant-general, TUAN Ch'ên, in command of an army to go and offer condolences. . . .

"In the T'ang period when an envoy was sent to a foreign country he was called 'an envoy to foreign countries' (ju-fan shih 入蕃使). . . .

"In the Sung period when an envoy was sent to a foreign country he was called 'an envoy with a state message' (kuo-hsin shih 國信使). The Emperor T'ai-tsu in 975 sent the Hsi shang ko mên shih (西上閣門使 Usher of the Upper Western Hall), HAO Ch'ung-hsin 郝崇信, on a mission to the Khitan, with the secretary of the Court of Sacrificial Worship as his assistant. From this time on, messengers were sent without interruption. . . .

"Under the Yüan in 1211 (the Emperor) sent an envoy to the kingdom of the Uigurs. Their ruler, I-tu-hu, was greatly pleased, and treated (the envoy) with very extensive ceremony. For this reason he sent an envoy to pay tribute. In 1260 (the Emperor, i.e. Kublai Khan) sent the Director of the Board of Ceremonies, MÊNG Chia

孟甲, and the Assistant Department Director Lɪ Chün 李俊, as envoys to Annam and Tali. In 1266 he sent the Vice-President of the Board of War, Hei-ti 黑的, as envoy to Japan. In 1291 he sent the President of the Board of Ceremonies, CHANG Li-tao 張立道, as envoy to Annam; in 1293 he also sent LIANG Tsêng 梁曾 and CHʻÊN Fu 陳孚 as envoys to Annam, to summon envoys to come to the Court; he also gave an imperial command that the son (of the ruler of Annam) should come for an audience.

"The reigning dynasty has united the whole empire into one. Various envoys have been sent out in order to show compassion to those at a distance. To such countries as Korea (Kao-li), Annam, and Champa imperial proclamations have been promulgated and the imperial commands have been sent to them. Furthermore by imperial command envoys have gone and conferred the imperial seal. The dynasty has also sent down fragrant presents in order to make sacrifices to the mountains and streams of these countries. Its purpose in soothing and subduing the barbarians of the four quarters is most complete. We now in detail set forth the ceremonies connected with the issue of imperial proclamations, the conferring of a seal, and the bestowals and gifts to form the section on 'Sending Envoys....'" [22]

From the official résumé just quoted, several things stand out. Relations between the Son of Heaven and his tributaries were on an ethical basis, and hence reciprocal. The tributaries were submissive and reverent, the Emperor was compassionate and condescending. These reciprocal relationships required formal expression. Presentation of tribute was a ritual performance, balanced by the forms of imperial hospitality and bestowal of imperial gifts. Hence the great importance of ceremonies, so complicated that they must be practiced under guidance beforehand. The detailed regulations given at length in official Chinese works [23] might fruitfully be compared with the feudal and ecclesiastical ceremonies of medieval Europe.

[22] *Ibid.* 32.1-3.
[23] Cf. *Wan-li hui-tien* 58, 8b line 9): "Reception by a foreign country of a seal and goods: ... the foreign king and his officials in a body all kneel. The envoy proclaims the imperial decree, reading, ' His Majesty the Emperor commands his envoy ——— (to be filled in by name) to take a seal and confer it on your country's king ———, and also confer ——— goods.' When this proclamation is finished, the envoy holds up in both hands the seal which is conferred and the ——— goods, and facing the west gives them to the foreign king. The foreign king kneels and receives them, and gives them to his attendants. When this is finished, the ceremonial conductor (yin-li

But, as in European experience, very practical results were achieved within this cloak of ritual. Mourning for the dead being a major ceremony in the Confucian life, the Emperor could properly send his envoys abroad on the death of a foreign ruler, at just the time when it was desirable to have information as to the new ruler and perhaps exert pressure upon affairs in the foreign state. TUAN Ch'ên, in going to offer condolences to the Hsiung-nu, incidentally took an army with him. Bestowal of an imperial seal upon a new ruler has obvious analogies to the recognition of new governments practiced in the West. Diplomatic courtesies of a sort were extended to tributary envoys, who traveled by government post and received state burial if they died in China. Other comparisons can be made to show that the tributary system functioned, among other things, as a diplomatic medium. The fact that the normal needs of foreign intercourse could be met in this egocentric manner tended to perpetuate it, and made any other system seem impossible. Hence the fatal tenacity with which the Manchu Court in the modern period tried to solve its foreign problems through the ancient tributary mechanism.

2. TRIBUTARIES OF THE LATE MING.

The foregoing essay has attempted to suggest certain lines of approach to this subject, any one of which might be made a topic in itself. The nature of the sources, however, seems to prescribe a certain order of investigation: studies of political theory and national psychology connected with tribute must wait upon a more complete understanding of the basic facts of the system, in particular upon an understanding of its economic basis,—what were the conditions of trade between the tributaries and China? This important commercial aspect, in turn, can be approached perhaps most easily through a study of the so-called tribute embassies themselves,—whence did they come and how often? This brings us to the immediate question, what places outside of China were actively tributary, and what fluctuations can be observed in their sending of embassies?

Students of the Ch'ing period are fortunate not only in their opportunities in a virgin field but also in the fact that a number of

引禮) calls out, 'Fall prostrate; rise (to a kneeling position); get up.' The official usher calls out the same (commands). The foreign king and his officials in a body all fall prostrate, rise (to a kneeling position), and get up . . ." etc. PAUTHIER 14-22 gives a not impeccable but useful translation of *Ta-ch'ing t'ung-li* 大清通禮 (edition 1756) ch. 43 on tributary ceremony in general.

eminent scholars have established, by their studies of the Ming period, certain *points d'appui* from which Ch'ing studies may take their start. Researches on the maritime expeditions under CHÊNG Ho are a case in point, to say nothing of those concerning medieval travelers in Central Asia. Since, moreover, the Manchus took over the Ming administration almost as it stood and altered it only by degrees, the Ch'ing system of government can really be understood only against its Ming background. We therefore begin with a glance at the tributary system of the late Ming period.

With the exception of certain aboriginal border tribes under the supervision of the Board of War, all Ming tributary relations were under the management of the Reception Department (Chu K'o Ssŭ 主客司) of the Board of Ceremonies.[24] We present below (table 1) the tributaries listed under the Reception Department in the last Ming edition of the *Collected Statutes* (1587).[25] It will at once be

[24] The *Statutes* open as follows (*Wan-li hui-tien* 105. 80, in ts'ê 7): " Reception Department: the Directors, Assistant Directors, and Second Class Secretaries share the charge of matters connected with the various barbarians' presentation of tribute at Court, and their entertainment and the bestowal of gifts upon them. They select their interpreters and attendants, and make known to them the prohibitory regulations. They also have control over gifts made, by imperial grace to the various officials (of the empire) and the tribute of local produce from the various provinces.

" Court tribute (ch'ao-kung): at the beginning of the dynasty the Court tribute (i. e. presented at Court) of the various foreign countries and of the tribal officials among the barbarians was clearly recorded in the *Administrative Duties* [chih-chang 職掌 for *Chu-ssŭ chih-chang* 諸司 (Administrative duties of the various offices), the first work listed in the bibliography given in *Wan-li hui-tien*, ts'ê 1, preceding chüan 1]. Thereafter those who longed to be transformed (i. e. civilized, mu-hua chê 慕化者) multiplied, the cases and precedents daily increased, and the Tribal Officials Office (t'u-kuan ya-mên) was set up. For this, see under the Board of War; matters concerning Court tribute are appended here.

" Barbarians of the east and south, part one: see the *Ancestral Instructions* [tsu-hsün 祖訓, for *Huang-Ming tsu-hsün* 皇明, another work listed in the bibliography just noted] and the *Administrative Duties*; there are altogether twenty countries. The *Ancestral Instructions* enumerate the unconquered barbarians as follows: Korea (Kao-li), Japan, Great and Small Liu-ch'iu, Annam, Cambodia, Siam, Champa, Samudra, Western Ocean (Hsi-yang), Java, Pahang, Pai-hua (Po-hua?), Palembang, Brunei,— altogether fifteen countries. In the *Duties of Administration* there are also recorded the countries of Chola, Western Ocean Chola, Lan-pang, Tan-pa, Samudra,—which is a bit different from the Ancestral Instructions." The *Statute* continues from here as quoted in note 26.

[25] *Wan-li hui-tien* 105-108. For comparative purposes we take this list from the *Ming hui-tien* as the most exact available description of the situation in 1587, a century before the first edition of the *Ch'ing hui-tien* in 1690. It may be compared

observed that this list includes those distant places visited by the fleets under CHÊNG Ho some two centuries earlier, with most of which formal relations had ceased as soon as the Chinese expeditions failed to reappear after 1433. It therefore gives a totally incorrect impression of the number of countries actively tributary in 1587; it is, rather, a list of all countries with which the Ming dynasty had ever had nominal tributary relations.[26] For the reader's guidance it may be totaled as follows, under the categories given in the *Statutes*:

COURT TRIBUTE:
[1]Barbarians of the east and south, part one: 18 (Korea through Tan-pa);
[2]Barbarians of the east and south, part two: 45 (Sulu through Cananore);
[3]Northern barbarians:
   Small princes toward the north: 3 entries (Mongol princes, et al.)
   Barbarians of the northeast: 2 entries (Jurchen, et al.)
   Western barbarians; part one: 4 entries (Hami etc.)
                                   38 countries of the Western Regions
                                   13 other western places.
[4]Western barbarians, part two: (Tibet, and aboriginal or border tribes, some 20 entries, not listed in this article.)

(Total entries listed below in this article: 123.)

The Chinese version of these place names and the mechanics of their identification we have confined to an index, part 8 below.

In anticipation of our second problem, how often these tributaries were recorded as sending tribute (which may indicate the frequency

with the quite similar list given in the *Ming History*, ch. 320-332, a survey of which was published by BRETSCHNEIDER in 1876 et seq. (see appendix 1).

[26] This fact is indicated by indirection in the opening passages of the Statute:

"At the beginning of the Hung-wu period (1368-1398) various envoys were sent with imperial proclamations to go and announce them to the various barbarians, with a view to establishing peace over the four seas (i. e. all the world). Frequently there were accompanying envoys (with the imperial envoys, on their return) who came to Court to present tribute. In 1375 it was imperially ordered that Annam, Korea, and Champa should send tribute to Court every three years, and when a king in those countries succeeded to the throne then the heir-apparent should appear (at Court). During the Yung-lo period (1403-1424) on several occasions there were troubles in the Western Ocean and (the Emperor) sent palace (i. e. eunuch) envoys with 30,000 seamen, taking gold and silks to bestow them as imperial gifts. There were sixteen envoys who accompanied (the Chinese, on their return) to present tribute at Court."

Nothing further is said concerning tribute presented during the century and a half which had preceded the publication of the *Wan-li hui-tien*.

of trade), we note after each place the dates [27] mentioned by the compilers of the *Statutes* in connection with each place as they listed it. These may be presumed to be important milestones at least in the opinion of the compilers. (The first seven states, Korea through Champa, sent tribute with comparative regularity, and the compilers of the *Statutes* gave certain additional facts which we indicate regarding the periodicity and route of their tribute embassies.)

TABLE 1. MING TRIBUTARIES AS OF 1587.

Country	Tribute Embassies	Periodicity	Route via
Korea (Chao-hsien)	1369 ff.	1372, every 3 yrs. or 1 yr.; after 1403, annual	Yalu R., Liao-yang, Shanhaikuan
Japan	1374 refused, accepted 1381 1403-1551 occasional	10 yrs.	Ningpo
Liu-ch'iu	1368 ff.	2 yrs.	Foochow
Annam	1369 ff.	3 yrs.	P'ing-yang chou, Kwangsi
Cambodia (Chên-la)	1371 ff.	Court tribute indefinite	Kwangtung
Siam	1371 ff.	3 yrs.	Kwangtung
Champa	1369 ff.	3 yrs.	Kwangtung
Java (Chao-wa)	1372, 1381, 1404, 1407	1443 every 3 yrs., later indefinite	

Country	Tribute Embassies	Country	Tribute Embassies
Pahang	1378, 1414	Chola (Hsi-yang so-li)	1370, 1403
Pai-hua	1378		
Palembang (San-fo-ch'i)	1368, 1371, 1373, 1375, 1377	Chola (So-li)	1372
Brunei (P'o-ni)	1371, 1405, 1408, 1414, 1425	Lan-pang	1376 (in periods 1403-24, 1426-35 joined a neighboring country in sending tribute)
Samudra (Hsü-wên-ta-na)	1383		
		Tan-pa	1377
Samudra (Su-mên-ta-la)	1405, 1407, 1431, 1435	Sulu	1417, 1421
		Ku-ma-la	1420

---

[27] In the *Collected Statutes* most events are dated by year only. The lunar Chinese year overlaps the Gregorian by about 34 days, say 10%. It follows that on the average one in ten of the year dates given in the *Statutes* will represent a time (in the western month of January) which is really in the succeeding year.

Country	Tribute Embassies	Country	Tribute Embassies
Calicut	1405, 1407, 1409	Maldive Is.	"
Malacca	(via Kwangtung) 1405, 1411, 1412, 1414, 1424, 1434, frequently 1445 ff., 1459	Burma (A-wa)	"
		Lambri (Nan-wu-li)	"
		Kelantan	"
Borneo (?So-lo)	1406	Ch'i-la-ni	"
Aru	1407 with Calicut et al.	Hsia-la-pi (Arabia?)	"
Quilon	1407 with Samudra et al.		
Bengal	1408, 1414, 1438	K'u-ch'a-ni	"
Ceylon	1411, 1412, 1445, 1459	Wu-shê-la-t'ang	"
Jaunpur	1420	Aden	"
Syria (Fu-lin)	1371	Rum, Asia Minor	"
Cochin	1404, 1412	Bengal (P'êng-chia-na)	"
Melinde	1414		
The Philippines (Lü-sung)	1372, 1405, 1576 (via Fukien)	Shê-la-ch'i	"
		Pa-k'o-i	"
Tieh-li	sent tribute with Java in 1405	Coyampadi (K'an-pa-i-t'i)	"
Jih-lo-hsia-chih			
Marinduque (Ho-mao-li)		Hei-ka-ta (also Pai-ka-ta in 1432)	"
Ku-li-pan-tsu (Pansur?)	1405	La-sa	"
Ta-hui	1405	Barawa, Africa	"
Hormuz	1405	Mogadisho	"
Coyampadi (Kan-pa-li)	1414	Lambri (Nan-p'o-li)	"
Cail	Yung-lo period (1403-1425)	Ch'ien-li-ta	"
		Cananore (Jurfattan)	
Djofar	"		

The list of tributaries in the *Wan-li hui-tien* then continues with the northern barbarians, chiefly the Wa-la (Oirats), as quoted below.[28]

---

[28] "Court Tribute, part three: Northern barbarians. Of the northern barbarians, the Tatars (ta-ta, Tartars) are the largest. Since the Mongolian Yüan (dynasty) retired into the Gobi, the remaining troublemakers for generations have called (themselves) Khans (k'o-han, kagan). On the east is Urianghai, on the west Hami, on the north Wa-la. The Wa-la (Oirats) became strong and several times defeated the Tatars. Thereafter Urianghai and Hami both tendered their allegiance. But Urianghai was then divided to form the three (military) districts of To-yen, etc. (i. e. To-yen, Fu-yü, and T'ai-ning). The chief of the Wa-la, Ma-ho-mu 馬哈木, was invested as Prince of Shun-ning 順寧. The Tatar chief of the Altai offered his allegiance and was invested as Prince of Ho-ning 和寧. Both sent envoys to present tribute. Thereafter they were rebellious and submissive in an uncertain manner. In the Ch'êng-hua period (1465-1487) the small princes also sent tribute. The tribute was without a

It then continues: "Western barbarians, first section: from Lanchow in Shensi one crosses the (Yellow) River and goes 1500 li to reach Su-chou. From Su-chou west 70 li is the Jade Gate (Chia Yü Kuan). Everything outside the Jade Gate is called the Western Regions. But to the south of Shensi everything beyond the frontier from Szechwan to Yunnan is called the Western Tribes (Hsi-Fan). In the Western Regions are seven districts: Hami, Anting, A-tuan (Khotan?), Ch'ih-chin Mongolia, Ch'ü-hsien, Han-tung, and Han-tung the Left, all west of the Gate, Hami being the farthest west 皆在關西而哈密又最西...."

Hami	tribute begun 1404, annual from 1465, every 5 yrs. from 1475	district of Han-tung	
district of Anting	begun 1374	Ch'ih-chin Mongolia district of Ch'ü-hsien	1404, every 5 yrs. from 1563 1437

"The tribute sent to the Court by the thirty-eight countries of the western regions all passes through Hami. As to their periods for tribute, it may be sent off perhaps once in 3 or once in 5 years. The (number of) men may not exceed 35." (The 38 countries are as follows:)

Herat	sent an envoy in 35th year of Hung-wu (1402), 1409, 1437	Ilibalik (and Bashibalik)	sent tribute 1391, 1406, 1413, 1418(?), 1437, continuous from 1457
Ha-san		Nieh-k'o-li	
Ha-lieh-erh		(or Mieh-k'o-li)	
Sha-ti-man		Badakshan	
Kashgar		(Pa-tan-sha)	
Ha-ti-lan (Khotelan?)		Balkh	
Sairam (Sai-lan)		Almalik?	
Sao-lan (Sairam?)		Togmak	

fixed period. In the Lung-ch'ing period (1567-1572) Anda 俺荅 was invested as Prince of Shun-i 順義. Every year he sends a tribute of horses and has traded (with China) to the present time uninterruptedly. The small princes extending toward the north (are as follows): The three princes of the Wa-la, [tribute begun 1403; annual, with interruptions, from 1458], the Prince of Shun-i [tribute annual from 1570], the districts of To-yen, Fu-yü, and T'ai-ning [1388, tribute twice a year from 1403]. The northeastern barbarians are as follows: [Jurchen et al., tribute irregular because of distance]. On the west of the sea (is) Chien-chou [annual tribute]."

BRETSCHNEIDER 2.159-173 gives an extensive critical account of the same subject-matter drawn from the *Ming History*, and a similar account appears in *JA* ser. 9, vol. 7 (1896).173-179.

Chalish	Ya-hsi
Kan-shih	Yarkand
Bukhara?	Jung (Western
P'a-la	barbarians?)
Shiraz	Pai
Nishapur	Wu-lun
Kashmir	Alani
Tabriz	Khotan? (A-tuan)
Kuo-sa-ssŭ	Yeh-ssŭ-ch'êng
Khodjend? (Huo-t'an)	K'un-ch'êng (Kunduz?)
Khodjend (Huo-chan)	Shê-hei
Kucha (K'u-hsien)	Pai-yin
Khodjend (Sha-liu-hai-ya)	K'o-chieh

(The list continues with further countries in the west as follows:)

Turfan	1430, 1497, 1509, 1510, after 1523 once in 5 yrs.	Medina	Hsüan-tê period (1426-1435)
including after 1430:		Khotan (Yü-t'ien)	1408
Karakhodjo (Huo-chou);	1409, 1430	Jih-lo	Yung-lo period (1403-1424)
Liu-ch'ên city	1430	Badakshan	
Samarkand	1387, 1389, 1391, etc.; after 1523 once in 5 yrs.	(Pa-ta-hei-shang) Andkhui Isfahan	" " "
Kingdom of Rum (Asia Minor)	after 1524 once in 5 yrs., via Kansu	Khorassan Ê-chi-chieh	1432 Chia-ching period
Arabia (Tien-fang, Mecca?)	Hsüan-tê period (1426-1435), 1517, in Chia-ching period (1522-1566) fixed to be once in 5 yrs.	Ha-hsin	(1522-1566) "

(The list concludes with Tibet (chüan 108), followed by a score of temples and tribes of the Tibetan border or the southwest.)

When compared with the lists recorded in other Ming sources, this one appears to be relatively complete,[29] enabling us to make the following tentative analysis:

---

[29] With this list from the *Hui-tien* of 1587 may be compared that given in the (pre-Ming) *Wên-hsien t'ung-k'ao* 文獻通考 ch. 324-332, which includes a total of 97 barbarian places or peoples. The Ch'ing supplement to this work (*Ch'in-ting hsü wên-hsien t'ung-k'ao*), ch. 239-250, the compilation of which was ordered in 1747, in a corresponding section lists some 125 places or peoples; this is chiefly for the Ming

Eliminating the first seven adjacent states and those entries which appear to be duplicates, there are some 50 tributaries communicating by sea (of which about 15 remain unidentified so far as we know). A dozen of these states are recorded as sending tribute *before* the period of the great Ming expeditions under CHÊNG Ho (c. 1403-1433). But only half a dozen are recorded as doing so *after* 1433 (Java 1443 ff., Samudra 1435, Malacca 1459, Bengal 1438, Ceylon 1459, Philippines 1576,—an exception, concerned with a reward for the seizure of pirates). Moreover, with the exception noted, not one of these maritime tributaries is recorded as arriving *after* 1460.

Turning to the tributaries communicating by land, if we pass over the Mongols and others on the north, and the western frontier districts such as Hami, we find a list of 38 tributaries of the western region which are said to communicate via Hami. These are listed without comment and are almost the same list, item for item, as that given in the *Ming History* (Cf. BRETSCHNEIDER 2. 314-15), also without comment. Almost half of these places are of doubtful identity, so far as we are aware, and the entire list, so closely and yet not exactly copied later in the *Ming History*, seems like a hand-me-down,— a traditional roll-call without validity for our purposes; perhaps its origin can be found in some work of an earlier period. By contrast, the dozen western places which conclude the list, and concerning which details are given, are plainly of historical importance, particularly Turfan, Samarkand, Rum, and Arabia. These four places, plus Ilibalik and the two obscure items at the end, appear to be the chief " tributaries " which functioned independently via Central Asia, all the others being grouped under Hami. They seem well suited to serve as the alleged or actual sources of merchants in caravan trade. It is significant that their tributary activity appears regularly established at the beginning of the Chia-ching period after 1522.

These observations warrant the hypothesis that the chief activity in the sending of tribute embassies under the Ming shifted from the

---

period and a great number of the entries are for aboriginal or border tribes or places really within the confines of nineteenth century China.

Another work, the *Ta-ming i-t'ung chih* 大明一統志 ch. 89-90,—used by BRETSCHNEIDER,—gives a list of 56 tributaries, all of which are included in the list given above. BRETSCHNEIDER 2.176-315 chiefly from the *Ming History* sections on foreign countries (*Ming-shih wai-kuo chüan*, ch. 329-332), lists 43 tributaries plus 38 smaller places (29 via Hami) all of which had intercourse with China from the west by land; a score of these are not in the list above, half of them being very obscure items.

southern sea-routes to the northwestern land-routes after the middle of the fifteenth century, just as the capital had been shifted from Nanking to Peking in 1421.

This general hypothesis is supported by reference to the lists of tribute embassies recorded at the end of each annual section in the annals of the *Ming History* (*Ming-shih pên-chi*). For analytical purposes we have constructed a chart of these embassies as recorded for the period 1369-1643. Publication of so voluminous a document does not seem feasible, particularly when there are so many problems of identification and the like still unsolved; but certain observations may be based upon it. Judging by the completeness with which the embassies from the Southern Sea and the Indian Ocean were recorded during the period of the great maritime expeditions,[30] this record given in the annals may be considered complete enough for survey purposes.[31]

1. First it is worth noting again that embassies from Southeast Asia began to come to the Ming capital from the very beginning of the dynasty, years before the first of the maritime expeditions under CHÊNG Ho were sent out. This is not surprising in view of the long growth of Chinese trade with this region and the Mongol expeditions which had already sailed through it. Thus in the period from 1369 to 1404 (CHÊNG Ho's first expedition occupied the years 1405-1407) tribute is recorded from Java (Chao-wa) in 11 different years, from Java (Shê-p'o) in 1378, from Brunei (P'o-ni) in 1371, from Pahang (P'êng-hêng) in 1378, from Samudra (Hsü-wên-ta-na) in 1383, from Palembang (San-fo-ch'i) in Sumatra 6 times, and from Chola (So-li) on the Coromandel coast of India in 1372. This agrees with the dates given in the *Collected Statutes* and noted above.

In this period embassies from states adjacent to China,—Korea (Kao-li, Koryŏ), Liu-ch'iu, Annam, Champa, Cambodia, Siam, Tibet (Wu-ssŭ-tsang),—are comparatively regular and frequent. It is note-

---

[30] PELLIOT (1) 317 n. states that all the South Sea embassies in the period of the Ming expeditions were recorded in the *Ming-shih pên-chi*. In the case of Central Asian embassies the *Hui-tien* seems to refer to some not recorded in the *Pên-chi*. This is not unexpected, judged by the example of the Ch'ing records analyzed in part 6 below. On the other hand nearly all the references to XV century embassies from Java and Champa collected by FERRAND 14. 5-11 are included in the *Ming History*.

[31] The annals (Chung-hua shu-chü edition) list some 36 tributaries arriving in the period 1369-1404, some 55 in the period 1405-1433, some 16 in 1434-1500, and some 14 in the long period 1500-1643.

worthy, however, that relatively few are recorded from Central Asia: Samarkand 3 times, Bashibalik once, and but few others.

2. During the much-studied period of the maritime expeditions up to 1433, when tribute embassies from the Indian Ocean graced the court frequently, the activity of embassies from Central Asia steadily increased. Beginning in 1421 the Wa-la (Oirats) are recorded in almost every year up to 1453. Meanwhile Badakshan, Shiraz, and Ispahan are recorded for 1419, Herat in 1415 and later, Ilibalik from 1426; and, most important, Hami, the funnel for Central Asian trade, begins to be regularly recorded in 1415, as does Turfan also.

3. During the remainder of the sixteenth century after the end of the maritime expeditions in 1433, Tibet and the other countries adjacent to China are recorded with a good deal of regularity with the exception of Korea (Chao-hsien) which appears in the record only a few times after 1397 (perhaps because it could be taken for granted), while Japan is recorded half a dozen times. Of the many countries from the Indian Ocean and the South Sea, only Java and Malacca (recorded 10 times between 1439 and 1481) continue with much regularity, Ceylon (Hsi-lan-shan) being recorded along with Malacca in 1445 and 1459. Meanwhile tribute embassies from Hami are noted in more than half the years of the period (1434-1500), Turfan and Samarkand less frequently, about one year in four, and Ilibalik half a dozen times. Thus there is a marked shift of tributary activity from the maritime south to the continental west.

4. During the sixteenth century there is a thinning out of the number of embassies noted in the annals. Liu-ch'iu appears 50 times, every other year on the average. Annam, however, appears only 19 times; Siam, only 9; Champa, 4 (to 1543); and Japan, 7. By way of contrast, the embassies recorded from Central Asia remain relatively numerous: Tibet, 26; Hami, 19; Turfan, 24; Samarkand, 16; Arabia (T'ien-fang), 13; and Rum (Lu-mi, in Asia Minor), 6.

5. In the last years of the dynasty, 1600-1643, the embassies from Central Asia wither away like those from elsewhere: Liu-ch'iu, 15; Annam, 7; Siam, 9; Tibet, 9; Turfan, 3; Hami, 3; Samarkand, Arabia, and Rum, each once (in 1618, with Hami and Turfan).

Certain implications of these data are discussed below in section 6.

3. THE LI FAN YÜAN (COURT OF COLONIAL AFFAIRS) UNDER THE CHʻING.

The inauguration of the Manchu dynasty led to a thorough reshuffling of the relations between China and Central Asia. The Manchus therefore divided their inheritance of tributaries from the Ming into two categories, those from the east and south, who continued to be under the Reception Department (Chu Kʻo Ssŭ) of the Board of Ceremonies, and those from the north and west, who were put under a new agency, the 理藩院 Li Fan Yüan. Since this article is concerned primarily with the former, among whom were included the maritime nations of Europe, we shall take only brief note of the Chʻing tributaries to the north and west.

The tributaries of the north and west were primarily the Mongols. So important were Mongol relations that a special department of the Manchu administration, a Mongolian Office (Mêng-ku Ya-mên), was set up, some years before the entrance into China. In 1638 this Mongolian Office was changed into the Li Fan Yüan,[32] the so-called Court of Colonial Affairs or Mongolian Superintendency,[33] which continued as an important part of the government of China under the Chʻing dynasty.

It is worth noting first of all that the Li Fan Yüan managed Manchu-Mongol relations through the forms of the ancient tributary system.[34]

---

[32] In the sixth month of 1638; cf. *Chʻin-ting li-tai chih-kuan piao* 欽定歷代職官表 (Table of offices and officials of successive dynasties), compiled by CHI Chün 紀昀 et al., Kuang-ya shu-chü 廣雅書局 edition, 17.5.

[33] Although the term " Colonial " seems unfortunate, we favor the translation of BRUNNERT (a) because some sort of translation is necessary for non-sinologists and (b) for the sake of conformity to a manual of titles. MAYERS 183 gives a descriptive translation, " The Mongolian Superintendency . . . which has sometimes been called the Colonial Office." P. HOANG, *Mélanges sur l'administration* (*Variétés sinologiques* no. 21, Chang-hai 1902) 135 gives a more literal version, " Cour suprême de l'administration des Vassaux." Dr. H. B. MORSE and many others have followed MAYERS. HSIEH Pao-chao (*The Government of China 1644-1911*, Balt. 1925) 322, under American influence, uses " Department of Territories."

[34] Here as everywhere the reader must remember that tribute was a *substitute* for more forceful domination, rather than an expression of such domination. In actual fact, as Owen LATTIMORE puts it, " control was by manipulation rather than by decree " (*The Mongols of Manchuria*, N. Y. C. 1934, 50).

HSIEH Pao-chao, *op. cit.*, not only thoroughly misrepresents the nature of the tributary system (pp. 235-7) but also fails to indicate its use in the government of Mongolia and Tibet (pp. 321-341).

The K'ang-hsi edition of the *Hui-tien* introduced this new department in these rapturous terms: [35]

"When our Dynasty first arose, its awe-inspiring virtue (tê) gradually spread and became established. Wherever its name and influence reached, there were none who did not come to Court. As to the leaders of the Mongolian tribes, those who first tendered their allegiance all submitted to our jurisdiction and are regarded as of one body (with the Manchus). Those who came later were a vast host; and all of them coming with their whole countries or with their entire tribes happily tendered their allegiance. Since the land was extensive, the people were numerous. Thereupon they were ordered each to preserve his own territory, and in the years for audience to present a regular tribute. The abundant population and the vast area,—from ancient times down to the present there had been nothing like them! Therefore, outside the Six Boards, there was established the Court of Colonial Affairs (Li Fan Yüan)...."

Thus the origin of tribute is affirmed to lie, as usual, in the all-pervading virtue of the Son of Heaven, while the cognate principles of imperial compassion and reverent barbarian submission are expressed in another introductory passage, on Court assemblies: [36] "Among the 49 banners, from the princes on down, annually or seasonally there must be some who come to the capital. They are made to divide the years (of their attendance) to represent each other, in order to save them labor and weariness, and hay and grain are given them, in order to relieve their exhaustion and fatigue. Thus the system of visiting (the Court) for audience and the benevolence (of the Emperor) in soothing and guiding them are both accomplished."

The general nature of the administration exercised by this new agency will appear from a recital of the main divisions of the K'ang-hsi *Statutes* concerning it. Successive sections dealt with the Ranks of Nobility among the Mongolian princes; the Assemblies, held triennially and concerned with judicial matters, fines being exacted for non-attendance; the Registers of Males, including all between 18 and 60, with penalties for false report; the Postal Transmission system, with regulations for the use of post-station horses and facilities; the system of Guard Houses, with prohibitions of unannounced movements, unauthorized trips to Kuei-hua to sell horses, overstepping of tribal boundaries, or use of others' pasture, and the like; a set of Strict Pro-

[35] *K'ang-hsi hui-tien* 142.   [36] *Ibid.*, 143. 1.

hibitions regarding Persons Absconding, with penalties; the Soothing and Reuniting of Persons who Absconded, with penalties for non-coöperation.[37] As Mr. Lattimore points out,[38] these regulations were in general designed to check the reuniting of the Mongol tribes under another Jenghis Khan, a process which could occur only when relationships in Mongolia were so fluid as to allow the concentration of many personal loyalties under one tribal leader. Further regulations then dealt with Assemblies at Court, Presentation of Tribute, Banquets, Court Tribute, and Bestowal of Rewards,—all in the traditional forms of the tributary relationship.[39]

The later Chʻing rulers appear to have covered the tributary relationship with a sugar coating heavy enough to make it decidedly palatable. On the one hand it was decreed that "the various ranks of princes among the Mongols at the New Year festival all in Court dress are to look toward the throne and perform the ceremony of the three kneeling and nine knockings of the head";[40] and there were further regulations for the presentation of tribute and the bestowal of gifts and banquets in return. Yet within the limits of these formalities the system was developed to allow a maximum of Manchu supervision and control with a minimum of irritation on the part of the Mongols. The nobility among the Inner Mongols, for example, were divided into three classes (pan), of which one came to Court each year in rotation, just before New Years. Limits were put on the number of retainers that each might bring to the capital and on the length of time they might stay, and they were required to practice the ceremonies on their arrival; but beneath all these details the fact stands out that considerable payments were made to and for them. The seven ranks of Mongol nobility each received annually from the imperial coffers an emolument (祿 lu) corresponding to his rank. In the case

[37] *Ibid.*, 142 *passim*.

[38] O. LATTIMORE, *Inner Asian Frontiers of China* 90. The Li Fan Yüan kept a record of boundaries, with maps, of ranks and titles, and of genealogies, revised every decade; it conferred patents of nobility, enforced regulations of the sort mentioned above, and had a hand in marriages. Among other things it is provided that Mongols who have had smallpox are to be received in audience at Peking while those who have not had it, and therefore might carry it, are to be received in audience at Jehol. Cf. *Kuang-hsü hui-tien* 64.10a. The *Huang-chʻao fan-pu yao-lüeh* 皇朝藩部要略 (A general survey of the feudatory tribes under the reigning dynasty) (18 chüan, piao 4 chüan, preface 1839, colophon 1845) gives a chronological summary of edicts on these matters of administration.

[39] *Kʻang-hsi hui-tien* 143-144.   [40] *Kuang-hsü hui-tien* 65.4.

of a first class prince, this stipend might come to Tls. 2000 in silver (fêng yin 俸銀) and 25 rolls of silks (fêng pi 幣) or satin (fêng tuan 緞). "Chieftains (Dzassak), hereditary nobles (Daidji), and Tabunang, have a stipend of Tls. 100 in silver and 4 rolls of satin."[41] Further, the expenses of the noble's suits were taken care of in Peking, provisions being due to them for as much as 40 days. Thus a chieftain, the lowest of the seven ranks, was allowed to have ten retainers and receive provisions while in Peking in the following amounts: every day, in silver Tls. 1.61, in rice 6.5 pints; for three riding horses and ten lead horses, every day for fodder Tls. 0.875511.[42] There were also the customary banquets and presents, and even a gift of travel expenses on departure. In contrast to all these imperial donations, the *statutory* tribute presented at Court, as recorded for the late nineteenth century, was purely nominal. "The annual tribute of Inner (Mongol) chieftains is not to exceed . . . one sheep and one bottle of milk-wine (koumiss).[43] (This use of the velvet glove does not imply that the Mongols did not contribute heavily elsewhere). In the nineteenth century the regulations for Outer Mongolia, including the lamaseries, and for East Turkestan (the moslems of the Hami and Turfan areas) were along the same lines.[44] The Dalai Lama and others in Tibet were likewise now included in the system.[45]

Enough has been said to indicate that the traditional system of tribute was applied to northern and western Asia, though in a form adapted to new circumstances. This success in using old bottles for new wine must have given strength to the continuing Manchu effort to keep the European traders bottled up at Macao and Canton.

As a second point it is noteworthy that the jurisdiction of the Li Fan Yüan was extended to Central Asia only gradually. Relations with Turfan were not under its control until sometime after 1732 (see

---

[41] *Ibid.*, 65.1.   [43] *Ibid.*, 4.
[42] *Ibid.*, 5b.   [44] *Ibid.*, chüan 68.
[45] Cf. *Kuang-hsü hui-tien* 67.12b-13b: "Tribute from Tibet arrives at fixed intervals: Tibet (Hsi Tsang, i. e. central Tibet, Lhasa) once every year sends an envoy to present tribute. Anterior Tibet (Ch'ien Tsang, i. e. eastern Tibet) and Ulterior Tibet (Hou Tsang, i. e. western Tibet) each send tribute once every third year. . . . The Po-k'o-pa-la Living Buddha of Chamdo (eastern Tibet) sends an envoy to present tribute once every five years. . . . The Gurkha Erdeni King (King of Nepal) sends an envoy to present tribute once in five years. . . ." Officers are deputed to escort these tributary envoys, who are often abbots; their suites are limited in size but they are allowed to use the postal stations, for which purpose the Board of War issues tallies, and so on.

Table 2 in section 4 below). It appears that the Manchu conquests which built up a great continental empire including Mongolia, Tibet, and Chinese Turkestan,—ending with the conquest of Kashgar by 1760,—led to a reorganization of the Li Fan Yüan and an extension of its activities.[46] This meant in turn that tributary relations and tributary trade with the continent to the north and west of China were put in a special category, removed from the inherited tributary administration under the Board of Ceremonies. Central Asian trade in the later Ch'ing period thus becomes a special study, connected with the administration of the Li Fan Yüan, and until extensive research is done upon the working of this new agency, Manchu relations with Central Asia cannot easily be fitted into our picture of the tributary commercial system as a whole. In particular, a correlation between tribute and trade, such as it may have been for the Ming period, becomes impossible for this area under the Ch'ing because tributary embassies ceased to be even a chief form of economic intercourse.

For this reason an examination of the tributary embassies from the north and west recorded at the end of each annual section in the *Draft History of the Ch'ing* (*Ch'ing-shih kao, pên-chi*, see Table 5 below) cannot yield results as significant as those gained in this way

---

[46] In the first two editions of the *Statutes* the Li Fan Yüan was divided into four departments, as follows: 1. Department of Records of Merit (Lu Hsün Ch'ing Li Ssŭ 祿勳), 2. Department of Guests (Pin K'o 賓客), 3. Department for Receiving Princes of Outer Mongolia (Jou Yüan 柔遠, BRUNNERT 495.4; lit. "for gracious treatment of persons from afar"), 4. Judicial Department (Li Hsing 理刑). In the third and later editions, that is, from 1764 on, there were six departments; these are named as follows in BRUNNERT 495.1-6, where further details may be found: 1. Department of the Inner Mongols, 2. of the Outer Mongols, 3. for Receiving Princes of Inner Mongolia, 4. for Receiving Princes of Outer Mongolia, 5. Department of Eastern Turkestan, 6. Judicial Department. There were in addition a Treasury, a Mongol Translation Office, a Tangut Studies Office, Inspectors, Secretaries, a Chancery, and so on. For the nineteenth century the Mongol tribes and banners may be tabulated as follows (for details see BRUNNERT pp. 442-464, which, however, omits a simple synoptic table such as this):

AREA	TRIBES	BANNERS
Inner Mongolia (So. of the Gobi)	24	49
Outer Mongolia (across the Gobi)	6	86
Kokonor (Ch'ing Hai Mongolia) (Kukunor)	5	28
Kobdo (between the Altai and the T'ien Shan, Oelots, Durbets, etc.)	11	34
Hami-Turfan (Moslems)	..	2

Cf. *Kuang-hsü hui-tien* 63-68 or, for details, *Ch'in-ting Li-Fan-Yüan tsê-li* 欽定理藩院則例 (1908 movable type edition, 64 chüan).

for the Ming period. The chart which we have constructed of these recorded embassies shows a vast profusion of Mongol tribes and dignitaries presenting tribute at various times up to the beginning of the K'ang-hsi period (1662). From that time on, however, places in the north and west practically disappear from the record; during the remainder of the dynasty the embassies listed are almost entirely from the south and east. The classification of Turfan as a tributary until after 1732 might be taken to indicate that up to that time it was serving as a funnel for caravan trade with regions to the west, as Hami had done under the Ming; but the tribute embassies recorded in the *Ch'ing-shih kao* as from Turfan are so very few as to leave the whole question in obscurity.

4. CH'ING TRIBUTARIES FROM THE SOUTH AND EAST — GENERAL REGULATIONS.

Before touching upon the status formally accorded to Europeans in the Ch'ing tributary system, we must look at the general scheme into which they were fitted. The Ch'ing regulations for the Reception Department of the Board of Ceremonies were modelled upon those which have been described, by Professors CHANG Tê-ch'ang, YANO Jinichi, T. C. LIN, UCHIDA Naosaku, and others, for the Ming period.[47] Needless to say, an understanding of these rules will explain many of the points of friction that arose when Sino-European diplomatic relations became intensified. We therefore quote at length the statement of administrative principles made in the 1690 (K'ang-hsi) edition of the *Collected Statutes*.[48] (We have ourselves numbered the sections of the text, to facilitate reference.)

"GENERAL REGULATIONS FOR THE PRESENTATION OF TRIBUTE AT COURT:

"The prosperity of the united country exceeds that of all previous ages. East, west, north, and south, those who declare themselves sub-

[47] See appendix 1.
[48] *K'ang-hsi hui-tien* 72 (Board of Ceremonies 33). 1-3b: "Reception Department: The Senior Secretaries, Second-class Secretaries, and Second-class Assistant Secretaries divide the charge of the barbarians that send tribute to the Court, the receiving and entertainment of them, and the bestowal of presents upon them. They examine their translated documents; they explain the prohibitory regulations, together with the Superintendent of the Residence for Tributary Envoys. All rewards bestowed upon officials and the local tribute of the various provinces are also under their control." (The general regulations then follow.)

missive feudatories and present tribute at Court are beyond counting. As to the Mongolian tribes, the Court of Colonial Affairs (Li Fan Yüan) has been especially established to control them. Likewise the various aboriginal tribes are under the control of the Board of War. As for those which are under the Reception Department and the Residence for Tributary Envoys,—the years when they present tribute come at certain intervals, the persons who come to Court are of a certain number, the local products (presented as tribute) are of a certain amount, the rewards bestowed are of certain categories. Here we put the general regulations first of all, and then the various countries in order according to their priority in presenting tribute:

1. "In the Ch'ung-tê period (1635-43) it was settled that on (the rulers of) all foreign countries which tendered their submission there should be bestowed an imperial patent of appointment (ts'ê-kao), and there should be conferred a noble rank, and thereafter whenever memorials and official despatches ought to be presented, they should all be dated by the Ta Ch'ing dynastic reign-title. On the occasion of imperial birthdays, New Years days, and winter solstices, they should present a memorial in the imperial presence and offer a tribute of local products, and present a (congratulatory) tablet to the Empress and the Heir-apparent and offer a tribute of local products, sending an official delegate to the Court congratulations.

2. "In the Shun-chih period (1644-61) it was settled that whenever foreign countries presented tribute to the Court with a memorial and local products as proof of the fact, the Governor-General and Governor concerned should examine their authenticity and then permit them to present a memorial and send the tribute to Court.

3. "Whenever foreign countries, in presenting tribute to the Court, send back the imperial seal granted them in the Ming period, the local authorities may be allowed to present a memorial (on their behalf).

4. "The officers and servants who bring tribute on any one occasion must not exceed a hundred men; only twenty officers and servants may enter the capital, all the rest remaining at the border to await their reward. The ships which bring tribute must not be more than three; each ship must not exceed a hundred men.

5. "Whenever a tribute envoy reaches the capital, the local products which he is presenting as tribute are reported by the Residence for Tributary Envoys to the Board of Ceremonies. The Superintend-

ON THE CH'ING TRIBUTARY SYSTEM 165

ent in charge of the said Residence goes to the Residence, examines the things, and sends officers and underlings to control them. The said Board memorializes for the Emperor's information. The tribute objects are handed in to the Imperial Household Department. Elephants are transferred to the Imperial Equipage Department; horses are transferred to the Palace Stud. Daggers, deer's skin, blue squirrel skin [ch'ing-shu p'i 青黍皮 for ch'ing-shu p'i 鼠] and such things are handed over to the Imperial Armory. All sulphur brought in is kept and given to the Governor-General and Governor concerned, to be stored.

6. "For foreigners to send presents to the Governor-General and Governor concerned (in their case) is forbidden in perpetuity.

7. "Whenever a foreign ship comes privately to trade without reason and not in a year when tribute is presented, the Governor-General and Governor concerned shall forthwith stop it and drive it away.

8. "Whenever a foreign country sends tribute, all those ships which take over charge of tribute and ships which keep watch on tribute, and the like, aside from the ships specified by the regulations, are to be stopped and sent back. They must not be allowed to enter.

9. "Whenever the principal tribute ship has not arrived, the ships which protect tribute or keep watch on the tribute are not allowed to trade.

10. "Whenever a foreign tribute envoy happens to die en route, the Board of Ceremonies shall memorialize to order the Inner Secretariat [49] to compose a funeral essay (to be recited and burned at the grave) and the Financial Commissioner on the the spot to prepare the sacrificial offerings. A High Official (T'ang Kuan 堂官, B 304) shall be sent to offer the sacrifices on one occasion, and also arrange for a cemetery, set up a stone, and confer an (imperial) inscription. If an envoy who came with (the deceased) volunteers to take back the corpse, he may do so. If (an envoy) reaches the capital and dies, a wooden coffin and red satin shall be supplied and an official of the Department of Sacrifices shall be sent to issue the imperial orders for the sacrifices. The carts and men which were to be supplied by the Board of War and the clothing and satins and such things which were to be presented (to the deceased) shall still be handed

[49] Nei Yüan 內院, presumably the Nei Mi Shu Yüan 祕書, one of the Nei San Yüan 三, in charge of correspondence with foreign countries.

137

over to the envoy who came with him, for him to take back and bestow. If an attendant of the tribute mission dies at the capital, a coffin and red silk shall be supplied; if he dies en route, (the mission) may proceed to bury him of its own accord.

11. "When a tribute envoy returns to his country, by regulation there is deputed a Ceremonial Usher of the Court of Colonial Affairs (Ssŭ Pin Hsü Pan 司賓序班, B 940) and there is issued to him an official express rider's tally (k'an-ho). He is sent along with the official post and on the way is watched over and urged on, and not allowed to loiter and cause trouble, nor to trade in goods forbidden by the regulations. (When the envoy) has been clearly handed over to the Governor concerned, (the Ceremonial Usher) at once returns (to the capital). The Governor-General and Governor concerned, according to the regulations, send (the tribute envoy) out of the frontier.

12. "In 1664 it was settled that whenever foreign countries admire (Chinese) civilization (mu-hua) and come with a tribute of local produce, it should be examined and accepted as they present it, without adhering too closely to the old regulations.

13. "In 1666 it was memorialized and sanctioned that when foreign countries present a memorial to the throne they need not give it to an envoy, sent to bring it along with him. They should be ordered to depute a special officer to give it to the Governor-General and Governor concerned, who will in turn memorialize on their behalf.

14. "In 1667 it was settled that whenever a foreign country tenders a document to the Governor-General and Governor (concerned in its case), the said officers should straightway open and examine the original document, deliberate, and memorialize the throne.

15. "No Governors-General, Governors, Provincial Commanders-in-chief, or other such officials may unauthorizedly and of their own accord send a communication (i-wên) to a foreign country.

16. "In 1669 it was memorialized and sanctioned that whenever the principal and assistant tribute envoys of a foreign country and the fixed number of their attendants come to the capital, their provisions en route and the men, horses, boats, and carts of the postal service are to be supplied, in accordance with the regulations, by the Governor-General and Governor concerned. They are to depute officials to accompany (the tribute mission), and troops to escort it to the capital. When the tribute envoy returns to his country, for

the provisions en route and the men and boats of the post service, the Board of War is to provide them with postal tallies. As to the men (of the mission) who have remained at the frontier, the local authorities concerned according to the regulations give them provisions and carefully guard them. Later when the tribute envoy returns to his country, they are sent along with him out of the frontier." [50]

Since foreign trade was technically tributary trade, we quote further the regulations of 1690 on foreign trade,[51] omitting an initial passage on commerce with Korea, and numbering the sections.

"THE TRADE OF FOREIGN COUNTRIES:

1. "... In the Shun-chih period (1644-1661) it was fixed that after foreign countries bringing tribute to Court have come to the capital and their rewards have been distributed to them, a market may be opened in the Residence for Tributary Envoys, either for three days or for five days. But Korea and Liu Ch'iu need not adhere to this time limit. The Board of Ceremonies shall communicate with the Board of Revenue, which shall ahead of time detach Wu-lin men [52] to do the receiving and buying. When the despatch in reply has passed through the Board (of Ceremonies) then they shall issue a notice (of the opening of the market) and despatch officials to superintend it. They shall give orders for just and fair trade. It is altogether prohibited to collect or buy works of history. As to black, yellow, purple-black, large flowered, Tibetan, or lotus satins; together with all forbidden implements of war, saltpetre, ox-horn, and such things,—all shopmen and hongists shall bring their goods to the Residence (for sale) and exchange them justly and fairly.

2. "Dying-cloth, thin silk, and such goods shall be handed back within fixed limits. If there are any who buy on credit and intentionally delay (payment), cheating or seeking " squeeze," with the result that the foreigners wait a long time, they, together with those who trade with them in private, will be condemned; and will be put in the

[50] *Ibid. Yung-chêng hui-tien* 104. 1-3b, aside from minor textual changes, is practically identical in connect with *K'ang-hsi hui-tien* 72. 1-3b, only one or two items having been added; the chief difference is that the earlier edition presents the material chronologically, the later edition under topic headings.

[51] *K'ang-hsi hui-tien* 73. 12-14b.

[52] 烏林人, a transliteration of the Manchu title for K'u Shih 庫使 Treasury Overseers. For this information we are indebted to Mr. S. POLEVOY.

cangue for one month in front of their shops. If there are foreigners who purposely violate the prohibitory regulations and secretly enter people's houses to trade, the goods dealt in privately will be confiscated. In the case of those who have not yet been given their (imperial) rewards (i. e. gifts), there will be consideration of a proportional diminution.

3. "All soldiers and commoners inside or outside the Residence or neighboring it on any side, who on behalf of foreigners deal in prohibited goods, will be condemned to the cangue for a month, and banished to the border for military service for life. If there are those who take contraband implements of war, copper or iron, or such things, and sell them to foreigners to get a profit, according to the law for taking military implements out of the border in secret and thereby revealing affairs (of military importance), the ringleaders' heads will be cut off and exposed as a warning to the multitude. At the time of trade, the Board of Ceremonies will issue a notice giving such official information.

4. "Whenever a foreign tributary envoy returns to his country, the officers and men who escort him on his way are not permitted to trade privately in contraband goods.

5. "In 1664 it was fixed that when a foreign country presents tribute, as to goods brought along at this opportunity, if the tributary envoy wishes himself to provide the porters and transportation in order to bring the goods to the capital for trade, he may do so. If he wishes to trade there (at the port or place of entrance) the Governor-General and Governor concerned shall select capable officers and depute them to superintend (the trade), so that no trouble may arise.

6. "In 1685 it was proposed and imperially sanctioned that, as to the goods brought in foreign tribute vessels, if there is a stoppage in the collection of their customs duties, the other (goods) brought privately for trade may be traded; and it is permitted that the officials of the Board (of Revenue) who have been deputed (to superintend), collect customs duties according to the regulations.

7. "It is also proposed and imperially sanctioned that when a foreign merchant's vessel returns to its country, in addition to contraband goods, it shall not be allowed to take people of the interior (i. e. Chinese passengers), nor to export secretly such things as big beams, iron nails, oil, or hemp for making ships. Of rice and grain it may only take (enough for) provisions; it is not allowed to carry more.

When trade is finished and it is time to return to their country, the Governor-General and Governor concerned shall select and depute virtuous and able officers who shall make a strict examination and put a stop to smuggling.

8. "Whenever people of the interior (i. e. Chinese) have strayed to foreign countries and wish to return by ship to their native place, they may be permitted to come back to their former territory; they shall report in detail to the local authorities concerned, who shall make an investigation and allow them to return to their native place.

9. "On the day when a foreign vessel completes its trade, the officers and men of the foreign country are all to be sent back; they must not linger at length within (China).

10. "Whenever a tribute vessel returns to its own country, the goods which it takes along are exempt from the collection of customs duties. It was also proposed and imperial agreement was given that 'heretofore implements of war have been prohibited and not allowed to be taken away for sale to foreign countries; but when merchants come and go on the high seas, if they have no military weapons with which to protect themselves, it is to be feared that they may be plundered; hereafter for merchants of the interior (China) engaged in trade, such things as the cannon and military implements which they carry with them, ought to be in proportion to the size of the ship and the number of men. The Governor-General and Governor concerned should deliberate and fix the number, and at the time when a voyage is begun, they should order the officers who collect customs duties on the seacoast and the officers who are defending the seaports, to examine clearly the numbers (of arms) and permit them to be taken along. When they return they shall make a further examination in comparison with the original numbers.'"[53]

The foregoing principles of administration were made more numerous and detailed in the Ch'ien-lung edition of the *Statutes*, which were thoroughly revised and expanded and set the standard for the last century and a half of the dynasty's existence. These Ch'ien-lung regulations of 1764 were in effect, for instance, at the time of the MACARTNEY and AMHERST embassies of the British and during the Dutch embassy of VAN BRAAM and TITSINGH in 1794-95. They help to explain the demands, such as that for the practice of the kotow, which so annoyed the European representatives. (For the reader's con-

[53] *K'ang-hsi hui-tien* 73. 12-14b.

venience we have italicized the topic headings, and given serial numbers to each section in the original text, some sections of which are omitted.)[54]

"CEREMONIAL FOR VISITORS (PIN-LI 賓禮), COURT TRIBUTE:

1. "*As to the countries of the barbarians on all sides (ssŭ-i) that send tribute to Court*, on the east is Korea; on the southeast, Liu-ch'iu and Sulu; on the south, Annam and Siam; on the southwest, Western Ocean (hsi-yang), Burma, and Laos. (For the barbarian tribes of the northwest, see under Court of Colonial Affairs.) All send officers as envoys to come to Court and present tributary memorials and pay tribute.

2. "*As to the imperial appointment of kings of (tributary) countries*, whenever the countries which send tribute to Court have a succession to the throne, they first send an envoy to request an imperial mandate at the Court. In the cases of Korea, Annam, and Liu-ch'iu, by imperial command the principal envoy and secondary envoy(s) receive the imperial patent (of appointment) and go (to their country) to confer it 奉勅往封. As for the other countries, the patent (of appointment) is bestowed upon the envoy who has come (from his country) to take it back, whereupon an envoy is sent (from that country) to pay tribute and offer thanks for the imperial favor.

3. "*As to the king of Korea*, (the patent) is bestowed upon his wife (fei 妃) the same as upon the king. When the son grows up, then he requests that it be bestowed upon him as the heir apparent. In all cases officials of the third rank or higher act as principal and secondary envoys. Their clothing and appearance, and ceremonial and retinue (i-ts'ung) in each case are according to rank. In the cases of Annam and Liu-ch'iu, officials of the Hanlin Academy, the Censorate, or the Board of Ceremonies, of the fifth rank or below, act as principal and secondary envoys; (the Emperor) specially confers upon them 'unicorn' (ch'i-lin) clothing of the first rank, in order to lend weight to their journey. In ceremonial and retinue (i-ts'ung) they are all regarded as being of the first rank. When the envoys return, they hand back their clothing to the office in charge of it.

[4. Periodicity of tribute, 5. Route of tribute envoys, see Table 3 below.]

[54] *Ch'ien-lung hui-tien* 56. 1-8b.

6 "*As to tribute objects*, in each case they should send the products of the soil of the country. Things that are not locally produced are not to be presented. Korea, Annam, Liu-ch'iu, Burma, Sulu, and Laos all have as tribute their customary objects. Western Ocean and Siam do not have a customary tribute. . . .

7. "*As to the retainers* (who accompany an envoy), in the case of the Korean tribute envoy there are one attendant secretary, three chief interpreters, 24 tribute guards, 30 minor retainers who receive rewards, and a variable number of minor retainers who do not receive rewards. For Liu-ch'iu, Western Ocean, Siam, and Sulu, the tribute vessels are not to exceed three, with no more than 100 men per vessel; those going to the capital are not to exceed 20. When Annam, Burma, and Laos send tribute, the men are not to exceed 100, and those going to the capital are not to exceed 20. Those that do not go to the capital are to be retained at the frontier. The frontier officials give them a stipend from the government granary, until the envoy returns to the frontier, when he takes them back to their country.

[8. Presentation of tributary memorials, after arrival at Peking.]

9. "*As to the Court ceremony*, when a tribute envoy arrives at the capital at the time of a Great Audience or of an Ordinary Audience, His Majesty the Emperor goes to the T'ai Ho 太和 palace and, after the princes, dukes, and officials have audience and present their congratulations, the ushers lead in the tributary envoys and their attendant officers, each of them wearing his country's court dress. They stand in the palace courtyard on the west in the last place. When they hear (the command of) the ceremonial ushers they perform the ceremony of three kneelings and nine knockings of the head [the full kotow]. They are graciously allowed to sit. Tea is imperially bestowed upon them. All this is according to etiquette (for details see under the Department of Ceremonies). If (a tribute envoy) does not come at the time of an Audience, he presents a memorial through the Board (of Ceremonies) asking for an imperial summons to Court. His Majesty the Emperor goes to a side hall of the palace (pien-tien) . . . etc.[55]

[10-13. There follow details concerning further ceremonies, with

[55] The practice of the ceremonies is charmingly described in Prof. DUYVENDAK's long article, (3) "The Last Dutch Embassy to the Chinese Court (1794-1795)."

performances of the kotow; banquets; and imperial escorts, including those provided for westerners because of their services as imperial astronomers.]

14. "*As to trade*,—when the tribute envoys of the various countries enter the frontier, the goods brought along in their boats or carts may be exchanged in trade with merchants of the interior (China); either they may be sold at the merchants' hongs in the frontier province or they may be brought to the capital and marketed at the lodging house (i. e. the Residence for Tributary Envoys). At the customs stations (lit. passes and fords) which they pass en route, they are all exempted from duty. As to barbarian merchants who themselves bring their goods into the country for trade,—for Korea on the border of Shêng-ching [Fengtien province], and at Chung-chiang 中江 [northeast of Chengtu, Szechwan], there are spring and autumn markets, two a year; at Hui-ning [southeast of Lanchow, Kansu], one market a year; at Ch'ing-yüan [in Chihli, now Chao-hsien], one market every other year,—(each) with two Interpreters of the Board of Ceremonies, one Ninguta (Kirin) clerk, and one Lieutenant to superintend it. After twenty days the market is closed. For the countries beyond the seas, (the market) is at the provincial capital of Kwangtung. Every summer they take advantage of the tide and come to the provincial capital (Canton). When winter comes they wait for a wind and return to their countries. All pay duties to the (local) officers in charge, the same as the merchants of the interior (China).

15. "*As to the prohibitions*,—when a foreign country has something to state or to request, it should specially depute an officer to bring a document to the Board (of Ceremonies), or in the provinces it may be memorialized on behalf (of the country) by the Governor-General and Governor concerned. Direct communication to the Court is forbidden. For a tribute envoy's entrance of the frontier and the tribute route which he follows, in each case there are fixed places. Not to follow the regular route, or to go over into other provinces, is forbidden. It is forbidden secretly (ssŭ 私, i. e. without permission) to buy official costumes which violate the regulations, or books of history, weapons, copper, iron, oil, hemp, or combustible saltpetre; or to take people of the interior or rice and grain out of the frontiers. There are boundaries separating the rivers and seas; to catch fish beyond the boundaries is forbidden. The land frontiers are places of

144

defensive entrenchments where Chinese and foreign soldiers or civilians have established military colonies or signal-fire mounds, or cultivated rice-fields and set up huts; to abscond and take shelter (on either side) is forbidden. It is forbidden for civil or military officials on the frontier to communicate in writing with foreign countries not on public business. When commissioned to go abroad, to receive too many gifts, or when welcomed in coming and going, privately to demand the products of the locality (i. e. as " squeeze ") is forbidden. Offenses against the prohibitions will be considered according to law.

[16. Charity and sympathy to be shown regarding foreign rulers' deaths, calamities, etc.]

17. "*As to the rescue* (of distressed mariners),—when ships of foreign merchants are tossed by the wind into the inner waters (of China), the local authorities should rescue them, report in a memorial the names and number of distressed barbarians, move the public treasury to give them clothing and food, take charge of the boat and oars, and wait for a wind to send them back. If a Chinese merchant vessel is blown by the wind into the outer ocean, the country there can rescue it and give it aid, put a boat in order and send them (the merchants) back, or it may bring them along on a tribute vessel so as to return them. In all such cases an imperial patent is to be issued, praising the king of the country concerned; imperial rewards are to be given to the officers (of the tributary country) in different degrees."

These regulations conclude with a section on the Residence for Tributary Envoys (Hui T'ung Ssŭ I Kuan), which was organized much as in the Ming period.[56]

The two following synoptic tables present essential data showing the vicissitudes of the Ch'ing tributary system.

---

[56] *Ch'ien-lung hui-tien* 56. 8b-11. Cf. *Wan-li hui-tien* 109. 99b; *K'ang-hsi hui-tien* 73. 14b; YANO (2) 133-150.

TABLE 2. REGULAR CH'ING TRIBUTARIES.

Table of regular tributaries as listed in the various Ch'ing editions of the *Collected Statutes*, in the order of listing. For data regarding each country, see the Index at the end of this article and Table 3 below.

K'ang-hsi 72. 4-19b (1690)	Yung-chêng 104. 4-38b (1732)	Ch'ien-lung 56. 1 (1764)	Chia-ch'ing 31. 2-4 (1818)	Kuang-hsü 39. 2-3 (1899)
Korea	Korea	Korea	Korea	Korea
Turfan	Liu-ch'iu	Liu-ch'iu	Liu-ch'iu	Liu-ch'iu
Liu-ch'iu	Holland	Sulu	Annam	Annam
Holland	Annam	Annam	Laos	Laos
Annam	Siam	Siam	Siam	Siam
Siam	The countries of the Western Ocean (viz. Portugal, the Papacy) [b]	The countries of the Western Ocean	Sulu	Sulu
Western Ocean country (73. 1a-12a)		Burma	Holland [a]	Burma
	Sulu	Laos	Burma	
The various monasteries of the Western Tribesmen (i. e. Eastern Tibet)	Turfan		Western Ocean (Portugal, I-ta-li-ya, Portugal, England) [c]	
	Monasteries of the Western Tribesmen (as in K'ang-hsi)		Countries having commercial relations [d]	
The Manchurian tribes (lit. the tribes of the eastern sea)	Barbarian Monasteries of the border region of Szechwan province			

(a). Holland was omitted in 1764, having been inactive since 1686, but reappears in 1818.

(b). Specific European countries were not listed by name, though easily identifiable.

(c) Portugal appears as two different countries with very similar names, see Index below. I-ta-li-ya was the Papacy.

(d). For the list of countries having commercial relations with China in the Chia-ch'ing (1818) edition of the Hui-tien (ch. 31. 3-4) see part 6 below. The list included Portugal (Kan-ssŭ-la), France (Fa-lan-hsi, or Fo-lang-hsi; stated to be the same as Fu-lang-chi, Portugal), Sweden, and Denmark.

146

ON THE CH'ING TRIBUTARY SYSTEM 175

TABLE 3. FREQUENCY AND ROUTES OF EMBASSIES.

Table of the statutory frequency, and the routes of regular tribute embassies, as listed in the various Ch'ing editions of the *Collected Statutes*.

Note: the phraseology is chiefly translated from the *Statutes*; the order of the countries varies in the different editions, see Table 2.

	K'ang-hsi 72. 3b-19b	Yung-chêng 104. 4-38b	Ch'ien-lung 56. 1	Chia-ch'ing 31. 4	Kuang-hsü 39. 3
KOREA	Has annual tribute and festival tribute, an annual custom; tribute route via Fêng-huang-ch'êng 鳳凰城.	Same as K'ang-hsi.	Comes annually, crossing the Yalu R. to enter the boundaries; via the land route from Fêng-huang-ch'êng, goes to Mukden, enters Shanhaikuan and proceeds to the capital.	Tribute four times a year, presented all together at the end of the year; tribute route from Fêng-huang-ch'êng to Mukden, entering Shanhaikuan.	Same as Chia-ch'ing
LIU-CH'IU	Fixed tribute period once in two years; tribute route via Min-hsien, Fukien 閩縣.	" " "	Comes every other year via Min-an-chên, Fukien.ᵃ	Tribute once every other year via Min-an-chên, Fukien 閩安鎮.	" " "
ANNAM	Tribute period at first fixed at once in three years; later changed to twice in six years; tribute route via P'ing-yang-chou, Kwangsi 憑祥州	" " "	Comes again after six years, via T'ai-p'ing-fu, Kwangsi 太平府.ᵇ	Tribute once in two years, sending an envoy to Court once in four years to present two tributes together; via P'ing-yang-chou in Kwangsi entering Chên-nan-kuan 鎮南關.	" " "
SIAM	Tribute period once in three years, tribute route via Kwangtung.	" " "	Three years, via Hu-mên (i.e. Bocca Tigris, Canton).ᵃ	Tribute once in three years, via Hu-mên, Kwangtung.	" " "

147

	K'ang-hsi	Yung-chêng	Ch'ien-lung	Chia-ch'ing	Kuang-hsü
HOLLAND	Tribute period at first fixed at once in eight years, later changed to once in five years; tribute route via Kwangtung, recently changed to Fukien.	" " "	Omitted	Tribute at no fixed period; the old regulations were for tribute once in five years; via Hu-mên, Kwantung.	omitted
WESTERN OCEAN	Because this place is distant, a tribute period was not fixed; tribute route via Kwangtung. Recently some of these people have remained to dwell at Macao.	The countries are distant and it is difficult to fix tribute periods; tribute objects also are not fixed in quantity; tribute route via Kwangtung.	A long route; tribute at no fixed period, via Macao, Kwangtung.[a]	Tribute at no fixed periods, via Macao, Kwangtung.	omitted
TURFAN	Tribute period once in five years; tribute route via Shensi-Kansu.	Same as K'ang-hsi.	omitted	omitted	omitted
LAOS (Nan-chang)	omitted	omitted	Comes once in ten years, via P'u-erh-fu, in Yunnan 普洱府.[b]	Tribute once in ten years, via P'u-erh-fu in Yunnan.	Same as Chia-ch'ing
SULU	omitted	(tribute began 1726), tribute route via Fukien.	Five years, via Amoy.[a]	Tribute once in five years or more, via Amoy.	Tribute once in five years, via Amoy, Fukien.
BURMA	omitted	omitted	A long route; tribute at no fixed periods, via Yung-ch'ang-fu in Yunnan 永昌府.[b]	Tribute once in ten years, via T'êng-yüeh-chou, in Yunnan 騰越州.	Same as Chia-ch'ing

(a). Regarding Liu-ch'iu, Sulu, Western Ocean, and Siam, the text reads " they all float their ships on the sea and pass through the ocean to enter the boundaries (of China)."

(b). Regarding Annam, Burma, and Laos, the text reads, " all travel by land and knock at the door (k'uan-kuan 款關) to enter the boundaries."

In comment on the foregoing tables it may be noted that until after 1732 relations with Turfan and certain places in E. Tibet were not yet under the jurisdiction of the Li Fan Yüan, while Russia was under it until 1858 [57] and so does not appear here. Spain and America (the United States) are not listed as countries. The Western Ocean (Hsi-yang) grows from one country in 1690 to several countries in 1732, and in the latter case is treated at some length, tribute objects being listed for each of the three countries incorrectly distinguished. Western Ocean is retained as a sort of catch-all for the Europeans until after 1818. Meanwhile Holland is in high favor in the first two editions, after its naval assistance to the imperial forces in the 1660s, but is dropped in the Ch'ien-lung period and reappears in 1818 presumably because of the embassy of 1794-95. The total of countries listed [58] is markedly less than for the Ming period, even deducting for the transfer of northern and western continental places to the Li Fan Yüan.

---

[57] Cf. *Chia-ch'ing hui-tien* 52 (Li Fan Yüan).23. The Imperial Agent at Urga was in charge of frontier affairs concerning Russia and correspondence with the Russian "Senate" (sa-na-t'ê ya-mên 薩那特衙門).

[58] See appendix 2: Additional lists of Ch'ing tributaries.

5. EUROPEAN COUNTRIES IN THE CH'ING TRIBUTARY SYSTEM.

Just as the ancient forms of tribute were adapted to provide a vehicle for Manchu-Mongol relations under the Li Fan Yüan, so a similar adaptation of the traditional system was achieved in the case of the Europeans who came by sea after 1500.[59] This modification was worked out during a period of two generations of conflict between the Ming and the Portuguese, and resulted in the middle of the sixteenth century in the Macao system whereby the Portuguese barbarians, already tributary in form, were made innocuous in fact by a sort of quarantine. They lived on the walled-off peninsula at Macao, paying a land rent to the local Chinese authorities and going to Canton only periodically to trade. Into this system the English East India Company fitted itself at the beginning of the eighteenth century, although by the end of that period Canton was becoming the real center of foreign activity. Until the third decade of the nineteenth century the effort at quarantine continued. Foreigners were restricted to the Canton factories, outside the city walls, until 1858; even the first treaties after 1842 had restricted them to the five treaty ports or a day's journey therefrom. This bare recital should suggest that the Ch'ing administration was by no means incapable of adaptation in the face of danger. Manchu foreign policy was blindly stubborn in support of the ancient system but not lacking in defensive makeshifts.

In the seventeenth century the Portuguese had been safely confined to Macao and the other western countries had not yet grown to be a menace. The K'ang-hsi edition of the *Statutes* expatiates upon their tributary activity, particularly that of Holland, with evident satisfaction. The record of European embassies is as follows; note the high degree of confusion which obtained in the case of Western Ocean country (Hsi-yang kuo).[60]

"THE COUNTRY OF HOLLAND: Holland is in the southeastern sea. In 1653 it asked (the privilege of) sending tribute. In 1656 it sent tribute . . . [for periodicity and route, see Table 3].

"In 1653 the country of Holland sent an envoy sailing across the sea requesting permission to cultivate (friendly relations) by sending tribute to Court. In 1655 the Governor of Kwangtung memorialized

[59] On the treatment of Europeans as tributaries in the Ming period see the study of the *Ming History* by CHANG Wei-hua.
[60] *K'ang-hsi hui-tien* 72. 12-14.

150

stating that the country of Holland had sent an envoy to offer a tributary memorial and local produce, and to ask (the privilege of) presenting tribute (at Court). The Board of Ceremonies replied giving permission that the Governor-General and Governor concerned should consider deputing officials and troops to escort him to the capital; the number of men coming to the capital should not exceed twenty. It was also ordered that the Governor-General and Governor concerned should select three or four men well versed in the language of Holland, to come along with them. In 1656 the envoys of Holland, Pieter VAN GOYER (and) Jacob VAN KEYSER (Pi-li-wo-yüeh-yeh-ha (or k'a)-kuei-jo 嗶哩哦嚕嚛哈哇噠),[61] and others reached the capital. They lodged at the Residence for Tributary Envoys and presented one memorial. The Board of Ceremonies replied, giving permission that tribute be presented once in five years, the route to be through Kwangtung; each time tribute was presented, the officers and subordinates should not exceed one hundred men, and those officers and subordinates entering the capital should be only twenty men; the rest should all wait and dwell in Kwangtung; the taotai of that region should guard them with great care; when the men who had gone to the capital returned, they should all together be sent back to their native country; they must not dwell permanently on the seacoast. An imperial rescript was received (reading): 'The country of Holland reveres righteousness and pays its allegiance by sailing across the sea to cultivate tributary (relations). We are mindful that the route is dangerous and long. Let them come once in eight years to Court, thus manifesting our compassionate sympathy for men from afar.'

" In 1663 the country of Holland sent an admiral [Balthasar BORT?; 出海王 ch'u hai wang] in command of warships to Min-an-chên [near Foochow], where they helped exterminate the sea rebels, and also asked permission to trade. An imperial rescript was received: 'Let them come to trade once in two years.' In 1664 the country of Holland sent the admiral to assist the (imperial) troops in exterminating pirates; they recovered Amoy and Chin-mên 金門 [in Fukien]. Two command-edicts (ch'ih-yü) were promulgated and officials and clerks of the Board of Ceremonies were sent to go there and offer them a reward, presenting them with silver and satin. Together with the Governor-General concerned they gave (these things) to the Hollanders to take back with them.

[61] For a list of western envoys to China, see below, table 4. Cf. ROCKHILL (4) 437-442, for a brief account of the Dutch Embassy of 1656.

"In 1666 Holland [Pieter van Hoorn?][62] presented tribute and traded. An imperial rescript was received: 'Since Holland sends tribute once in eight years, let its biennial trade be permanently suspended.' In 1667 it was memorialized and imperial agreement was received 'Holland has broken the regulations and come via Fukien to present tribute. Aside from the present occasion, which will not be discussed, hereafter in a year when they send tribute they must enter via Kwangtung; they must not be allowed to enter by other routes.'

"In 1686 it was agreed and imperially sanctioned that 'the time for Holland's presentation of tribute originally was fixed at once in eight years. Now the king of that country, having been moved by the receipt of the imperial benevolence, again asks a fixed time (for tribute). He should be permitted (to send tribute) once in five years. The places of trade may only be in the two provinces of Kwangtung and Fukien. On the day when (trade) is completed, straightway order them to return to their own country.' It was further ordered that the tribute route of Holland be changed to come via Fukien. Further, it was agreed and imperially sanctioned that 'the route from Holland is dangerous and long. To navigate the seas and present tribute is grievous toil. Hereafter, as to the local produce presented as tribute, let the (fixed) amount be considered and reduced.'

"Western Ocean Country (Hsi-yang kuo): Western Ocean is in the southeastern sea ... [for tribute period and route, see Table 3].

"In 1667 the Governor of Kwangtung memorialized stating that Western Ocean country [i.e. Portugal] had sent an official to present tribute, with one principal tribute vessel and three escorting vessels. In 1668 it was memorialized and imperially sanctioned that when Western Ocean sent tribute thereafter the ships must not exceed three, and each ship must not exceed one hundred men. In 1669 it was memorialized and imperially sanctioned to order the principal and secondary envoys and their retinue, twenty-two persons, to come to the capital. The subordinates detained at the border were to be given provisions by the local authorities concerned, and also to be carefully guarded. In 1670 the tributary envoy of Western Ocean country, Manoel de Saldanha (Ma-no-wu-sa-la-ta-jo 嗎諾吻薩喇噠嗒) arrived at the capital, presented a tributary memorial, and offered tribute. After he had been rewarded with gifts and a banquet, an Usher of the Court of Colonial Affairs (Li Fan Yüan) was deputed

---

[62] See table 4 below, for this and later names inserted in text.

to escort him back to Kwangtung and hand him over to the Governor-General there, who should depute an officer to escort him out of the frontier. The tributary envoy of Western Ocean country, Manoel DE SALDANHA (Ma-no-sa-erh-ta-nieh 瑪訥撒爾達聶)[63] traveled as far as the region of Shan-yang in Kiangnan [i. e. Huai-an, Kiangsu] and died of illness.[64] The Board of Ceremonies memorialized and it was imperially sanctioned that the Inner Secretariat [of the Nei San Yüan] should compose a funeral address and the local Financial Commissioner prepare the sacrificial offerings; a high official of the Board should be sent to offer sacrifices one time and also arrange a place for burial, erect a stone tablet and confer an (imperial) inscription; if the tributary envoy accompanying (the deceased) wished to take the remains back with him, he should be allowed to suit his own convenience.

" In 1678 the king of Western Ocean country, Alfonso [A-fêng-su 阿豐肅, i.e. Alfonso VI of Portugal] sent an envoy [Bento Pereyra DE FARIA] who presented a tributary memorial, offered a lion (as tribute), and came to the capital. The Board of War supplied him en route with provisions and with the men and boats of the postal stations. The Board of Ceremonies again sent an official to escort him back to Kwangtung, to hand him over to the Governor-General and Governor there, who deputed an official to escort him out of the frontier." [65]

In these accounts the manner in which the European envoys are assimilated to the traditional system, even to Confucian sacrifies for the dead Portuguese envoy, are so striking as hardly to require comment. Whatever the facts, the official record is preserved perfectly intact.

The Ch'ien-lung edition of the *Hui-tien* (1764), regulations from which were quoted in the preceding section, made no detailed reference to European countries in its section on tribute,[66] although the voluminous *Tsê-li* published simultaneously of course contain much material, into which we have gone not gone.[67]

---

[63] Plainly the same person as above, but here given entirely different characters, which are different again in the Yung-chêng edition 104. 30b line 6.

[64] This is in conflict with Prof. PELLIOT's statement (4) 424 that SALDANHA " mourut en revenant à Macao, à la fin de 1670 ou dans le courant de 1671." Note that this case was treated according to the regulation translated above, following note 49.

[65] *K'ang-hsi hui-tien* 72. 12-14.   [66] *Ch'ien-lung hui-tien* 56.

[67] A great mass of material, on the subjects touched upon in the regulations translated above, is included in the *Hui-tien tsê (shih)-li*; cf. *Kuang-hsü hui-tien shih-li*

The Chia-ch'ing edition completed in 1818 is for our purposes by far the most interesting version of the *Statutes*. This formed the last real revision,—the Kuang-hsü edition of 1899 being modeled closely upon it,—and in it there is preseved the same agreement with traditional tributary forms as in the earlier editions. Here the countries of Europe which are about to beat down the gates are complacently listed alongside Sungora, Kelantan, Trengganu, Ligor, and similar small places of the Malay peninsula. European geography and peoples are still in shadowy confusion and relegated to obscurity. Perhaps we must assume that the official compilers by 1818 really knew the situation more fully but disdained to give the European invaders their due prominence. In that case we have at least an indication of stubborn prejudice and wishful thinking. At all events, these descriptions remained official, and were no doubt for a time consulted by the bureaucracy, until the publication of the last edition of the *Collected Statutes* in 1899. In the 1899 edition all reference to these western countries was omitted, although the other passages on Korea, Annam, etc., already out of date, were reprinted verbatim. We give these official summaries at length below so that the references to Europeans may be seen *in situ*.[68]

" THE COUNTRIES OF THE BARBARIANS THAT SEND TRIBUTE TO COURT ARE (AS FOLLOWS):

"KOREA (Chao-hsien): Korea is the same as ancient Kao-li (Koryŏ). During the period of Ming Hung-wu (1368-98) LI Ch'êng-kuei 李成桂 (Kor. I. Sŏnggye) established himself as king and changed the name of the country to Korea (Chao-hsien). In 1637 King LI Tsung 李倧 (Kor. I. Chong) put his whole country forward to offer its allegiance and was appointed by imperial command [69] King of

502-514, 219, 251, 307. DUYVENDAK (3) illustrates the great possibilities of this material (also JAMIESON 99-109, but quite unreliably).

[68] *Chia-ch'ing hui-tien* 31. 2-4; except where otherwise noted, this text reads the same as *Kuang-hsü hui-tien* 39. 2-3.

PAUTHIER (*Histoire* 178-182) published various extracts from this chüan in 1859. JAMIESON in 1883 in the *China Review*, 12. 96-98, published a very rough translation of this passage, which was made without benefit of PAUTHIER's work, omitted or confused a number of passages, and failed in many identifications. DUYVENDAK (3) 52 translates the main headings given in *Kuang-hsü hui-tien* 39, but not this passage.

[69] Ch'ih-fêng 勅封 which we translate here and below as " appoint by imperial command," and ch'ih-yü 諭, " command-edict," used below for Laos and Sulu, both appear to correspond in a general way to the conferring of " letters patent " in the west. We avoid the western term because it would over-simplify the Chinese situation.

Korea. This country's border on the north is the Ch'ang-pai mountains, on the northwest it is the Yalu river, on the northeast it is the Tumen river, on the east, south, and west it is the seacoast.

"LIU-CH'IU: Liu-ch'iu at the beginning of the Ming consisted of Chung-shan 中山, Shan-nan 南, and Shan-pei 北 (lit. the central mountains, south of the mountains, and north of the mountains), each having a king. Subsequently Shan-nan and Shan-pei were absorbed by Chung-shan. In 1654 the eldest son of the King of Liu-ch'iu, SHANG Chih 尚質, handed in the patent and seal of the late Ming period, whereupon an imperial command appointed him King of Chung-shan. This country is in the great southeastern sea to the east of Fukien.

"ANNAM (Yüeh-nan): Yüeh-nan is the ancient Chiao-chih. Its old name was Annam. In 1666 the eldest son of (the king of) Annam, LI Wei-hsi 黎維禧, handed in the patent and seal of the Ming period, whereupon he was appointed by imperial command King of Annam. In 1789 the Li family lost the throne. The country chose JUAN Kuang-p'ing 阮光平 to be head of the country (kuo-chang). He came (lit. knocked at the gate) to offer allegiance and also asked that he might come to Court. Thereupon JUAN Kuang-p'ing was appointed by imperial command King of Annam. In 1802 JUAN Kuang-tsuan 纘 again lost the throne. The head of the state of Nung-nai 農耐 [Nung was in Tongking-Kwangsi], JUAN Fu-ying 福映, sent an envoy to present (at Court) a memorial and tribute. He also tied up and sent escaped pirates from the seas of Fukien and Kwangtung and presented the patent and seal formerly received by Annam. The Emperor Jên-tsung (Chia-ch'ing period) approved his respectful submissiveness and issued a proclamation changing the name of the country to Yüeh-nan, whereupon by imperial command he appointed JUAN Fu-ying King of Yüeh-nan. This country's northern border is Kwangsi, its western, Yunnan; on the east and south, the coast of the great sea (ta-hai). Over the sea to the south is the ancient territory of Jih-nan 日南 [southern part of Annam]; it also was absorbed in Yüeh-nan.

LAOS (Nan-chang): Nan-chang is the same as Lao-chua. In 1730 the king of the country, Su-ma-la-sa 素馬喇薩, first sent an officer to present a memorial and bring tribute. By imperial proclamation a command-edict (ch'ih-yü) was bestowed on the king of the said country. In 1795 an imperial command first appointed him King of Nan-chang. This country is beyond the frontier of the southernmost part of Yunnan.

SIAM (Hsien-lo): Siam in ancient times was two countries, Dvaravati (Lopburi, Lo-hu 羅斛) and Haripunjaya (Hsien 暹). Later Haripunjaya was absorbed by Dvaravati and thereupon they made the country of Siam. In 1653 it first sent an envoy requesting (the privilege of tribute). In 1673 an imperial command first appointed Sênlieh-p'o-la-chao-ku-lung-p'o-la-ma-hu-lu-k'un-ssǔ-yu-t'i-ya-p'u-ai 森列拍臘照古龍拍臘馬嘩陸坤司由堤雅普埃 King of Siam.[70] In 1766 (the country) was crushed by Burma. In 1781 a native of the country, CHÊNG Chao 鄭昭, recovered the territory and took revenge. The king of the country had no progeny and chose CHÊNG Chao to be head of the country. He sent an envoy to present tribute. In 1786 an imperial command appointed CHÊNG Hua 華 king of the country. This country is south of Burma, cut off from China. Its southern coast is on the great sea, and all intercourse with it is by the sea-route.

SULU: Sulu in 1726 first sent an envoy to present tribute. In 1727 by imperial proclamation a command-edict [71] was conferred on the king of that country. It is in the southeastern sea.

HOLLAND:[72] Holland, also called the red-haired barbarians (hung-mao fan) in 1653 first communicated a tribute.[73] In 1664 they assisted the imperial troops in attacking and capturing Chin-mên [outside Amoy]. An edict was imperially proclaimed to praise them. This country is in the southwestern sea. Later they seized Java (Ka-la-pa) and thereupon divided their people and inhabited it, but still governed at a distance through Holland.

BURMA: Burma (Mien-tien) is the same as Ava (A-wa). In 1750 the king, Mang-ta-la 蜯達喇, first sent an officer to present a memorial and offer tribute. In 1790 an imperial command appointed Mêng-yün 孟隕 King of Ava and Burma (a-wa mien-tien). This country is beyond the frontier barriers of T'ien-ma 天馬 and Hu-chü 虎踞 in the department of T'êng-yüeh, Yunnan.

WESTERN OCEAN: (Hsi-yang):[74] the countries of the Western Ocean consist of:

PORTUGAL (po-êrh-tu-chia-li-ya): In 1670 the king Alfonso [A-,

---

[70] Unidentified.

[71] Note that appointment is conferred on the rulers of Laos and of Sulu by a less exalted form of document (ch'ih-yü).

[72] This section was omitted from the Kuang-hsü edition.

[73] Evidently refers to preliminary correspondence regarding the embassy of 1656, cf. the K'ang-hsi account translated above.

[74] Omitted from Kuang-hsü edition. Paragraphing inserted by us under this heading.

fêng-su, Alfonso VI] first sent an officer [Manoel DE SALDANHA] to present a memorial and bring tribute.

I-TA-LI-YA: In 1725 the king, Benedict [Po-na-ti-to 伯納第多, Pope Benedict XIII at Rome] first sent officers [GOTHARD and ILDEPHONSE] to present tribute.

PORTUGAL (po-êrh-tu-ka-êrh): In 1727 the king, John [Jo-wang 若望, John V] first sent an officer [A. M. DE SOUZA Y MENEZAS] to present tribute.

ENGLAND: In 1793 sent an officer [Lord MACARTNEY] to present tribute. In each case an imperial proclamation was conferred on the kings of the said countries. These countries all are in the southwestern sea.

"The remaining countries have commercial intercourse (with China):[75] The trading countries are as follows: JAPAN, that is, the dwarfs (wo-tzŭ). It is in the eastern sea and trades with China at the island of Nagasaki in that country; it and P'u-t'o [i.e. Puto shan, the sacred Buddhist site in the Chusan Archipelago] are opposite peaks on east and west. From here (Puto) to there the water route is forty watches. From Amoy to Nagasaki, with a north wind one enters via the Goto Archipelago (wu-tao), with a south wind one enters T'ien-t'ang.[76] The water route is seventy-two watches.

CHIANG-K'OU KUO (Siam?) is in the southwestern sea. It has traded since 1729. From that country one traverses the Paracel Islands (and the ocean?)[77] to arrive at Lu-wan-shan,[78] and entering port via the Bocca Tigris one reaches the border of Kwangtung. The route is estimated at 7200 li; from Amoy the sea route is 160 watches. CAMBODIA, the ancient Chên-la, is in the southwestern sea between Annam and Siam. The route from the Bocca Tigris into port is the same

---

[75] All this section was omitted from the Kuang-hsü edition.

[76] 天堂. Hsü Chi-yü's atlas of 1848, *Ying-huan chih-lüeh* 1.15b (map), in a highly abstract manner shows Nagasaki behind an island, evidently the Goto Archipelago; the southern entrance so formed is labelled Wu-tao mên, "Goto Archipelago entrance," and the northern is labelled T'ien-t'ang mên.

[77] 七洲大洋. FUJITA (WANG 66) identifies Ch'i-chou as the Paracel Is. off the east coast of Indo-China. *Hai-kuo wên-chien lu* 41b (map) shows 七洲洋 off the southeast tip of the Indo-Chinese peninsula. Perhaps this phrase should be taken as the "great ocean of the Paracels."

[78] 魯萬山. Lu Wan Shan, according to the *Hai-lu* 1.1, is the same as Wan Shan, a mountainous island in the sea outside Canton which served as the navigator's final landmark on the voyage home. *Hai-kuo wên-chien lu* 2.55 (map) shows Lao Wan Shan 老 in the sea south of Lintin Is. between the present Hongkong and Macao.

as for the country of Chiang-k'ou. The water route from Amoy is 170 watches. Adjoining (Cambodia) is the country of YIN-TAI-MA (Chantebun?). The water route to it from Amoy is 140 watches. The country of SUNGORA is in the southwestern sea. It is a dependency of Siam and has traded (with China) continuously since 1729.[79] The water route to this country from Amoy is 180 watches. Adjoining Sungora are the three countries of JAYA (Ch'ih-tzǔ), LIGOR, and PATANI. Jaya borders upon Sungora on the northeast. The water route from Amoy to this country is the same as to Sungora. Ligor on the east borders upon Jaya. The water route from Amoy is 150 watches. Patani (Ta-ni) is also called Ta-nien. On the northeast it borders upon Ligor. The water route from Amoy is the same as for Ligor. These three countries have all traded (with China) continuously since 1729. JOHORE is in the southwestern sea. It has traded continuously since 1729. Across the ocean it is 9,000 li to the border of Kwangtung; they enter port through the Bocca Tigris. From Amoy the water route is 180 watches. Dependencies of Johore are the three countries of TRENGGANU, TAN-TAN, and PAHANG. From Trengganu to the border of Kwangtung the route is estimated at 9,000 li. From Amoy to Tan-tan by sea is 130 watches. Pahang and Johore adjoin one another. ACHIN is in the southwestern sea. It is traditionally said to be the old country of Samudra. The country of LÜ-SUNG (lit. Luzon, i. e. the Philippines) is situated in the southern sea, southeast of Fêng-shan sha-ma-chi,[80] Formosa. The water route to Amoy is 72 watches. In the Ming period it was taken by the Fo-lang-chi [Spanish or Portuguese]. The name of the country was retained (by them). In 1717 an edict was handed down putting a stop to trade with the southern (? text blurred) ocean. After 1727 there was trade as before. The country of MANG-CHÜN-TA-LAO (Mindanao?) is in the southeastern sea. It has traded continuously since 1729. The water route from Amoy is 150 watches. The country of KA-LA-PA originally was the old land (? text blurred) of Java. It was taken over by Holland; the

---

[79] The reference here and below to the official resumption of trade with southeast Asia about 1729 adds one more question to the many that already present themselves concerning administrative reforms in the Yung-chêng period. The era 1723-35 stands out as one of reorganization along many lines; and deserves intensive study.

[80] 在台灣鳳山沙馬崎東南. *Hai-kuo wên-chien lu* 1.60 (map of T'ai-wan) shows Fêng-shan on the west coast near the south tip and Sha-ma-ch'i-t'ou 沙馬崎頭 at the south tip; WADA 153-4 (quoting *T'ai-wan-fu chih*) gives Sha-ma-chi-t'ou 磋 shan as equivalent to the present Mao-pi-t'ou Cape.

name of the country was retained. It is in the southern sea, and has traded continuously since 1727. The water route from Amoy is 280 watches. PORTUGAL (Kan-ssŭ-la) is in the northwestern sea near England. FRANCE (Fa-lan-hsi 法蘭西), also called Fu-lang-hsi 弗郎西 is the same as the Portugal (Fo-lang-chi 佛郎機) of the Ming period, in the southwestern sea; after absorbing the Philippines (Lü-sung), they divided their people and lived there, still governing it at a distance from France (Fa-lan-hsi). Also the people of this country from the late Ming period have come in and lived at Macao in Heung-shan. The present dynasty continued the previous arrangement and every year orders them to pay a land-rent in silver. But their people are forbidden to enter the provincial capital (Canton). The sea route from this country to China is more than 50,000 li. SWEDEN (Jui-kuo) is in the northwestern sea; the sea-route is calculated to be over 60,000 li to Kwangtung. They have traded since 1732. DENMARK (Lien-kuo) is in the northwestern sea. The route to Kwangtung is the same as for Sweden. After they came to Kwangtung for trade in the Yung-chêng period (1723-1735), it became an annual affair."[81]

The amazing confusion exhibited in these entries was nothing new and had come down from the eighteenth century or earlier, when the Franks, the Portuguese, the French, Italy, the Spanish, the Philippines, and even Holland in the course of time had all become pretty thoroughly mixed up together in Chinese geographical writings. The important thing is not that such errors had arisen but that they persisted so long in the Ch'ing period. The degree of confusion existing in the middle of the eighteenth century is well illustrated in the *Illustrations of the Regular Tributaries of the Imperial Ch'ing (Dynasty)*, a compilation of drawings of barbarians of all countries, with explanatory text, illustrating the costume of the sexes and of various social classes in each case.[82] The material for this imperial work was collected by the high provincial authorities and sent to the Grand Council for presentation to the Emperor. Yet in the explanatory text the following statements occur: 1.23, I-ta-li-ya presented tribute in 1667 (actually Holland) and the Pope came to do so in 1725; 1.47, England is a dependency of Holland; 1.49, France is the same as Portugal; 1.51, Sweden is a dependency of Holland; 1.61, Sweden

[81] *Chia-ch'ing hui-tien* 31.3-4.
[82] *Huang-Ch'ing chih-kung t'u* compilation imperially ordered 1751, Palace edition 1761, 9 chüan.

TABLE 4. EARLY EUROPEAN EMBASSIES TO THE COURT OF PEKING.

Note: dates refer to western calendar years in which an embassy was in Peking. Unless otherwise noted, all these embassies appear actually to have arrived at the capital and to have had audience of the Emperor. For each embassy we have tried to note the chief research recently published with reference to it. Lists of embassies, none completely accurate, are given by PAUTHIER, L. PFISTER (*Notices biographiques et bibliographiques sur les Jésuits . . .*, p. 506, also p. 610, completed by Havret), and S. COULING (*The Encyclopaedia Sinica*, p. 160, from PFISTER).

PORTUGAL	HOLLAND	RUSSIA [8]	PAPACY [9]/BRITAIN
1520-21 Thomé Pires sent by Emmanuel [1]	1656 Pieter van Goyer and Jacob van Keyser	1656 Féodor Isakovitch Baikov by Alexis I Mikhailovitch	
1670 Manoel de Saldanha by Alfonso VI [2]	1665? Pieter van Hoorn [5]	1676 Nicolas G. Spathar Milescu by Alexis I	
1678 Bento Pereyra de Faria [3]	1686 [6]	1689 Féodor Alexiévitch Golovin by regent Sophia (to Nerchinsk, not to Peking)	
		1693-94 Isbrand Ides by Peter I	
			1705 Patr. T. Maillard de Tournon by Clement XI
		1720-21 Leon Vassiliévitch Izmailov by Peter I	1720 Patriarch Mezzabarba by Clement XI
		(1721-25 Laurent Lange trading agent)	1725 PP. Gothard and Ildephonse by Benedict XIII
1727 A. Metello de Souza y Menezas by John V [4]		1726-27 Sava Vladislavitch ("Ragu-zinski") by Catherine I	
		1767 Capt. I. Kropotov by Catherine II	
1753 F.-X. Assis Pacheco y Sampayo by Joseph I		1805-6 Count Golovkin by Alexander I (turned back at Urga)	1793 Lord Macartney by George III [10]
	1795 Isaac Tithsing [7]		
		1808, 1820 (no audiences)	1816 Lord Amherst by George III

160

[1] CHANG T'ien-tsê 43-44 states that the King left the choice of an ambassador to the Governor of India, who chose PIRES; see also CHANG Wei-hua 張維華, P'u-t'ao-ya ti-i-tz'ŭ lai-hua shih-ch'ên shih-chi k'ao 葡萄牙第一次來華使臣事蹟考 "The First Portuguese Embassy to China," SHNP 1 no. 5 (Aug. 1933). 103-112; YANO (2).

[2] PELLIOT (4).

[3] K'ang-hsi hui-tien 72.18b cites this embassy as sent by Alfonso (A-fēng-su). (Although Alfonso VI had been exiled in 1667, his brother Pedro ruled in his name until 1683.)

[4] PFISTER 610 gives data concerning the arrival of this embassy.

[5] DUYVENDAK (5) 337 n. 4, 338 n. 1 states that this embassy was in 1665 and that references to 1666 in a Chün Chi Ch'u memorandum of 1794 and to 1667 in the Kuang-hsü hui-tien shih-li, are incorrect. Similarly the Ch'ing-shih kao, pên-chi, records the embassy under 1667, the K'ang-hsi hui-tien under 1666 (see text above), and COULING p. 150 as of 1668. Prof. DUYVENDAK's masterly treatment of the last Dutch embassy naturally arouses the hope that he will deal similarly with these early ones.

[6] K'ang-hsi hui-tien 72.13b (see text above after note 62), and DUYVENDAK (5).337-8 refer to this embassy, but we have not noticed much material concerning it. Ch'ing-shih kao also lists it, as from William of Orange.

[7] DUYVENDAK (3), (4), and, (5).

[8] A number of minor Russian emissaries reached Peking whom we have not listed, some of them, like BAIKOV, being merely "agents." COULING 160, following PFISTER, lists 11 Russian embassies; but on pp. 491-2 for the same period COULING lists a total of 18 "Russian representatives and envoys to China." The latter list, obviously from a different (though unnamed) source, includes a mission "received by the Chinese emperor" (MILOVANOV and KOBIAKOV 1670) which is not in PFISTER's list; and at the same time it omits embassies of 1808 and 1820 which are listed by PFISTER. Meanwhile both lists omit a certain BRATISHCHEV, cited by STANTON, who was sent to seek a treaty in 1754, and actually received a letter from the Li Fan Yüan. Much further work along the lines laid down by Dr. STANTON is plainly required. On the whole subject see J. F. BADDELEY, Russia, Mongolia, China . . ., London 1919; G. CAHEN, Histoire des relations de la Russie avec la Chine . . . (1689-1730), Paris 1911; J. W. STANTON, "Russian Embassies to Peking during the eighteenth century," University of Michigan Historical Essays (1937), pp. 97-112; and LIU Hsüan-min, "Russo-Chinese Relations up to the Treaty of Nerchinsk," Chinese Social and Political Science Review 23 (1940). 391-440.

[9] Papal relations are referred to by PFISTER, passim, among others.

[10] E. H. PRITCHARD, The Crucial Years of Early Anglo-Chinese Relations, 1750-1800, Pullman 1936, ch. 5-10 gives an invaluable treatment from the British records.

(Jui) and England (Ying-chi-li) are shortened names for Holland; 1.71, the Spanish in the Philippines (Lü-sung) are the Portuguese (Fo-lang-chi) who took Malacca and Macao. (This exaggerated impression of Holland evidently stems from the seventeenth century.)

As the most striking commentary on this persistent confusion it may be noted finally that in November 1844 the Imperial Commissioner Ch'i-ying 耆英, who had just finished the negotiation of treaties with Great Britain, the United States, and France and was presumably the highest authority in China on the subject of western countries, reported to the Emperor that France (Fo-lan-hsi 佛嚂哂) was the Fo-lang-chi (Portugal) of the Ming period, whence derived the French interest in Christianity; after the arrival of Matteo Ricci, he explained, "the Frenchmen suddenly yielded Macao to Portugal, themselves returning to their own country; that those barbarians should be ten times as powerful as Portugal and yet willingly give up the place was (due to) their submission to the teaching of Matteo Ricci."[83] Plainly the ideology of the tributary system with all its implications survived in the nineteenth century in large part because of pure ignorance,—an ignorance so profound that the growth of a conscious Chinese foreign policy was seriously inhibited.

The above table of European embassies to Peking, in compiling which we are much indebted to the assistance of Prof. C. S. Gardner, is offered here as an aid to further study. These embassies illustrate all the problems of the tributary system in its decline,—the growth of trade unconnected with formal tribute, the European dislike of the kotow and demand for equal status, the tragic Chinese ignorance of the west. It is amazing that a larger number of systematic studies have not been made of these successive experiments in Sino-western relations.

6. Ch'ing Tribute Embassies and Foreign Trade.

The successive editions of the *Collected Statutes* reflect a changing situation but do not reveal its realities in any detail. As a first step toward the study of the real activity of individual tributaries we submit the following table of embassies recorded in the period 1662-1911. The years 1644-1661 are omitted because in that period are recorded well over a hundred Mongol tribes and others, many of which we

---

[83] *IWSM-TK* 73. 3b.

have been unable to identify, and almost none of which are recorded after the beginning of the K'ang-hsi period in 1662,—evidently because their activity under the Li Fan Yüan by that time was considered as in a different category from that of the traditional tributaries remaining under the Board of Ceremonies.

No one source, unless it be the 1200 odd unindexed volumes of the Ch'ing shih-lu,[84] gives a complete list of tribute embassies to the Court of Peking under the Manchus. The following table has been compiled from the annals of the Draft History of the Ch'ing (Ch'ing-shih kao, pên-chi) and the Tung-hua lu.[85] Both these sources at the end of each annual section usually give a list of tribute embassies, and usually they agree, particularly in the first half of the nineteenth century (Chia-ch'ing and Tao-kuang periods, excepting 1829-31). But sometimes one records embassies which the other does not, and sometimes embassies are recorded in the text of an annual section in either work but not in the summary list at the end of the section. Thus embassies from Nepal and the Dzungars are often recorded only in the text, not at the end. We have distinguished among these sources within sources by numerals:

1 = recorded at the end of the annual section of the Ch'ing-shih kao, pên-chi.
2 = at the end of Tung-hua lu.
3 = in the text of the Ch'ing-shih kao.
4 = in text of Tung-hua lu.

We have searched 3 (the text of the Ching-shih kao) during most of the period covered, particularly for the Ch'ien-lung era when summaries at the end were usually omitted in both sources. The more extensive text of the Tung-hua lu (4) has been searched only for the first decade after 1662 and elsewhere spasmodically. Each item represents a reference to actual tribute (kung 貢) and has been checked,

[84] Ta-Ch'ing li-ch'ao shih-lu 大清歷朝實錄, Tokyo (1937), 1220 vols. Cf. K. BIGGERSTAFF, Some Notes on the Tung-Hua Lu and the Shih-Lu, HJAS 4.101-115. Prof. BIGGERSTAFF 112 points out that even this collection is by no means complete in its coverage of edicts.

[85] Shih-i-ch'ao tung-hua lu 十一朝東華錄, compiled by WANG Hsien-ch'ien and P'AN I-fu (cf. BIGGERSTAFF loc. cit.), Kuang-pai-sung-chai 廣百宋齋 edition, Shanghai 1891. Our copy of the Ch'ing-shih kao contains prefaces by CHAO Êrh-hsün dated 1927 and by CHIN Liang dated 1928, making it of the first or Peking edition [cf. C. H. PEAKE, A comparison of the various editions of the Ch'ing Shih Kao, TP 35 (1940). 354-363].

although not double-checked; further references can doubtless be found in these sources but not, we believe, in numbers sufficient to change the general picture here presented.

On the other hand, the more complete record available in the mountain of documents compiled to form the *Ch'ing shih-lu* upsets to some degree calculations based upon the *Ch'ing-shih kao*; for the *Shih-lu* contains numerous annual references to the presentation of tribute (from Mongol tribes, Tibet, and such places) not mentioned in the *Ch'ing-shih kao*. This appears from an examination of the *Shih-lu* for 1644, 1654, 1664, and so on at ten year intervals through 1834. This discrepancy might be explained on the theory that reference to ordinary tribute from places under the jurisdiction of the Li Fan Yüan came to be regularly excluded from the *Ch'ing-shih kao*. But it appears that the exclusion went even further, and sometimes applied to embassies from the south and east. Thus the *Shih-lu* for 1664 (3rd year of K'ang-hsi, ch. 11.3b, 12.24b) records tribute from Annam and Liu-ch'iu, while the *Ch'ing-shih kao, pên-chi*, for the same year, does not. The *Shih-lu* for 1674 (13th year of K'ang-hsi, ch. 45. 10b) records tribute from Annam, while the *Ch'ing-shih kao, pên-chi*, for the same year, does not. Other examples could be cited to indicate that the annals of the *Ch'ing-shih kao* present an incomplete record of tribute embassies.[85a] It is hardly surprising that the compilers of the Ch'ing history, working in the twentieth century, should give an imperfect record of the functioning of an institution which really perished long before the dynasty itself. As a result it would appear that a relatively complete record of Ch'ing tribute embassies can be secured only through a page by page examination of the twelve hundred odd volumes of the *Ch'ing shih-lu*. This we have not attempted, but we hope someone else will do so. Until this happy event, the data given below appear to be the best available.

[85a] For example, Cʜ'ɪ Kun 齊鯤 and Fᴇɪ Hsi-chang 費錫章, *Hsü Liu-ch'iu kuo chih-lüeh* 續琉球國志略 (Supplement to the Brief Gazetteer of Liu-ch'iu), latest date in text 1809, dated in Harvard catalogue 1808, in ch. 2 for the period 1757-1809 record tribute sent from Liu-ch'iu for ten years not recorded in our table; the latter, on the other hand, records tribute from Liu-ch'iu in six years not recorded in this work. Again, the *Yüeh-hai-kuan chih* 21.17-45 during the period 1665-1839 refers to the tributary activity of Siam in a score of years in which Siamese tribute is not recorded in our table, while the latter records tribute in a dozen years when this work does not. Some of these discrepancies may of course be explained by the difference in place of the variant observers; tribute recorded at Canton or Liu-ch'iu may have reached Peking in a different year or not at all.

TABLE 5. TRIBUTE EMBASSIES 1662-1911.

Reign Title	Reign Year	Calendar Year	KOREA 朝鮮	LIU-CH'IU 琉球	ANNAM 安南	SIAM 暹羅	BURMA 緬甸	LAOS 南掌	SULU 蘇祿	NEPAL 廓爾喀	DZUNGARS 準噶爾	RUSSIA 俄羅斯	(EUROPEAN)	(MISC.)
K'ang-hsi	1	1662	*12	...	...	...	...	...	...	...	...	...	...	...
	2	1663	*1	...	...	...	...	...	...	...	...	...	*34[a] HOLL.	...
	3	1664	*12	*2	*4	...	...	...	...	...	...	...	...	...
	4	1665	*12	*12	...	*12	...	...	...	...	...	...	...	...
	5	1666	*12	*12	...	...	...	...	...	...	...	...	...	...
	6	1667	*12	...	...	...	...	...	...	...	...	...	*12 HOLL.	...
	7	1668	*12	...	*12	*12	...	...	...	...	...	...	...	...
	8	1669	*12	*12	...	...	...	...	...	...	...	...	...	...
	9	1670	*12	...	...	...	...	...	...	...	...	...	*24 PORT.	...
	10	1671	*12	*12	...	...	...	...	...	...	...	...	...	...
	11	1672	*12	...	...	*4	...	...	...	...	...	...	...	*4[b]
	12	1673	*12	...	*1	*2	...	...	...	...	...	...	...	...
	13	1674	*12	*12	...	...	...	...	...	...	...	...	...	...
	14	1675	*12	...	...	...	...	...	...	...	...	...	...	...
	15	1676	*12	...	...	...	...	...	...	...	...	*34	...	...
	16	1677	*12	...	...	...	...	...	...	...	...	...	...	...
	17	1678	*12	...	...	...	...	...	...	...	...	...	*12 PORT.	...
	18	1679	*12	*12	*12	...	...	...	...	...	...	...	...	...
	19	1680	*12	*12	...	...	...	...	...	...	...	...	...	...
	20	1681	*12	*2	...	...	...	...	...	...	*13[c]	...	...	...
	21	1682	*12	...	*12	...	...	...	...	...	...	...	...	...
	22	1683	*12	*12	...	...	...	...	...	...	...	...	...	...
	23	1684	*12	*2	...	*12	...	...	...	...	...	...	...	...
	24	1685	*12	*12	...	...	...	...	...	...	*1[c]	...	...	...
	25	1686	*12	...	*12	...	...	...	...	...	...	...	*12 HOLL.	*12[b]
	26	1687	*12	...	...	...	...	...	...	...	...	...	...	...
	27	1688	*12	*12	...	...	...	...	...	...	...	...	...	...
	28	1689	*12	*2	...	...	...	...	...	...	...	...	...	...
	29	1690	*12	...	...	...	...	...	...	...	...	...	...	...
	30	1691	*12	*12	*1	...	...	...	...	...	...	...	...	...
	31	1692	*12	...	...	...	...	...	...	...	...	...	...	...
	32	1693	*12	*12	...	...	...	...	...	...	...	...	...	...
	33	1694	*12	...	...	...	...	...	...	...	...	...	...	...
	34	1695	*12	*12	...	...	...	...	...	...	...	...	...	...
	35	1696	*12	...	...	...	...	...	...	...	...	...	...	...
	36	1697	*12	*12	*12	...	...	...	...	...	...	...	...	...
	37	1698	*12	...	...	...	...	...	...	...	...	...	...	...
	38	1699	*12	*12	...	...	...	...	...	...	...	...	...	...
	39	1700	*12	...	...	...	...	...	...	...	...	...	...	...
	40	1701	*12	*12	...	...	...	...	...	...	...	...	...	...
	41	1702	*12	*1	...	...	...	...	...	...	...	...	...	...

[a] "The country of Holland sent an envoy who presented tribute and requested permission to assist the imperial army in carrying on the war against Formosa; an exceptional reward was bestowed upon him." Presumably refers either to BORT or to VAN KAMPEN and NOBEL, none of whom reached Peking?

[b] Turfan.

[c] O-lu-t'ê 厄魯特, i.e. Oëlot (Western Mongols), later followed by the Dzungars. M. COURANT, *L'Asie Centrale aux XVIIe et XVIIIe siècles*, Paris 1912, summarizes Manchu-Mongol relations in this period as recorded in the *Tung-hua lu*.

Reign Title	Reign Year	Calendar Year	Korea	Liu-ch'iu	Annam	Siam	Burma	Laos	Sulu	Nepal	Dzungars	Russia	(European)	(Misc.)
K'ang-hsi	42	1703	*12	*12	*12	...	...	...	...	...	...	...	...	...
	43	1704	*12	...	...	...	...	...	...	...	...	...	...	...
	44	1705	*12	*12	...	...	...	...	...	...	...	...	...	...
	45	1706	*12	...	...	...	...	...	...	...	...	...	...	...
	46	1707	*12	*12	...	...	...	...	...	...	...	...	...	...
	47	1708	*12	...	...	*2	...	...	...	...	...	...	...	...
	48	1709	*12	*12	...	...	...	...	...	...	...	...	...	...
	49	1710	*12	...	*12	...	...	...	...	...	...	...	...	...
	50	1711	*12	*12	...	...	...	...	...	...	...	...	...	...
	51	1712	*12	...	...	...	...	...	...	...	...	...	...	...
	52	1713	*12	*12	...	...	...	...	...	...	...	...	...	...
	53	1714	*12	...	...	...	...	...	...	...	...	...	...	...
	54	1715	*12	*12	...	...	...	...	...	...	...	...	...	...
	55	1716	*12	...	*12	...	...	...	...	...	...	...	...	...
	56	1717	*12	...	...	...	...	...	...	...	...	...	...	...
	57	1718	*12	*12	*12	...	...	...	...	...	...	...	...	...
	58	1719	*12	*12	...	...	...	...	...	...	...	...	...	...
	59	1720	*12	*12	...	...	...	...	...	...	...	...	...	...
	60	1721	*12	*12	*12	...	...	...	...	...	...	...	...	...
	61	1722	...	...	...	...	...	...	...	...	...	...	...	...
Yung-chêng	1	1723	*12	*12	...	...	...	...	...	...	...	...	...	...
	2	1724	*1	...	*1	*1	...	...	...	...	...	...	...	...
	3	1725	*1	*12	...	...	...	...	...	...	...	...	*12 Pope	...
	4	1726	*1	*1	...	...	...	...	*12	...	...	...	...	...
	5	1727	*1	...	...	...	...	...	...	...	...	*1	...	...
	6	1728	*1	...	...	...	...	...	...	...	...	...	...	...
	7	1729	*12	*12	...	...	...	...	...	...	...	...	...	...
	8	1730	*1	...	*12	...	...	*1	...	...	...	...	...	...
	9	1731	*1	*12	...	...	...	...	...	...	...	...	...	...
	10	1732	*1	...	...	...	...	...	...	...	...	...	...	*1 d
	11	1733	*1	...	*1	...	...	...	*1	...	...	...	...	...
	12	1734	*1	*12	...	...	...	...	...	...	...	...	...	...
	13	1735	*2	...	...	...	...	...	...	...	*3	...	...	...
Ch'ien-lung	1	1736	*12	...	*12	*12	...	*12	...	...	...	...	...	...
	2	1737	*12	*12	*23	...	...	*23	...	...	...	...	...	...
	3	1738	*23	*23	*23	...	...	...	...	...	*3	...	...	...
	4	1739	*23	...	...	...	...	...	...	...	...	...	...	*3 e
	5	1740	*23	*23	...	...	...	...	...	...	...	...	...	...
	6	1741	*2	*23	...	...	...	*23	...	...	...	...	...	...
	7	1742	*23	*3	...	...	...	...	...	...	*3	...	...	...
	8	1743	*23	*23	*23	...	...	...	*23	...	*3	...	...	...
	9	1744	*23	*2	...	...	...	...	...	...	...	...	...	...
	10	1745	*23	...	...	...	...	...	...	...	*3	...	...	...
	11	1746	*23	...	...	...	...	...	...	...	*3	...	...	...
	12	1747	*2	...	...	...	...	...	*3 e	...	...	...	...	...
	13	1748	*23	*23	...	...	...	...	...	...	...	...	...	...
	14	1749	*2	...	...	*2	...	*3	...	...	...	...	...	...
	15	1750	*23	*2	...	...	*23	...	...	...	...	...	...	...
	16	1751	*2	*2	...	...	*3	...	...	...	...	...	...	...

d Pa-pu-êrh kuo 巴布爾國. Cf. 巴布 Parbuttiya, i.e. Nepal, Brunnert 907.
e Presentation of tribute not specifically mentioned.

ON THE CH'ING TRIBUTARY SYSTEM

Reign Title	Reign Year	Calendar Year	KOREA	LIU-CH'IU	ANNAM	SIAM	BURMA	LAOS	SULU	NEPAL	DZUNGARS	RUSSIA	(EUROPEAN)	(MISC.)
ien-lung	17	1752	...	...	...	...	...	*3	...	*3	...	*3 PORT.	*3 g
	18	1753	*2	...	...	...	...	...	*3	...	*3 f	...	*3 PORT.	...
	19	1754	*2	*23	*23	...	...	*23	...	...	...	...	...	...
	20	1755	*23	*23	...	...	...	...	...	...	...	...	...	...
	21	1756	*2	*2	...	*23	...	...	...	...	...	...	...	...
	22	1757	*123	*123	...	*123	...	...	...	...	...	...	...	*3 h
	23	1758	*23	...	...	...	...	...	...	...	...	...	...	*3 h
	24	1759	*2	...	...	...	...	...	...	...	...	...	...	...
	25	1760	*12	...	...	...	...	*12	...	...	...	...	...	...
	26	1761	*2	...	...	...	...	*3	...	...	...	...	...	...
	27	1762	*23	...	...	...	...	...	...	...	...	...	...	*13 i
	28	1763	*2	...	...	...	...	...	...	...	...	...	...	...
	29	1764	*23	...	...	...	...	...	...	...	...	...	...	...
	30	1765	*23	...	...	...	...	...	...	...	...	...	...	...
	31	1766	*12	*12	...	...	...	...	...	...	...	...	...	...
	32	1767	*2	...	*2	...	...	...	...	...	...	...	...	...
	33	1768	*2	*2	...	...	...	...	...	...	...	...	...	...
	34	1769	*2	...	...	...	...	...	...	...	...	...	...	...
	35	1770	*2	*2	...	...	...	...	...	...	...	...	...	...
	36	1771	*2	...	...	...	...	*2	...	...	...	...	...	...
	37	1772	*2	*2	...	...	...	...	...	...	...	...	...	...
	38	1773	*12	...	*12	...	...	...	...	...	...	...	...	...
	39	1774	*12	*12	...	...	...	...	...	...	...	...	...	...
	40	1775	*2	*2	...	...	...	...	...	...	...	...	...	...
	41	1776	*2	...	...	...	*3	...	...	...	...	...	...	...
	42	1777	*2	...	...	*3	...	...	...	...	...	...	...	...
	43	1778	*23	*23	...	...	...	...	...	...	...	...	...	...
	44	1779	*2	...	...	...	...	...	...	...	...	...	...	...
	45	1780	*23	*2	...	...	...	...	...	...	...	...	...	...
	46	1781	*23	...	*2	*23	...	*23	...	...	...	...	...	...
	47	1782	*2	*2	...	*2	...	...	...	...	...	...	...	...
	48	1783	*23	...	...	...	...	...	...	...	...	...	...	...
	49	1784	*12	*12	*12	*12	...	...	...	...	...	...	...	...
	50	1785	*12	...	...	...	...	...	...	...	...	...	...	...
	51	1786	*12	*12	...	*12	...	...	...	...	...	...	...	...
	52	1787	*2	...	...	...	...	...	...	...	...	...	...	...
	53	1788	*2	*2	...	*3	...	...	...	...	...	...	...	...
	54	1789	*2	...	*23	...	...	...	...	...	...	...	...	...
	55	1790	*23	*23	*23	*3	*23	*23	...	...	...	...	...	...
	56	1791	*23	...	*2	*2	*23	...	...	...	...	...	...	...
	57	1792	*2	...	*23	*2	...	...	...	*23	...	...	...	*3 k
	58	1793	*2	*2	*23	...	*2	...	...	...	...	...	*23 ENG. j	...
	59	1794	*2	...	...	...	...	...	...	*3	...	...	*23 HOLL.	...
	60	1795	*2	*12	*12	*12	*12	*12	...	*1	...	...	*12 ENG. j	...

f Tribute ordered permanently stopped; in the following year the Dzungars surrendered.
g 布魯克巴之額爾德尼第巴 The Erdeni Regent of the Sakya, or Brugba, i. e. Tibet. Cf. BRUNNERT 906.
h Kirghiz (Ha-sa-k'o).
i 庫爾勒伯克 K'u-êrh-lê Beg; and also Afghanistan (Ai-wu-han).
j 1792: permission for tribute embassy (MACARTNEY) given; 1793: embassy; 1795: tribute not presented at Court.
k 霍罕額爾德尼伯克那爾巴圖 The Ho-han Erdeni Beg, Na-êrh-pa-t'u?
l Annam (An-nan) became Yüeh-nan.

Reign Title	Reign Year	Calendar Year	Korea	Liu-ch'iu	Annam	Siam	Burma	Laos	Sulu	Nepal	Dzungars	Russia	(European)	(Misc.)
Chia-ch'ing	1	1796	*12	...	...	...	...	...	...	...	...	...	...	..
	2	1797	*12	*12	...	*12	...	...	...	...	...	...	...	..
	3	1798	*12	*12	...	*12	...	...	...	...	...	...	...	..
	4	1799	*12	...	...	*12	...	...	...	...	...	...	...	..
	5	1800	*12	*12	...	...	...	...	...	...	...	...	...	..
	6	1801	*12	...	...	*12	...	...	...	...	...	...	...	..
	7	1802	*12	...	...	...	...	...	...	...	...	...	...	..
	8	1803	*12	...	*12 [1]	...	...	...	...	...	...	...	...	..
	9	1804	*12	...	...	*12	...	...	...	...	...	...	...	..
	10	1805	*12	...	...	...	...	...	...	...	...	...	*123 Eng.	..
	11	1806	*12	*12	...	...	...	...	...	...	...	...	...	..
	12	1807	*12	*12	...	...	...	*12	...	...	...	...	...	..
	13	1808	*12	*12	...	...	...	...	...	...	...	...	...	..
	14	1809	*12	*12	*12	*12	...	*12	...	...	...	...	...	..
	15	1810	*12	...	...	*12	...	...	...	...	...	...	...	.•
	16	1811	*12	*12	...	*12	*12	...	...	...	...	...	...	.•
	17	1812	*12	...	...	*12	...	...	...	...	...	...	...	.•
	18	1813	*12	*12	*12	*12	...	...	...	...	...	...	...	.•
	19	1814	*12	*12	...	...	...	...	...	...	...	...	...	.•
	20	1815	*12	*12	...	*12	...	...	...	...	...	...	...	.•
	21	1816	*12	*12	...	...	...	...	...	...	...	...	*123 Eng.	.•
	22	1817	*12	*12	*12	...	...	...	...	...	...	...	...	.•
	23	1818	*12	*12	...	...	...	...	...	...	...	...	...	.•
	24	1819	*12	*12	*12	*12	...	*12	...	...	...	...	...	.•
	25	1820	*12	*12	...	...	...	...	...	...	...	...	...	.•
Tao-kuang	1	1821	*12	*12	*12	...	...	...	...	...	...	...	...	.
	2	1822	*12	*12	...	*123	...	...	...	...	...	...	...	.
	3	1823	*12	*12	...	*12	*12	...	...	*3 e	...	...	...	.
	4	1824	*12	*12	...	...	...	...	...	...	...	...	...	.
	5	1825	*12	*12	...	*12	*12	...	...	...	...	...	...	.
	6	1826	*12	*12	...	...	...	...	...	...	...	...	...	.
	7	1827	*12	*12	...	*12	...	...	...	...	...	...	...	.
	8	1828	*12	*12	...	...	...	...	...	...	...	...	...	.
	9	1829	*23	*2	*2	*2	*23	...	...	...	...	...	...	.
	10	1830	*2	*2	...	*23	...	...	...	...	...	...	...	.
	11	1831	*23	*2	*2	*23	...	...	...	...	...	...	...	.
	12	1832	*12	*12	...	*12	...	*12	...	...	...	...	...	.
	13	1833	*12	*12	*12	...	*12	...	...	...	...	...	...	.
	14	1834	*12	*12	...	*12	*12	...	...	...	...	...	...	.
	15	1835	*12	*12	...	...	...	...	...	...	...	...	...	.
	16	1836	*12	...	...	*12	...	...	...	...	...	...	...	.
	17	1837	*12	*12	*12	*12	...	...	...	...	...	...	...	.
	18	1838	*12	*12	...	*12	...	...	...	...	...	...	...	.
	19	1839	*12	*12	...	...	...	...	...	...	...	...	...	.
	20	1840	*12	...	...	...	...	...	...	...	...	...	...	.
	21	1841	*12	*12	...	...	...	*12	...	...	...	...	...	.
	22	1842	*12	*12	...	...	...	...	...	*1	...	...	...	.
	23	1843	*12	...	...	*12	*12	...	...	...	...	...	...	.
	24	1844	*12	...	...	*12	...	...	...	...	...	...	...	.
	25	1845	*12	...	*12	...	...	...	...	...	...	...	...	.
	26	1846	*12	*12	...	...	...	...	...	...	...	...	...	.
	27	1847	*12	*12	...	...	...	...	...	...	...	...	...	.
	28	1848	*12	*12	*12	*12	...	...	...	...	...	...	...	.
	29	1849	*12	*12	*12	...	...	...	...	...	...	...	...	.
	30	1850	*14	*14	...	...	...	...	...	...	...	...	...	.

Reign Title	Reign Year	Calendar Year	Korea	Liu-ch'iu	Annam	Siam	Burma	Laos	Sulu	Nepal	Dzungars	Russia	(European)	(Misc.)
n-fêng	1	1851	*1	*1	...	...	...	...	...	...	...	...	...	...
	2	1852	*1	...	...	*1	...	...	...	...	...	...	...	...
	3	1853	*1	*1	*1	*1	*1	*1	...	...	...	...	...	...
	4	1854	*14	*1	...	...	...	...	...	...	...	...	...	...
	5	1855	*1	*1	...	...	...	...	...	...	...	...	...	...
	6	1856	*1	...	...	...	...	...	...	...	...	...	...	...
	7	1857	*1	*1	...	...	...	...	...	...	...	...	...	...
	8	1858	*14	*1	...	...	...	...	...	...	...	...	...	...
	9	1859	*1	*1	...	...	...	...	...	...	...	...	...	...
	10	1860	*1	...	...	...	...	...	...	...	...	...	...	...
	11	1861	*3	...	...	...	...	...	...	...	...	...	...	...
g-chih	1	1862	*12	*12	...	...	...	...	...	...	...	...	...	...
	2	1863	*12	...	...	...	...	...	...	...	...	...	...	...
	3	1864	*12	*12	...	...	...	...	...	...	...	...	...	...
	4	1865	...	...	...	...	...	...	...	*3	...	...	...	...
	5	1866	*12	*12	...	...	...	...	...	...	...	...	...	...
	6	1867	*12	*12	...	...	...	...	...	...	...	...	...	...
	7	1868	*12	...	...	...	...	...	...	...	...	...	...	...
	8	1869	*12	*12	*12	...	...	...	...	...	...	...	...	...
	9	1870	*12	...	...	...	...	...	...	...	...	...	...	...
	10	1871	*12	*12	*12	...	...	...	...	...	...	...	...	*2 m
	11	1872	*12	...	...	...	...	...	...	...	...	...	...	...
	12	1873	*1	...	...	...	...	...	...	...	...	...	...	...
	13	1874	...	...	...	...	...	...	...	...	...	...	...	...
ng-hsü	1	1875 p	*1	*1	...	...	*1	...	...	...	...	...	...	...
	2	1876	...	...	...	...	...	...	...	...	...	...	...	...
	3	1877	...	*3 n	*3	...	...	...	...	...	...	...	...	...
	4	1878	*1	...	...	...	...	...	...	*1	...	...	...	...
	5	1879	*1	...	...	...	...	...	...	*1	...	...	...	...
	6	1880	*1	...	...	...	...	...	...	*1	...	...	...	*3 o
	7	1881	*1	...	*1	...	...	...	...	...	...	...	...	...
	8	1882	*1	...	...	...	...	...	...	...	...	...	...	...
	9	1883	*1	...	*1	...	...	...	...	...	...	...	...	...
	10	1884	*1	...	...	...	...	...	...	...	...	...	...	...
	11	1885	...	...	...	...	...	...	...	...	...	...	...	...
	12	1886	*1	...	...	...	...	...	...	...	...	...	...	...
	13	1887	*1	...	...	...	...	...	...	...	...	...	...	...
	14	1888	...	...	...	...	...	...	...	...	...	...	...	...
	15	1889	*13	...	...	...	...	...	...	...	...	...	...	...
	16	1890	...	...	...	...	...	...	...	...	...	...	...	...
	17	1891	...	...	...	...	...	...	...	...	...	...	...	...
	18	1892	*1	...	...	...	...	...	...	...	...	...	...	...
	19	1893	...	...	...	...	...	...	...	...	...	...	...	...
	20	1894	*1	...	...	...	...	...	...	...	...	...	...	...
	21	1895 r	...	...	...	...	...	...	...	...	...	...	...	...
	34	1908	...	...	...	...	...	...	...	*3	...	...	...	...
an-t'ung	1	1909	...	...	...	...	...	...	...	...	...	...	...	...

m Japan.
n Liu-ch'iu tribute to China stopped by Japan; tribute envoy to China sent back.
o 察木多帕克巴拉胡土克圖. The Po-k'o-pa-la Living Buddha of Chamdo, Tibet.
p Only sources 1 and 3 are used after 1874.
q Three khans from Tibet 西藏巴爾布部庫庫木顏布葉楞三汗.
r Nothing recorded from here through 1907.

The picture presented above in Table 5 may be summarized as follows for the two centuries from 1662 to 1860:

Korea—tribute embassies every year with only one or two exceptions;

Liu-ch'iu—embassies every other year on the average, actually in some 115 years out of the two centuries mentioned, and annually in the period 1813-1835,—this has significance for the trade between China and Japan;

Annam—some 45 years in the two centuries mentioned, of which 24 were in the second century,—a slight (recorded) increase in the latter part of the period;

Siam—some 48 years during the two centuries mentioned, of which 11 were in the first century and 37 in the period from 1780 to 1860,—a marked (recorded) increase in the latter part of the period;

Burma—some 16 years between 1750 and 1853, of which 12 were after 1789,—i. e. chiefly in the nineteenth century;

Laos—some 17 years between 1730 and 1853, rather evenly scattered about ten years apart;

Sulu—some 7 years between 1726 and 1754.

The remaining tributaries listed after 1662 are either European, or from the north or west; the latter total a dozen miscellaneous items, including Nepal (the Gurkas) on ten occasions between 1792 and 1908, the Western Mongols (Oëlots, Dzungars) on at least ten occasions, and Tibet, Turfan, and certain tribes, all very occasionally. Nepal sent tribute before the 1818 edition of the Statutes but was not regularly enrolled in it.

From these indications, such as they are, it would appear that, in the latter of the two centuries between 1662 and 1860, embassies from Korea continued regularly, those from Liu-ch'iu and from Annam increased in frequency, and those from Siam and Burma showed a marked increase. According to this table, recorded embassies totalled 216 in the first century and 254 in the second (1762-1860 inclusive). Leaving Korea out of account, as a constant factor, the average number of embassies per year 1662-1761 was 1.16, whereas in the years 1801-1860 it was 1.68. It therefore appears that embassies increased as the dynasty grew older,—that the height of Ch'ing power in the eighteenth century saw less tributary activity than the period of decline in the first half of the nineteenth century.

There is as yet no way of passing final judgment upon the completeness of the references recorded in the sources upon which this conclusion is based. It is conceivable that as the dynasty grew weaker an effort was made to maintain prestige by recording tributary embassies more completely. Judging by the regularity of the bureaucratic scribal activity under the Ch'ing, so far as we know it, this seems unlikely. In any case this evidence, even if it be a mere selection of data, must be reckoned with as it stands until an index has been made for the *Shih-lu*, and it or other sources have yielded further references. What are we, then, to make of this evidence?

The most obvious suggestion is that this increase in the sending of embassies was prompted by commercial motives. The alternative explanation would seem to lie in the realm of international politics. Under the latter heading, if it can genuinely be separated from economic interests, might lie the increase of Burmese and Nepalese activity, following the Chinese campaigns against these countries in 1765-69 and 1792, respectively. The activity of Sulu and of Laos do not seem to fit any particular pattern of explanation. That of Siam and of Liu-ch'iu, however, particularly the latter, might be tentatively ascribed to an increased interest in commerce. Whether the embassies were themselves commercial or merely auxiliary to trade remains to be investigated. But at least in the case of Liu-ch'iu a strong argument may be advanced for the commercial explanation, since Liu-ch'iu was the entrepôt for Sino-Japanese trade; and as a matter of fact a good deal (almost a third) of the recorded increase in the total of embassies is due to Liu-ch'iu. By statute this kingdom should have sent tribute every second year, but it was recorded in 45 years between 1806 and 1860. We summarize below a rather interesting report written by the British Vice-consul at Foochow in 1851 describing at first hand the process of tributary trade.[85b]

[85b] For the conduct of the Liu-ch'iu trade at Foochow, ten Chinese brokers were named for life, being collectively responsible for each other like the old Cohong at Canton. These monopolists similarly had a semi-official status, which was practically hereditary; they reported to the government on the trade and through their monopoly were able to profit extensively from it.

The procedure was described as follows: the tributary envoy from Liu-ch'iu on his arrival called on the Taotai and Financial Commissioner of the province and was in turn given an entertainment, which the Financial Commissioner did *not* attend, the Marine Magistrate (Hai-fang?) usually doing the honors. He then handed in a list of the tribute presents and of the import cargo and the armament of his two vessels,— which being approved, he started on his journey to Peking under official escort and

The suggestion that embassies, at least in some cases, increased in number to provide a vehicle for an expanding commerce naturally raises the whole question of the relation between trade and tribute in the modern period. Having already raised a good many more problems

his ships were allowed to break bulk. After examining the list of imports, the official brokers, each undertaking to dispose of a certain share of the total, would state to the Liu-ch'iu traders the prices they were prepared to give for imports and to demand for exports. The Liu-ch'iu traders on their part brought specie to cover the extra cost of their exports; this was in the form of small Japanese gold coins containing a good deal of alloy, which the Chinese brokers could easily transport to Canton or Soochow for sale if it could not be converted into sycee locally. The Liu-ch'u traders' sole compensation while in the hands of the monopolists was the fact that they were freed from all official customs duties, although not from the unavoidable presents to Chinese officials.

The Liu-ch'iu trade flourished because at least one half of it was for re-export to Japan on the occasion of the annual Liu-ch'iuan tribute missions there, and goods were brought to Foochow from Liu-ch'iu on credit repayable in two to five months, after transfer of goods to the Japanese trade could be completed. Even though freed from customs duties, the Liu-ch'iu cargoes were not accurately reported to the Foochow customs; following " old custom " the same imports would be reported year after year with but slight variation, so that less than half the cargo was really reported, most of it being smuggled by the brokers with the knowledge of the authorities. The Consul suspected that this was done to obviate some statutory limit placed upon the size of the trade.

When the tributary envoy returned from Peking, all accounts were closed. The envoy again called on the Financial Commissioner and received another entertainment under the heading, says the Consul, of " tender mercies and hospitality to strangers from afar " which the Chinese were so fond of quoting. The envoy also received Tls. 500 from the Financial Commissioner to defray the expenses of his late journey to Peking. Finally as a parting ceremony, dressed in full Liu-ch'iu costume, he performed a grand kotow to the Emperor on an elevated platform at the custom house, in gratitude for the exemption of his ships from duty.

The Liu-ch'iuans like all foreigners were classed as I, barbarians. At Foochow they were restricted to the suburbs, where the residence for the tributary envoy was situated, and they were not allowed without authorization to enter the city walls or the interior. In 1851 the new King of Liu-ch'iu was still a minor, aged 17, his father having died two or three years before, and was due to be installed in his kingship in the following year (1852), when an imperial commissioner would be sent to Liu-ch'iu with an imperial document and presents of silks and satins. Customarily this high official was selected from Fukien and departed from Foochow with 500 picked troops in two large war junks. " It is calculated, what with presents to the Ambassador and his escort, their maintenance, and the cargo which the Loochooans are forced to purchase at heavy prices from the members of the Embassy, that it will cost Loochoo no less than thirty thousand Taels of silver." (Vice-consul SINCLAIR, Foochow, no. 26 to Sir George BONHAM, June 18, 1851, *British Consular Archives*, Foochow.)

172

than have been solved, we venture to put forward a brief interpretation of tributary trade in general.

1. It is a truism that in the modern period Chinese exclusiveness was broken down by maritime trade with the west, which increased to a point where it could not be confined within tributary channels. This process was most spectacular in the case of the opium trade in the nineteenth century which provided the lubrication for the entire Anglo-American commercial penetration, and which rapidly increased the flow of Sino-western commerce built up by the eighteenth century tea trade under the East India Company. It was this continued growth of trade which brought on the fatal trial of strength between the tributary system and Great Britain, from which stemmed the débacle of the later nineteenth century. The subject has already been much studied.

2. By contrast, the expansion of Chinese native trade in the Ch'ing period has been relatively neglected. The junk trade from Amoy and Canton to the East indies and Malaya [86] has been tacitly accepted as the logical background of the spectacular Ming expeditions under CHÊNG Ho, but scholarly studies of that period of Chinese imperial expansion have been largely devoted to unavoidable textual problems rather than to its economic history. After the expeditions ceased in 1433 Chinese commerce with Southeastern Asia remains obscure until after the arrival of the Portuguese at Malacca in 1511, when the story of European penetration begins as noted in the preceding paragraph.

It is generally accepted that the Portuguese at Malacca, in the Moluccas, and elsewhere entered into an east-west trade which had previously been flourishing under Arab domination. It is an obvious next step to posit that the Portuguese and their successors the Dutch and English also entered into a north-south trade, which was already

---

[86] The existence of this great southern trade of Chinese junks from Canton and Amoy was recognized in the following passage in *Chia-ch'ing hui-tien* 31.15 (omitted in Kuang-hsü edition), in a section listing native products of trading countries: " As to the various countries which are near the northwest, such as Portugal (Kan-ssŭ-la), Sweden, and Denmark, in all cases the barbarian merchants of those countries come to China (nei-ti) to trade. They come in summer and go back in winter. As to the various countries in the southeastern sea,—Cambodia, Sungora, Johore, Trengganu, Achin, and so on,—and the countries in the South Sea,—the Philippines (Luzon) and others,—in all cases the merchants of our own harbors of Kwangtung and the merchants of Chekiang and Fukien in the winter and spring go to these various countries to trade, and in summer and autumn then come back. . . ."

flourishing beteen China and Southeastern Asia and was conducted largely by the Chinese. This may be taken as a truism. A recent student of the Spanish in the Philippines,[87] for example, points out that Manila prospered chiefly as an entrepôt between China and America, the China-Manila trade being conducted by the Chinese. In other words, early European trade with eastern Asia was grafted onto the Chinese junk trade which already flourished there. Native Chinese commercial expansion stemming from the Mongol period, or probably much earlier, paved the way for the European invasion of China by sea. Should we not assume that it also for a time kept pace with the growth of western Commerce?[88]

3. The vitality of the Chinese junk trade with Malaya in the early nineteenth century is clearly reflected in the list of countries recorded in the 1818 edition of the *Collected Statutes* as having commercial rather than tributary intercourse with China. From the account of these countries, translated in section 4 above, the following table may be constructed:

TABLE 6. NON-TRIBUTARY TRADING COUNTRIES 1818.

Place	No. of "watches" (ching 更)[89] distant from Amoy	No. of li distant from Canton; remarks
Siam? (Chiang-k'ou)	160 to Amoy	7200 to Canton
Cambodia (Tung-pu-chai)	170 " "	same route to Canton as Chiang-k'ou
Yin-tai-ma (Chantebun?)	140 " "	(adjoins Cambodia)
(Malay Peninsula begins here?)	......	......
Ligor	150 " "	(adjoins Jaya)
Jaya (Ch'ih-tzŭ)	same as Sungora (180)	(adjoins Sungora)

---

[87] W. L. SCHURZ, *The Manila Galleon*, New York, 1939.

[88] This early Sino-western commercial competition in Malaya is touched upon in an article by Prof. CHANG Tê-ch'ang 張德昌, Ch'ing-tai ya-p'ien chan-chêng ch'ien chih Chung-hsi yen-hai t'ung-shang 清代鴉片戰爭前之中西沿海通商 (Sino-western coastal trade in the Ch'ing period before the Opium War), *CHHP* 10 (1935), 97-145.

[89] The length of one sea watch (kêng, Pek. ching) appears to be as uncertain as the length of one li on land. WANG Ta-hai (*Hai-tao i-chih*, see under section 7 below) 479 gives one watch as 50 li 每更五十里, while a nineteenth century source, YEH Ch'iang-yung (*Lü-sung chi-lüeh*) 3, states flatly that one ching is 100 li 凡海中記里, 以一百里爲一更. At this rate he figures 124 ching as 12,400 li and estimates the distances Shanghai-Ningpo as 12 ching, Ningo-Amoy as 40, Amoy-Lü-sung as 72. For the Ming period 300 to 400 years earlier, however, MILLS 7 describes a "Kêng"

ON THE CH'ING TRIBUTARY SYSTEM 203

Place	No. of "watches" (ching)[89] distant from Amoy	No. of li distant from Canton; remarks
Sungora	180 to Amoy	......
Patani	same as Ligor (150)	(adjoins Ligor?)
(Siamese-Malayan border comes here?)	......	......
Trengganu	......	9,000 to Kwangtung border
Tan-tan	130 to Amoy	......
Pahang	......	(adjoins Johore)
Johore	180 to Amoy	9,000 li to Kwangtung border
(end of Malay peninsula)	......	......
(revert to eastern route)	......	......
Lü-sung (P. I.)	72 to Amoy	......
Mang-chün-ta-lao (Mindanao?)	150 to Amoy	......
Java (Batavia?)	280 to Amoy	......

A glance at the *Atlas van Tropisch Nederland*, Blad. 10b, or any good map of the region [90] will show how plainly these places form a chain of ports of call on the coastal trade route from Amoy to the Straits. That this list is an accurate contemporary record is confirmed in a pleasantly unexpected manner by the report of a British empire-builder, Captain Francis LIGHT, the chief founder of Penang, who sent home about the year 1788 a list of places in Malaya entitled "A Brief Account of the several countries surrounding Prince of Wales's Island with their production." [91] The places of trade listed by Capt. LIGHT are as follows; note the nearly perfect correspondence with the Chinese

(ching) or watch as 2.4 hours in Chinese navigation; and WADA 152 states that one ching equalled 60 li, say 20 miles, 10 ching being covered in 24 hours with a favorable wind. These statements demand careful investigation of nineteenth century practice. MILLS' calculations are of course borne out by the facts.

MILLS 43 calculates that Chinese junks of the Ming period according to the sailing directions used by them appear to have traveled 2.93 miles an hour in shore waters, and to have averaged 6.25 miles an hour in open waters; whereas a modern junk might go at most 8.5 miles an hour.

[90] Hsü Chi-yü's geography of 1848, 1.23b, 2.1b (maps of S. E. Asia), gives nearly all this list of places.

[91] Communicated by C. E. WURTZBURG (originally enclosed in CORNWALLIS to DUNDAS, Jan. 7, 1789), *J. of the Malayan Branch of the R. A. S.*, vol. 16 part 1 (July 1938). 123-126.

175

list published 30 years later: Siam, Chantebon, Chia, Sangora, Pattany, Ligore, Tringano, Pahang, Jahore, Rheo, ... (5 items) ... Acheen....

Considering the wealth of place names and points of trade recorded in Malaya at earlier periods, the relatively close correspondence of these two sources would indicate that they mirrored the same situation, i. e. that the Chinese list of 1818 was based on fact. Confirmation may be found in other Chinese works.[92]

4. The most important thing about this list is the fact that it was frankly labelled " trading countries " 互市諸國, not " tributaries." In the Ming period Kelantan, Pahang, and Johore had been officially enrolled as tributaries. Now they were not. Evidently this was a tardy acknowledgment of the situation created in the fifteenth century when tribute embassies from Southeastern Asia, with the chief exception of Malacca, ceased to arrive at Peking just as soon as CHÊNG Ho stopped coming to get them,—although trade with Southeast Asia continued.

In this context the voyages of CHÊNG Ho may be regarded as an effort to bring the sources of Chinese maritime trade into the formal structure of the tributary system. Foreign places communicating by land were by official tradition regarded as tributary and were so enrolled, as were those foreigners who came by sea. But the effort to extend this system to keep up with the expansion of Chinese maritime trade was too costly and after 1433 it was given up. The tributary system no longer worked by sea, and the compilers of 1818 finally acknowledged the fact.

5. It is not difficult to see why this should be so. Like the Chinese state as a whole, the tributary system had developed upon the land without experience of the sea; and in accord with the position of the Middle Kingdom as the center of eastern Asiatic civilization, it had functioned passively. The barbarians came to China, the Chinese had no reason to go abroad. During the first two millennia of Chinese history the tributary system had continued to be based upon land frontiers, and whenever the government was even moderately strong the trade which crossed these territorial boundaries could be controlled. The Jade Gate was merely the most notable of many points of control.

---

[92] Cf. the following passage from the *Hai-kuo wên-chien lu* (block print ed., preface 1730, 1.25b; we quote SCHLEGEL's translation in *TP* [1898].298): " South from Siam are Chaya, Lakon (Ligor) and Sungora which are all tributary states of Siam. Patani, Kelantan, Tringano, and Pahang all follow each other in succession along the (central) mountainridge."

On the land frontiers there appears to be ample evidence that the traditional system functioned, in its own peculiar way, down to the end of the Ming period and even later. The "tributary envoys" who came to China from the defunct Kingdom of Rum in 1618 may have been great liars but they did no more violence to the system than their ancestors from "Constantinople" had done.

Moreover, the ancient caravan trade across Central Asia had been necessarily limited in volume and inclined to concentrate upon luxury goods of little weight and high value. Such goods could find their best market at the capital. Merchants bound for the metropolis found it easy to come in the train or in the guise of a tribute embassy. Even if they stopped at the frontier, they could still be enrolled as part of an embassy. Similarly trade and tribute from a state like Korea, coming by land over a fixed route to the market and the throne at Peking, retained a natural connection,—particularly when the foreign ruler himself monopolized the trade.

6. It was far different with sea trade, which presented new problems of regulation. Staple cargoes reaching a southern Chinese port could not possibly be transported to Peking and only a token or luxury trade accompanied the envoy to the capital. The development of a staple trade, made possible by the use of ships, obliged foreign merchants to reside in the seaports of South China, and resulted in the Arab communities at Zayton and Canton. This called forth an adaptation of the tributary system which has already been noted. The foreign community was quarantined in its own quarter under its own headman. The adaptation was successful and was applied after 1500 to Macao and the Thirteen Factories, the theoretical connection between trade and tribute being kept alive spasmodically by embassies from some of the new maritime trading countries. Like the Russians in the north, the Europeans and their trade who came to the south were kept under control at certain places on the frontier for the cognate purposes of safety and profit.

The real problem was presented by the expansion of maritime trade in Chinese hands to which we have already referred. The junk fleets of Amoy and Canton conducted a foreign trade not only outside the capital but even outside the frontiers of China, quite beyond control through tributary forms. Countries which remained passively abroad while the Chinese went to them could no longer be enrolled as tributaries attracted irresistibly by the civilization of the Middle Kingdom. Finally the connection of foreign trade and tribute, always an idea but not always a fact, was dealt another blow when countries like the United States, Sweden, and Denmark began to trade prosperously at Canton without ever sending to Peking anything that could be called a tribute embassy. Tribute had at last been eclipsed by trade.

7. If in these circumstances our suggestion is correct, that embassies grew more frequent in the early nineteenth century in order to facilitate a generally expanding trade in eastern Asia, then the tributary system had indeed fallen upon evil days and was being prostituted by the tributaries and no doubt by Chinese merchants as well. This had happened before, but now it served most inopportunely to increase the inadaptibility of the Chinese state and preserve a useless official myth. For insofar as the traditional system seemed to be confirmed by these embassies, the Chinese were left to face the western maritime invasion with an outmoded foreign policy suited only to the land and the far past.

This interpretation points to two lines of study, in the history of trade and of ideas, as most pressingly needed to explain the dichotomy in China's reaction to the west a century ago,—on the one hand, the intellectual inadaptability of the Chinese scholar-bureaucracy; on the other, the activity of Chinese merchants as abettors of the western invasion. Source materials for these lines of study are suggested below.

7. A Selected List of Ch'ing Works (1644-1860) on Maritime Relations.

This selection is arranged in a roughly chronological order and includes official compilations, gazetteers, and private works and essays, all of which provide source material for one or both of two main types of investigation: for students of economic history, information as to maritime trade routes, ports, ships, goods, and trading places; for students of intellectual history, examples of Chinese thought and knowledge concerning the maritime countries and their trade in the period covered. Within the limits of this period,—that is, the Ch'ing dynasty before the Westerners had penetrated inland to dwell at Peking and in the Yangtze valley and so become known at first hand, —we have tried to indicate certain works of primary and certain others of typical value. We have excluded works on Japan, Liu-ch'iu, and land-frontier countries; works written by foreigners in Chinese, including primarily those of western missionaries; works referring nominally to an earlier period, like the *Ming History* or the *Hsü wên-hsien* t'ung-k'ao;[93] and works containing material drawn from the period but compiled later, such as the *Kuo-ch'ao jou-yüan chi* 國朝柔遠記 of WANG Chih-ch'un 王之春 (1896). It need hardly be remarked that no study of Chinese knowledge of the west can be conducted without reference to Matteo RICCI and his successors among the Jesuits at Peking. The declining influence of RICCI's world-map has been studied in a very interesting article by Mr. Kenneth CH'ÊN,[94] following the lead of Prof. HUNG.[95] Several items by Jesuits or showing such influence may be found in the huge and fundamental collection of Ch'ing works on geography compiled by WANG Hsi-ch'i in 84 volumes.[96] Aside from one or two illustrative items, we have excluded materials to be found in this collection, which fortunately has been indexed in the new classified catalogue of the Chinese-Japanese Library of the Harvard-Yenching Institute (Cambridge 1938—).[97]

In the Ch'ing period three works on the maritime nations and their trade, judging by the quotations of other scholars, appear to have had more than usual influence. They were compiled at intervals of a little

---

[93] For a bibliography of Ming works on barbarian relations, cf. CHU Shih-chia 朱士嘉, Ming-tai ssŭ-i shu-mu 明代四裔書目, *Yü-kung* 5 no. 3-4 (April 11, 1936). 137-158.

[94] Kenneth CH'ÊN, "Matteo Ricci's contribution to, and influence on, geographical knowledge in China," *JAOS* 59 (1939). 325-359; refers to a number of early Ch'ing works, several of which are included in the present list. For the original Chinese version of this article see CH'ÊN Kuan-shêng 陳觀勝 in *Yü-kung* 5 no. 3-4. 51-72.

[95] HUNG Wei-lien 洪煨蓮 (William HUNG), K'ao Li-ma-tou ti shih-chieh ti-t'u 考利瑪竇的世界地圖 (A study of the world-map of Matteo RICCI), *Yü-kung* 5. no. 3-4 (April 11, 1936). 1-50.

[96] WANG Hsi-ch'i 王錫祺 *Hsiao-fang-hu-chai yü-ti ts'ung-ch'ao* 小方壺齋輿地叢鈔 (Collected copies of works on geography, from the Hsiao-fang-hu study), preface dated 1877, type print, Shanghai; second supplement preface dated 1897. Contains a total of 1438 titles, including the two supplements, in 84 volumes (ts'ê), some 6000 pages. Cited below as *Hsiao-fang-hu-chai* with number of chih 帙, ts'ê, and page where possible.

[97] Another important collection from which we cite several works is the *Chao-tai ts'ung-shu* 昭代叢書 originally compiled by CHANG Ch'ao 張潮, enlarged by YANG Fu-chi 楊復吉 and revised by SHÊN Mou-tê 沈楙德, first pub. 1697, revised ed. 1833, re-printed 1876.

Several items in this list are also noted in A. WYLIE, *Notes on Chinese Literature* . . . , London 1867, with which our findings sometimes differ.

Since completing this article, we have seen the valuable contribution of Mr. Fêng-t'ien CHAO, An Annotated Bibliography of Chinese Works on the First Anglo-Chinese War, *Yenching Journal of Social Studies*, 3 no. 1 (October 1940). 61-103, which gives further data concerning half a dozen of the items listed below.

over a century. The first was the *Tung-hsi-yang k'ao* 東西洋考 of CHANG Hsieh 張燮 completed in 1617,[98] sections from which are translated by GROENEVELDT and which has more recently been studied by WADA. The other two, which fall within the period here considered, were the *Hai-kuo wên-chien lu* completed in 1730 (no. 8 below) and the *Hai-kuo t'u-chih* completed in 1842-52 (no. 32 below). Both these works deserve monographic attention.

For the study of Chinese maritime trade the materials appear to become unusually rich in the early nineteenth century just before the crisis over foreign trade at Canton. The brief first-hand account of a blind linguist entitled simply *Hai-lu*, "A record of the sea" (no. 20), was taken down in 1820; the enlargement of the gazetteer of Kwangtung province, edited by the great scholar JUAN Yüan, was completed about the same time (no. 21); a nautical guidebook, *Hai-wai chi-yao*, was completed in 1828 (no. 23); Prof. Hsü Ti-shan has unearthed at Oxford a manuscript describing the Chinese side of western trade up to 1832 (no. 24); the gazetteer of Amoy (no. 25), home port of Chinese junk trade with the Straits, was completed in the 1830's followed by the valuable gazetteer of the Canton maritime customs (no. 26). All of this was done before the hectic awakening precipitated by the first war with England and these works must in some sense be regarded as forbears of the famous geographies of the world compiled in the 1840's by WEI Yüan (no. 32) and Hsü Chi-yü (no. 33). If to such sources as these there could be applied the same high scholarship which has been bestowed upon earlier and more fashionable periods, one main door to the understanding of modern Chinese economic history could be unlocked. Though recent, these materials do not lack for textual conundrums and problems of identification. These geographical works in turn are no more than background material for the study of Chinese policy as reflected in the collected writings of officials (see, e. g., no. 29).[99]

1. KU Yen-wu 顧炎武, T'ien-hsia chün-kuo li-ping shu 天下郡國利病書 (A critical account of the divisions and states of the Empire), 120 chüan, author's preface dated 1662, republished 1816, later editions 1831, 1879.

---

[98] (A study of the eastern and western ocean [routes]), 12 chüan, in the *Hsi-yin-hsien ts'ung-shu,* ts'ê 18-21.

[99] See appendix 3 for an author and title index to the following list, which is itself arranged roughly chronologically.

A critical geographical work by an outstanding Chʻing scholar. Ch. 119 is devoted to the various barbarians beyond the seas (Hai-wai chu-fan) and discusses Japan, Liu-chʻiu, and countries of the southeast including Fo-lang-chi. Ch. 120 discusses the tribute and trade of these maritime countries (Ju-kung hu-shih), including reference to trade routes and to the history of the administration of foreign trade, down through the Ming and in some cases into the Chʻing period.

2. CHANG Yü-shu 張玉書 (1642-1711), **Wai-kuo chi** 外國紀 (A record of foreign countries), pp. 13, in *Chao-tai tsʻung-shu*, tsʻê 104; and *Chang Wên-chên Kung chi* 張文貞公集 (Block-print edition of 1792) 8.19-29. (Reference to 1675 in text).

By a famous scholar, editor-in-chief of the *Kʻang-hsi Dictionary* and the *Pʻei-wên yün-fu* and one of the editors of the *Ming History*. Deals with various tributary tribes in Manchuria and Mongolia, plus Korea, Russia, Siam, Holland, Liu-chʻiu, Annam, and Hsi-yang, with references to Christianity.

3. Yu-tʻung 尤侗 (1618-1704), **Wai-kuo chu-chih tzʻu** 外國竹枝詞 1 chüan (29 pp.), n. d., in *Chao-tai tsʻung-shu*, tsʻê 3, and *Tʻan-chi tsʻung-shu*, tsʻê 11.

This is a verse narration, with notes in prose, of the usual Ming list of countries and places; about one page or less to an item, rather miscellaneously arranged, e. g. Europe succeeds Hami. Does not appear important, except to indicate the knowledge possessed by a famous essayist concerning foreign countries.

4. LU Tzʻŭ-yün 陸次雲, **Pa-hung i-shih** 八紘譯史 4 chüan, 2 tsʻê, author's preface dated 1683. Published separately, as well as in the *Lung-wei mi-shu* 龍威祕書, tsʻê 75, and *Shuo-kʻu* 說庫, tsʻê 44.

Deals with more than a hundred tributary or trading countries or places, grouped (often incorrectly) by the four points of the compass. Ch. 2 includes references to several European countries. In several cases includes transliterations of native languages.

Note also by the same author: **I-shih chi-yü** 譯史紀餘 4 chüan, n. d. Usually published together with the preceding.

Supplementary to the *Pa-hung i-shih*, including descriptions of seas and their products, poems of Chinese envoys, illustrations of foreign coins, and copies with translations of the credentials (kuo-shu) of Korean and Mohammedan envoys.

5. Lu Ying-yang 陸應暘 (original author), **Kuang-yü chi** 廣輿記 (A record of the broad world), revised edition by Ts'ai Fang-ping 蔡方炳, 24 chüan, 7 ts'ê, preface by Ts'ai dated 1686, block-print edition 1707.

A systematic survey of the provinces, which in chüan 24 takes up the conventional Ming list of tributaries but appears to add little if anything from the Ch'ing period.

6. Lan *Ting-yüan* 藍鼎元 (1680-1733), **Lun Nan-yang shih-i shu** 論南洋事宜書 (A discussion of a proper policy regarding the Southern Ocean), in his *Lu-chou ch'u-chi* 鹿洲初集 3. 1-6 (first published 1732, republished 1880), also in Chu K'o-ching 朱克敬, *Jou-yüan hsin-shu* 柔遠新書 3. 14-17, and in *Hsiao-fang hu-chai*, ts'ê 54. Arranged by the compiler as of 1724.

A brief note by a well-known scholar urging abolition of the ban on maritime trade. He argues that trade with the Southern Ocean would benefit China, ridicules the ignorance of his contemporaries, and gives a brief survey of foreign countries.

7. **Ch'in-ting ku-chin t'u-shu chi-ch'êng** 欽定古今圖書集成 10,000 chüan, presented to the Emperor in 1725.

The great Ch'ing encyclopaedia in the geography section on border barbarians, *Fang-yü hui-pien, Pien-i tien* 方輿彙編, 邊裔典, chüan 83-106 in particular, contains material on southern and western places. Thus chüan 85, 97-101, 103-6 include tributaries of the Ming period, maritime and continental mixed together. Ch. 87 under "unidentified countries" (wei-hsiang 未詳) includes Spain, America, and others like Damascus (?), while ch. 108 lists also as "unidentified countries" I-ta-li-ya, Sicily, Mexico, and Banjermassin among others,—all of which raises the question of the influence of Ricci.

8. Ch'ên Lun-ch'iung 陳倫炯, **Hai-kuo wên-chien lu** 海國聞見錄 (A record of things seen and heard among the maritime nations), 1 chüan, maps 1 chüan, author's preface 1730, other prefaces 1743, 1744, wood-block reprint 1793; also in *I-hai chu-chên* 藝海珠塵, ts'ê 10, and *Chao-tai ts'ung-shu*, ts'ê 55.

A well-known and systematic treatment of the maritime nations. The author's father had had experience in the Southern Ocean on missions in search of Koxinga's remnants after the subjugation of Formosa, and finally became Manchu Brigade General at Canton in 1718. The author himself became a Brigade General in Formosa after 1721, traveled in Japan, and made extensive inquiries. The maps, old style, are of value, and the book appears to have remained a standard work down into the nineteenth century.

9. YIN Kuang-jên 印光任 and CHANG Ju-lin 張汝霖, **Ao-mên chi-lüeh** 澳門紀略 (A brief record of Macao), 2 chüan, prefaced dated 1751, reprinted 1800.

The authors were successively officials in the Macao area. In ch. 2 they first describe the maritime trading countries of the southeast for some 15 pages, including the rivalry of the Portuguese and the Dutch, and then concentrate upon the Portuguese at Macao, their way of life in much detail, concluding with accounts of the western calendar and language.

10. **Huang-Ch'ing chih-kung t'u** 皇清職貢圖, 9 chüan, (Illustrations of the regular tributaries of the Imperial Ch'ing) compiled by TUNG Kao 董誥 and others under imperial auspices: ordered 1751, completed 1760, Palace edition 1761.

Illustrations of some 300 aboriginal or border tribes or countries, with explanatory text; ch. 1 refers to several European countries. See above, note 82.

11. **Ta-ch'ing i-t'ung chih** 大清一統志 (Gazetteer of the Ch'ing Empire), compiled by CHIANG T'ing-hsi 蔣廷錫 and others under imperial auspices, imperial preface dated 1744, slightly revised in 1764, reprinted in 1849.

Chüan 353-356 at the end deal with tributary states. See App. 2.

12. **T'ai-wan-fu chih** 臺灣府志 (Gazetteer of T'ai-wan-fu, Formosa), 26 chüan, first compiled 1694, revised 1741 and 1774. Harvard has a block-print edition of 1888 reprinted from the 1872 edition.

Ch. 19. 37-49 on foreign islands (wai-tao) refers to Liu-ch'iu, Japan, Java (Ka-la-pa), Western Ocean, Holland, Siam, etc., and sea-routes and trade regulations.

13. **Ch'ing t'ung-tien**: *Huang-ch'ao t'ung-tien* 皇朝通典, 100 chüan, ordered compiled under imperial auspices in 1767. Covers the period 1644-1785.

Chüan 97-99 on border defense, Pien-fang 邊防, discuss the tributaries in general plus Japan and Liu-ch'iu, the maritime nations of the south, and those of the west, respectively. Several identifications of countries (e. g. Chêng-ch'ien, Ching-hai, and Hu-lu, 98. 18b-20b) are recorded.

14. **Ch'ing t'ung-k'ao**: *Huang-ch'ao wên-hsien t'ung-k'ao* 皇朝文獻通考 compilation ordered 1747, completed 1786 or 1787, covering material to 1785, Chekiang Shu-chü edition 1882.

Ch. 293-300 describe the barbarians at length. See App. 2.

15. WANG Ta-hai 王大海, Hai-tao i-chih 海島逸誌 (A treatise on the islands of the sea), 6 chüan, pub. 1791, in *Hsiao-fang-hu-chai*, ts'ê 54, chih 10, pp. 479-489.

Describes a score or more of the islands in the Southern Ocean, Chinese immigration, products, etc. The author had made a voyage to some of the islands he describes.

16. **Fu-chien t'ung-chih chêng-shih-lüeh** 福建通志政事略 (A survey of administrative affairs, for the Gazetteer of Fukien province), bound MSS., 15 chüan in 17 ts'ê, n. d., worm-eaten and with some marginal corrections; the text refers to the year 1794, if not later.

Ch. 14 gives a brief survey of the regulation of foreign trade since the Sung and the countries concerned. Ch. 15 consists of 8 pages on barbarian trade, referring to Liu-ch'iu, Sulu, and Holland, i.e. those tributary via Foochow.

17. HUNG Liang-chi 洪亮吉 (1746-1809), **Ch'ien-lung fu-t'ing-chou-hsien t'u-chih** 乾隆府廳州縣圖志 (Gazetteer of administrative areas, Ch'ien-lung period) 50 chüan, completed 1803.

A private compilation similar to the *Ta-ch'ing i-t'ung chih* but more condensed. Tributary and trading countries are described in the last chüan, classified by location. The author was well known as a historian. See App. 2.

18. YEH Ch'iang-yung 葉羌鏞, Lü-sung chi-lüeh 呂宋紀略 (A brief description of the Philippines), 3½ pp., in *Hsiao-fang-hu-chai*, ts'ê 76, chih 10, chüan 8, item 5 from end.

Notes on the customs, products, language, and commerce of the Philippines. One date in the text refers to 1812.

19. **Chia-ch'ing ch'ung-hsiu i-t'ung chih** 嘉慶重修一統志 (Gazetteer of the empire, revision of the Chia-ch'ing period), 560 chüan, a revision under imperial auspices of the *Ta-ch'ing i-t'ung chih* of the Ch'ien-lung period, (q. v.), the material extending to 1820; lithophotographic edition from the Palace manuscript, published by the Commercial Press, Shanghai, 1934.

The last few chüan deal with 43 foreign countries from Korea to

France, touching upon their location, history, products, and relations with China.

20. Hsieh Ch'ing-kao 謝清高 (1765-1821), Hai-lu 海錄 (A maritime record), 2 chüan.

(1) Wood-block edition, preface by Yang Ping-nan 楊炳南, T. Ch'iu-hêng 秋衡, of Chia-ying 嘉應 (Kwangtung), as author, describing how he obtained the information in 1820 from Hsieh, who had traveled abroad for 14 years, learned the languages and customs of the Southern Sea, and finally lost his eyesight and became an interpreter at Macao,—an unusual repository of first-hand information. (Wylie 53 makes no reference to Hsieh by name and gives the publication date as 1842).

(2) Another edition in the Chinese-Japanese Library at Harvard, revised and with notes by Lü T'iao-yang 呂調陽, preface by him dated 1870, is assigned to Hsieh as author without reference to Yang Ping-nan. This later edition appears to be the better known, e. g. Chang Wei-hua 109. It differs from the former in having western style maps and extensive notes, largely condensed from the original edition.

> This work merits extensive attention as a first-hand source on Chinese southern trade in the early nineteenth century. It gives sailing directions for and brief descriptions of more than 60 countries or places, from the Malay peninsula around to the coasts of India, and through the East Indies, including references to Europe. Its eye-witness quality is indicated, for example, when the writer, Yang, states that Japan is omitted because the narrator, Hsieh, had not gone there on his travels. A work entitled *Hai-lu chu* 注 by Fêng Ch'êng-chün has been advertised. Note also Prof. Fêng's discussion of this work in *Yü-kung* 6 (no. 8-9). 113-114.

21. Kuang-tung t'ung-chih 廣東通志 (Gazetteer of Kwangtung province), Wylie 36 refers to a first edition of 1683;

(1) Yung-chêng edition: 64 chüan, preface dated 1731.
   Ch. 58 on the outer barbarians (wai-fan) gives an historical survey and an orthodox Ming list of 31 countries with comments.

(2) Juan Yüan 阮元 edition: 334 chüan, compiled in 1818, Juan being editor-in-chief as well as then Governor-General at Canton, published 1822, reprinted 1864, the blocks having been burned in 1857.
   Ch. 170. 36-42 lists Siam, Holland, Western Ocean, England, etc.

as tributaries, the account being based partly on the archives (tang-ts'ê). Ch. 180 gives an historical summary of maritime trade and customs administration. Ch. 330. 32-62 discusses some 90 maritime countries or places, including the Europeans, using both standard accounts and local records, e.g. 61b the country of Pi-li-shih 吡唎啡 (Britain?) is recorded simply as having "entered port" (chin-k'ou) in 1752. (A common source can no doubt be established for parts of this work and of the *Yüeh hai-kuan chih*.) Ch. 100. 52b has a passage on Macao. The high scholarship of the chief editor, as well as its extensive detail, make this a work of importance.

22. Ho Chang-ling 賀長齡), compiler, **Huang-ch'ao ching-shih-wên pien** 皇朝經世文編 (A collection of essays of the reigning dynasty, of practical value), 120 chüan, compiler's preface 1826.

Ch. 83. 37-39 contains LAN Ting-yüan's essay on southern maritime trade (noted above, no. 6), followed by a similar item, and others on coastal defense, Formosa, suppression of piracy, and the like. These essays have value as reflecting the thought of the times. Unfortunately a supplementary collection (*Huang-ch'ao ching-shih-wên hsü-pien*) compiled by Ko Shih-chün 葛士濬 and published in 1888 contains material chiefly post-1860.

23. LI Tsêng-chieh 李增階, **Hai-wai chi-yao** 海外紀要 (A record of essentials concerning the outer seas), postface 1828, in CH'ÊN K'un 陳坤, compiler, *Ts'ung-chêng hsü-yü-lu* 從政緒餘錄, 7 chüan, preface 1881, forming ts'ê 19-22 in *Ju-pu-chi chai hui-ch'ao* 如不及齋彙鈔

A handbook of information and advice for sailing captains, divided into 23 sections on sheltered harbors (23 places listed); on the armament of ships, choice of pilots, and sea-fighting; on the itineraries for sailing vessels from Canton up the coast to Shanghai, from Amoy to Formosa and the Philippines, and from Amoy to the Straits and beyond, with times required (e.g. 12-13 days to Palembang); plus extensive tables for use in navigations, calculation of tides, and the like. Careful study of this work should yield invaluable conclusions regarding Chinese maritime (junk) trade in the early nineteenth century.

24. HSÜ Ti-shan 許地山 ed., **Ta-chung-chi** 達衷集, Commercial Press, Peiping, 1931, pp. 237.

A valuable collection of documents transcribed by Prof. Hsü from a MSS. found in the Bodleian Library, dealing (1) with the voyage of the East India Company ship *Lord Amherst* up the China coast in 1832 under H. H. LINDSAY to test out the market (petitions to the local authorities and proclamations and replies from them); and (2) correspondence at Canton between the Chinese authorities, the Hong merchants (HOWQUA and others), and the English, dating from the late XVIII and early XIX centuries. This material is of first rate value as illuminating the Chinese side of the correspondence summarized in Dr. H. B. MORSE's *Chronicles of the East India Company*.

25. Hsia-mên chih 廈門志 (Gazetteer of Amoy), compiled by CHOU K'ai 周凱 and others, 16 chüan, completed 1832, last preface 1839.

Ch. 5 contains interesting details regarding shipping, including Chinese vessels in oceanic trade (yang-ch'uan, p. 27) and barbarian vessels of various types (31-5). Ch. 6-7 on Formosan imports and customs administration are followed in ch. 8 by a systematic discussion of 31 maritime trading nations, their location, harbors, products, etc. evidently based in part on original data in addition to such works as the *Tung-hsi-yang k'ao* and *Hai-kuo wên-chien lu*; Amoy being a chief port in southern trade, the use of this material should yield unusually valuable results.

26. LIANG T'ing-nan 梁廷枏, Yüeh-hai-kuan chih 粵海關志 (Gazetteer of the maritime customs of Kwangtung), 30 chüan, reference to 1839 in text; Ch. 1-4, 21-25, and 26-30 (ts'ê 1, 7, and 8) reprinted Peiping 1935 et seq. in the *Kuo-hsüeh wên-k'u* 國學文庫 series.

Of the three volumes of this rare work so far published, the second and third deal with tributary trade and the barbarian merchants at Canton, ch. 21-24 in particular describing tributary relations with Siam, Liu-ch'iu and European states, and trade relations with 24 maritime countries including America and certain obscure places recorded as having " entered port " at one time. A valuable primary source based partly on archives.

27. LIN Tsê-hsü 林則徐, trans., Hua-shih i-yen 華事夷言 (Barbarian statements concerning Chinese affairs), 1 chüan, 3 pp., *Hsiao-fang-hu chai* ts'ê 77, chih 11, ch. 9, item 3.

Evidently a fragment of the work done by Commissioner LIN's corps of Chinese translators at Canton, probably in 1839 (cf. Gideon CH'ÊN, *Lin Tsê-hsü*, Peiping 1934, pp. 7-10). Miscellaneous content including references to the Thirteen Factories, Hong Merchants, interpreters, Russia, Chinese population, opium, currency, etc. The western originals should not be hard to find, perhaps in the *Chinese Repository*.

28. Ho Ta-kêng 何大庚, Ying-i shuo 英夷說 (A treatise on the English barbarians), in *Hsiao-fang-hu-chai*, ts'ê 77, chih 11, chüan 9, item 4. Follows LIN Tsê-hsü's *Hua-shih i-yen* and consists of five lines expatiating on the danger of British expansion in Malaya. N. d., post 1819 by reference to Singapore in text.

29. CHANG Shu-shêng 張樹聲, Yang-wu ts'ung-ch'ao 洋務叢鈔 (A miscellaneous collection on foreign affairs) pub. 1884.

Contains 11 works on military and foreign affairs, chiefly post-1860 but including LIN Tsê-hsü on Russia, and YAO Ying 姚瑩 (1785-1853) on Anglo-Russian relations. The papers of YAO Ying (*Chung-fu-t'ang ch'üan-chi* 中復堂全集 pub. 1867) contain a work reflecting his experience as an official in Formosa during 1838-1843 and his views on foreign policy (ts'ê 5-9, entitled *Tung-ming wên hou-chi* 東溟文後集, 14 chüan). This is of course but one of many such collections.

30. WANG Ch'ing-yün 王慶雲 (1798-1862), Shih-ch'ü yü-chi 石渠餘紀 also entitled Hsi-ch'ao chi-chêng 熙朝紀政, 6 chüan, 6 ts'ê, n. d., 1890 wood-block edition.

Useful notes on various aspects of administration by an official who rose to be President of the Board of Works. Ch. 6 contains material on maritime trade (shih-po), plus edicts on the MACARTNEY and AMHERST embassies.

31. *Fu-chien t'ung-chih* 福建通志 (Gazetteer of Fukien province), 278 chüan, first compiled 1737, revised several times, particularly in 1835 (date of preface); published with some further revision (material dated 1842) in 1871.

Ch. 269 discusses the barbarians tributary through Foochow,—Liu-ch'iu, Holland, Sulu,—with Japan also. Ch. 270 surveys the official regulation of maritime trade, quoting edicts, from the Sung down to 1842, followed by a list of foreign trading countries (pp. 18-19).

32. WEI Yüan 魏源, Hai-kuo t'u-chih 海國圖志 (An illustrated gazetteer of the maritime countries), 100 chüan; the preface to the 1876

edition states that it was completed in 1842 in 60 chüan, 40 more being completed in 1852 to make 100 chüan; reprinted in 100 chüan in 1876 (Harvard has only the 1852 and 1876 editions, each 100 chüan). Gideon CH'ÊN (*Lin Tsê-hsü* . . . 24) names three editions: 50 chüan in 1844, 60 chüan in 1847, and 100 chüan in 1852, and gives a valuable appraisal of changes in later editions of the work and LIN Tsê-hsü's probable connection as author of part of it.

> A monumental and historically important survey of foreign countries and the barbarian menace compiled at the time of the first war with England. (WYLIE 53 condemns the author as not impartial). Ch. 5-18 deal with countries of southeast Asia, followed by India at some length; ch. 37-58 deal with Europe; ch. 71 begins a description of the western religions, calendar, customs, armament, astronomy, and the like. The work had widespread influences, and justice cannot be done it here.

Note also by the same author: **Shêng-wu chi** 聖武記 (A record of imperial military activities), 14 chüan, preface to first edition 1842, 3rd and revised edition 1846, in *Ssŭ-pu pei-yao* edition of the Chung Hua Book Co.

> A famous work narrating the military campaigns of the Ch'ing, including those into Mongolia, Sinkiang, Tibet, Nepal; against Russia, Korea, Burma, Annam and the border tribes of the southeast; and concerning Formosa, the suppression of coastal pirates, and of internal rebels in the early nineteenth century,—only in small part on maritime relations. A valuable supplementary section deals with military organization and history. A section was translated by E. H. PARKER as *A Chinese Account of the Opium War*, Shanghai 1888; Gideon CH'ÊN (*Lin Tsê-hsü* . . . 28) points out that the account of this war is omitted in several editions of the work.

Hsiao-fang-hu-chai contains a number of brief items by WEI Yüan, e. g. **Ying-chi-li hsiao-chi** 英吉利小記 (A brief account of England), pp. 1½, (ts'ê 77, chih 11, chüan 9, item 8). A brief survey touching on finances, the non-use of opium, religion, quaint customs, etc.

33. Hsü Chi-yü 徐繼畬, Ying-huan chih-lüeh 瀛環志略 (A brief description of the oceans roundabout), 10 chüan, title page and prefaces dated 1848. Another edition, somewhat revised and dated 1873, contains prefaces dated 1849.

> A universal geography, by the barbarian-relations expert of Fukien who had been directly connected with the opening of the treaty

ports in that province and became governor of it in 1847 (cf. *IWSM-TK* 78). Other high officials lent their names to the title page, the plates were preserved at the (Governor's) yamen 本署藏板 and the work is plainly an invaluable reflection of the knowledge possessed by the Chinese authorities appointed after the first treaties to stem the western invasion. Chüan 1-3 concern Asia, 4-7 Europe, and 8-10 Africa and America. Hsü confesses in the directions to the reader (fan-li) that " place names of foreign countries are very difficult to distinguish; if ten persons make translations, all ten will be different." Hsü made careful use both of Chinese works, such as the *Hai-kuo wên-chien lu* of a century before, and of western maps, noting many differences in transliteration between the two. His text is punctuated, place names are marked, and sources cited.

Hsiao-fang-hu-chai contains several brief items by Hsü Chi-yü 徐繼畬, e.g. (1) **Wu-yin-tu lun** 五印度論 (ts'ê 54, chih 10, p. 413). Deals briefly with the British in India.

(2) **Ti-ch'iu chih-lüeh** 地球誌略 (A general description of the earth), two pages (ts'ê 1, chih 1, p. 7-8). Largely geographical, concerning the poles, equator, continents, etc; references to Antarctic explorations conducted two years previously by France, England, Spain, and the United States,—evidently those of D'Urville (1837-40), Wilkes (1839-40), and Ross (1841-43),—date this fragment as probably just previous to Hsü's universal geography of 1848.

34. Hsia Hsieh 夏燮, pseud. Chiang-shang-chien-sou 江上蹇叟 (lit. " the lame old man on the river "), **Chung-hsi chi-shih** 中西紀事 (A record of Sino-western affairs), 24 chüan in 8 ts'ê, first preface 1851 (Tao-kuang 30th year, 12th month), second preface to revised edition 1859, last preface 1865; extra title-page bears date Oct. 1868.

An important survey of Chinese relations with the West, throughout the modern period down to the 1860's (in the later editions); apparently well based on documents, contemporary sources, and even some western books, with chapters divided according to periods, concentrating on the post-treaty era.

Material of probable value, which we have not been able to examine: **Hai-wai fan-i lu** 海外番夷錄, compiled by Wang Yün-hsiang 王藴香 and published in a wood-block edition in 1844 by the Ching-tu shu-liu-hsüan 京都漱六軒, Peking, 4 ts'ê.

ON THE CH'ING TRIBUTARY SYSTEM 219

This collection contains an item by WANG Wên-t'ai 汪文泰, Hung-mao-fan Ying-chi-li k'ao-lüeh 紅毛番英吉利考略 (A study of the red-haired English barbarians?), listed by WYLIE 53 as published in 1841.

8. INDEX OF TRIBUTARIES LISTED IN SIX EDITIONS OF THE COLLECTED STATUTES

The identification of places mentioned above is concentrated here in order to disencumber the text and to provide a minimum reference list of places important in Ch'ing economic relations, also to indicate certain places still requiring identification. A number of items from the Ming period are obscure and probably unimportant, others have been recognized and discussed at length by scholars of several generations. Ming names of course frequently persist in the Ch'ing literature, such as that noted in the preceding section, at the same time that new forms are recorded. It is much to be hoped that expert attention will be devoted to the place names appearing in texts of the modern period down to 1860. No doubt many items not traced by us can be elucidated by workers better versed in this difficult specialty.

Note: This list includes all places listed as tributary in the following: *Wan-li hui-tien* 105. 80-107. 88b (Li-Pu, chüan 63-65); *K'ang-hsi hui-tien* 72. 4-19b; *Yung-chêng hui-tien* 104. 4-38b; *Ch'ien-lung hui-tien* 56. 1; *Chia-ch'ing hui-tien* 31. 2-4; *Kuang-hsü hui-tien* 39. 2-3; a few items are added. Nearly all these tributaries are listed as countries (kuo) in the sources. Variants are noted but not indexed unless they appear in the above sources; cross references are suppressed when they would form an adjoining item. Authorities are cited by abbreviations, as in Appendix 1 below. Note that the Mongol tribes and others under the Court of Colonial Affairs (Li Fan Yüan) in the Ch'ing period, and a few Tibetan monasteries in *Wan-li hui-tien* 108 are omitted.

Abbreviations: B = BRUNNERT (see App. 1 below), H = HERMANN, P = PLAYFAIR. Ctry. = country, Tn. = Town, Tr. = Tribe. ** = listed as tributary in one or more editions of the *Ta-Ch'ing hui-tien*. * = listed as having commercial relations in the 1818 edition.

Arrangement: place-name, location, *Hui-tien* reference, identification.

*ACHIN (Acheen, Acheh, Atjeh): Ya-chi 亞齊. No. tip of Sumatra. *Wan-li* 106. 84b; *Chia-ch'ing* 31. 3b.

GROENEVELDT 92 gives Atjeh, corrupted by Europeans to Achin or Acheen. *Ch'ing t'ung-k'ao* 297. 17b follows the *Ming History* in stating that this was the name given in the Wan-li period to what was formerly called Su-mên-ta-la; but the latter is now identified by PELLIOT (3) 214, also MILLS 11, as "Samudra harbour, near Pasai on the north coast of Sumatra; this port (says MILLS) was also the starting point of the voyage to the Nicobar Islands and Ceylon." See under Lambri below, also Samudra.

ADEN: A-tan 阿丹. Arabia. *Wan-li* 106.84b.
  ROCKHILL (1) 76.

AFGHANISTAN: Ai-wu-han 愛烏罕 (Mod. A-fu-han). *Kuang-hsü* 68.8.

ALANI (Aas, Aorsi): A-su 阿速. Tr., in the Caucasus. *Wan-li* 107.87b.
  BRETSCHNEIDER 2.84-90; H: 50D2.

ALMALIK?: An-li-ma 俺力麻. Tn., in No. Sinkiang. *Wan-li* 107.87b.
  Cf. BRETSCHNEIDER 2.33-39; FÊNG (2) 2: A-li-ma-li 阿力麻里.

A-LU KUO see Aru

ANDIJAN (Andedjan): An-chi-yen 安集延. Anc. Ferghana. *Ch'ing t'ung-k'ao* 299.7b.
  FÊNG (2) 2; H: 17 II C½.

ANDKHUI (Andkhoi): An-tu-huai 俺都淮. Tn., W. of Balkh, Bukhara. *Wan-li* 107.88b.
  BRETSCHNEIDER (2) 275: P: 119.

AN-LI-MA see Almalik?

AN-CHI-YEN see Andijan

****ANNAM** (Yüeh-nan): An-nan 安南. Ctry. *Wan-li* 105.81b; *K'ang-hsi* 72.14; *Yung-chêng* 104.24; *Ch'ien-lung* 56.1; *Chia-ch'ing* 31.2a; *Kuang-hsü* 39.2a. Name changed officially to Yüeh-nan in 1803.

AN-TING 安定. District in Kansu. *Wan-li* 107.87.
  TS'ÊN 166: modern Harashar (Ha-la-sha-erh); BRETSCHNEIDER 2.205-208.

AN-TU-HUAI see Andkhui

ARABIA (1): T'ien-fang 天方. *Wan-li* 107.88a.
  DUYVENDAK (1) 9: Mecca; H: 54D3: Arabia; PELLIOT (2) 296: Arabie, La Mecque.

?(2): Hsia-la-pi 夏剌比. *Wan-li* 106.84b.
  (?) TING 28: same as Arabia.

ARU: A-lu 阿魯 also 亞魯. Ctry., N.E. coast of Sumatra. *Wan-li* 106.84.
  H: 54F4; ROCKHILL (1) 75.

A-SU see Alani

A-TAN see Aden

A-TUAN see Khotan?

A-WA see Burma

BADAKSHAN (Badakashan): (1) Pa-ta-hei-shang 八答黑商. Ctry. and Tn., No. of Kabul, C. Asia. *Wan-li* 107.88b.
  BRETSCHNEIDER 2.276-8; Fêng (2) 4.
(2) Pa-tan-sha 把丹沙. *Wan-li* 107.87b.
  BRETSCHNEIDER 2.272.

BALKH: Pa-li-hei 把力黑. Tn., So. C. Asia. *Wan-li* 107.87b.
  BRETSCHNEIDER 100; Fêng (2) 4.

BANJERMASSIN: Ma-ch'ên 馬辰. So. coast Borneo. *Ch'ing t'ung-k'ao* 293.1b.
  Cf. Hsü Chi-yü 2.2 (map): Ma-shên 神; *Huang-Ch'ing chih-kung t'u* 1.55: same as Wên-lang-ma-shên in the southeastern sea 文郎馬神,—a scribal error for Wên-chi-ma-shên 即.

BARAWA: Pu-la-wa 不剌哇. Tn., So. of Mogadisho, Africa. *Wan-li* 106.84b.
  H: 54D4; FÊNG (2) 6.

BASHIBALIK: Pieh-shih-pa-li 別失八里. Tn., ancient Urumtsi (Tihwa), Sinkiang; anc. country of Moghulistan. *Wan-li* 107.87b.
  BRETSCHNEIDER 2.225-244.

BENGAL: (1) Pang-ko-la 榜葛剌. Ctry. *Wan-li* 106.84.
  ROCKHILL (1) 436; FÊNG (1) 12.
(2) P'êng-chia-na 彭加那. *Wan-li* 106.84b.
  ROCKHILL (1) 68, 435: P'êng-chia-la 剌; FÊNG (2) 5.

BILLITON: Ma-yeh-wêng 麻葉甕. Island E. of Sumatra. *Ch'ing i-t'ung chih*, Ch'ien-lung ed., 356.36.
  WU Han 174; FÊNG (1) 15.

BOLOR: Po-lo-êrh 博羅爾. Tn. and Ctry., E. of Badakshan in the Hindu Kush. HUNG Liang-chi 50.18b.
  FÊNG (2) 6. 洛.

BORNEO: So-lo 娑羅, presumably a scribal error for P'o-lo 婆, mod. form 婆羅洲 P'o-lo-chou. (P'o-lo does not appear in the *Hui-tien* text). *Wan-li* 107.84: "In 1406 the eastern king and the western king each sent an envoy to present tribute at Court."
  GROENEVELDT 101: Borneo.

BRUNEI (Bornui): (1) P'o-ni (Sung-Yüan form) 浡泥 Ctry., N. W. Borneo. *Wan-li* 105.82b.
  ROCKHILL (1) 66. Also written 渤.

(2) Wên-lai 文萊 (Ming form)

Wu Han 137; *Huang-Ch'ing chih-kung t'u* 1.57 identifies Wên-lai with P'o-lo (Borneo), erroneously, as do Chang Hsieh and the *Ming Shih*; Wada 127-8 suggests that P'o-ni was recorded from the western (hsi-yang) trade route while Wên-lai (or P'o-lo) came through the eastern (tung-yang) route.

BUKHARA?: Pu-ha-la 卜哈剌. *Wan-li* 107.87b.

Fêng (2).6 from the *Yüan* History quotes 卜哈兒 and 不花剌.

**BURMA: (1) A-wa 阿哇. Ctry. *Wan-li* 106.84b. (2) A-wa 瓦; *Kuang-hsü* 39.2b: same as Mien-tien. (3) Mien-tien 甸緬; *Ch'ien-lung* 56.1; *Chia-ch'ing* 31.3; *Kuang-hsü* 39.2b.

BURUT (Black Kirghiz, Kara-Kirghiz): Pu-lu-t'ê 布魯特. Tr., No. C. Asia. Hung Liang-chi 50.17.

Mayers no. 532; H: 66CD2/3; *Ch'ing t'ung-k'ao* 299.3, 5: moslem tribe S. W. of the Dzungars, with Eastern (Tung) and Western (Hsi) divisions.

CAIL: Chia-i-lê 加異勒. So. India, opposite Ceylon. *Wan-li* 106.84b.

Duyvendak (2) 386.

CALICUT: Ku-li 古里. Ctry., S. W. coast of India. *Wan-li* 106.83b.

Groeneveldt 44; H: 54E4: Ku-li-fo

*CAMBODIA: (1) Chên-la 眞臘; *Wan-li* 105.81b. (2) Chien-pu-chai (sai) 柬埔寨; *Chia-ch'ing* 31.3. (3) Tung-pu-chai 東, common error for Chien-pu-chai; e.g. *Ch'ing t'ung-k'ao* 293.1. This variant is discussed by Pelliot (Memoires sur les coutumes de Cambodge), BEFEO 2.127.

CANANORE (Jurfattan): Sha-li-wa-ni 沙里灣泥. S. E. Coast India, No. of Calicut. *Wan-li* 106.84b.

Fêng (1) 12, 16; Wu Han 168: Jurfattan; *ibid.* 174: Sha-li-pa-tan 八丹 Jarfattan, mod. Cananore. Pelliot (2) 287: Jurfattan?

CEYLON: Hsi-lan-shan 錫 (or 細) 蘭山. *Wan-li* 106.84.

H: no. 927-28

CHALISH: Ch'a-li-shih 察力失. Tn., near Ilibalik, Sinkiang. *Wan-li* 107.87b.

H. 55F2.

CHAMPA: Chan-ch'êng 占城 (Variants: Chan-pu-lao 占不勞, Chan-po 波, Chan-la 臘). *Wan-li* 105.82.

Pelliot (3) 216: Chinese name for native Chan 佔

CHAO-HSIEN see Korea

CHAO-NA-P'U-ERH see Jaunpur

CHAO-WA see Java

CHÊNG-CH'IEN 整欠.(?). HUNG Liang-chi 59.9. *Ch'ing t'ung-tien* 98.18b: located 1000 *li* outside P'u-êrh fu (Yunnan), sent tribute in 1775.

CHÊN-LA see Cambodia

CHIA-I-LÊ see Cail

*CHIANG-K'OU see Siam

CHIEN-CHOU 建州. District in E. Manchuria. *Wan-li* 107.86b.
H: 55H2; T. C. LIN (2) 867: a center of the Jurchen.

CH'IEN-LI-TA 千里達. *Wan-li* 106.84b.
Cf. ROCKHILL (1) 67: Ch'ien-li-ma 馬. Unidentified; possibly near northern Maldive Is.

CHIEN-PU-CHAI see Cambodia

CH'IH-CHIN-MÊNG-KU 赤斤蒙古. Milit. district in Kansu (Yü-mên hsien 玉門縣). *Wan-li* 107.87b.
BRETSCHNEIDER 2.211-215; P: 995

*CH'IH-TZǓ see Jaya

CH'I-LA-NI 奇剌泥. Unidentified. *Wan-li* 106.84b.

CHI-LAN-TAN see Kelantan

CHING-HAI 景海. (?). HUNG Liang-chi 50.9b.
Ch'ing t'ung-tien 98.19: sent tribute 1775 with Chêng-ch'ien, q.v.

CHIU-CHIANG see Palembang

CHOLA: (1) So-li 瑣里. Ctry., on the Coromandel coast, S. E. India. *Wan-li* 105.83.
PELLIOT (1) 328-329: same as (2).
(2) Hsi-yang so-li 西洋. *Wan-li* 105.83: a country on the seacoast near So-li.
GROENEVELDT 44 gave W. Soli; CHANG Wei-hua 175-6 shows the two to be identical.

CH'Ü-HSIEN 曲先. District in Kansu. *Wan-li* 107.87b.
H: 55F3; BRETSCHNEIDER 2.210

COCHIN: K'o(Ko)-chih 柯枝. Ctry. on the Malabar coast, S. W. India. *Wan-li* 106.84b.

COIMBATORE see Coyampadi

COYAMPADI (Coimbatore): (1) K'an-pa-i-t'i 坎巴夷替. S. E. India, No. of Cochin. *Wan-li* 106.84b.

FÊNG (1) text 42.

(2) Kan-pa-li 甘把（or 巴）里.
　　DUYVENDAK (2) 386 suggests "Coyampadi?"; PELLIOT (2) 290, 296: probably "Koyampadi (Coimbatore)"; FÊNG (1) 11.

*DENMARK: Lien-kuo 嗹國. *Chia-ch'ing* 31.4.

DJOFAR (Dufar, Zufar): Tsu-fa-êrh 祖法兒. Tn., So. Arabia or Tso-fa-êrh 左. *Wan-li* 106.84b.
　　ROCKHILL (1) 611n.

Ê-CHI-CHIEH 額卽瓜. Unidentified. *Wan-li* 107.88b.

**ENGLAND: Ying-chi-li 英吉利. *Chia-ch'ing* 31.3.

Ê-LO-SSŬ see Russia

EUROPE: Not formally listed, see Western Ocean

FA-LAN-HSI (France) see under Portugal

*FRANCE: Fa-lan-hsi, confused with Portugal, q. v.

FU-LIN see Syria

FU-LO-CHÜ 芙洛居, presumably an error for Mei-lo-chü, see Molucca.

FU-YÜ see To-yen

HA-HSIN 哈辛. Unidentified. *Wan-li* 107.88b.
　　TING Chien 2.30: in W. Persia

HA-LIEH see Herat

HA-LIEH-ERH: 哈烈兒. Unidentified. *Wan-li* 107.87b.
　　TING Chien 2.28b: same as Ha-lieh (Herat)

HAMI: Ha-mi 哈密. Tn., Sinkiang. *Wan-li* 107.87.
　　P: 1907

HA-SAN 哈三. Unidentified. *Wan-li* 107.87b.
　　TING Chien 2.28b.

HAN-TUNG 罕東. District in Kansu (Tun-huang hsien). *Wan-li* 107.87b.
　　P: 1980; BRETSCHNEIDER 2.218

HA-SHIH-HA-ERH see Kashgar

HA-TI-LAN 哈的蘭. (?). *Wan-li* 107.87b.
　　BRETSCHNEIDER 2.315: probably Khotelan

HEI-KA-TA 黑葛達. Unidentified. *Wan-li* 106.84b.

HEI-LOU see Khorassan

HERAT: Ha-lieh 哈烈. Tn., Afghanistan. *Wan-li* 106.87b.
　　P: 1906; BRETSCHNEIDER 2.278-290; FÊNG (2) 13.

HOLLAND: Ho-lan 荷蘭. *K'ang-hsi* 72.12a; *Yung-chêng* 104.22; *Chia-ch'ing* 31.3.

> Popularly known as the "Red-haired foreigners (barbarians)," Hung-mao fan 紅毛蕃, a term also used for the English, cf. CHANG Wei-hua 107-8. In the Ming period written 和蘭, cf. DUYVENDAK (3). 30n.4.

HO-MAO-LI or **HO-MAO-WU**, see Marinduque

HORMUZ (Ormuz): Hu-lu-mo-ssŭ 忽魯謨斯 or Hu-lu mu-ssŭ 母思 Tn., Persian Gulf. *Wan-li* 106.84b.

> GROENEVELDT 44.

HSIA-LA-PI see Arabia?

HSIAO-KO-LAN see Quilon

HSIEN-LO see Siam

HSI-LAN-SHAN see Ceylon

HSI-PAN-YA see Spain

HSI-PU-LU-T'Ê see Burut

HSI-YANG see Western Ocean.

HSI-YANG SO-LI see Chola

HSÜ-WÊN-TA-NA see Samudra

HU-LU: 胡盧 or 葫蘆. HUNG Liang-chi 50.8b.

> Lit. "bottle-gourd country"? Cf. ROCKHILL (1) 91 under Chan-ch'êng; *Ch'ing t'ung-tien* 98.20b: located 18 stages outside Yung-ch'ang fu, Yunnan,—sent tribute in 1746.

HU-LU-MO-SSŬ see Hormuz

HUNG-MAO FAN see Holland

HUO-CHAN see Khodjend

HUO-CHOU see Karakhodjo

HUO-T'AN see Khodjend

ILIBALIK: I-li-pa-li 亦力把力. Sinkiang near mod. Kuldja. *Wan-li* 107.87b.

> H: 55F2; BRETSCHNEIDER 2.225: later name for Bashibalik.

ISFAHAN (Ispahan): I-ssŭ-fu-han 亦思弗罕. Tn., Persia. *Wan-li* 107.88b.

I-TA-LI-YA see under Portugal

JAPAN: Jih-pên 日本 or Wo-nu 倭奴. *Wan-li* 105.80b; *Chia-ch'ing* 31.3.

JAUNPUR: Chao-na-p'u-êrh 沼納撲兒. Mid-India near Benares. *Wan-li* 106.84b.

    FÊNG (1) 17-18. Same as old Fo-kuo 佛國.

***JAVA**: (1) Shê-p'o 闍婆, Chinese pre-Mongol transcription; (2) Chao-wa 爪哇, post-Mongol (Fukien) transcription, Groeneveldt 45. *Wan-li* 105.82.

    ROCKHILL (1) 66: Majapahit.

    (3) Ka-la-pa 噶喇吧 or 葛剌. *Chia-ch'ing* 31.3b.

    WANG Kuo-wei 54; CHANG Wei-hua 110: old Chinese name for Batavia, hence for Java as a whole.

***JAYA** (Chaya, Jaiya): Ch'ih-tzŭ 赤仔. W. Siam. *Chia-ch'ing* 31.3b. *Hai-kuo wên-chien lu* 1.25b gives 斜 Hsieh (hsia)-tzŭ, translated by SCHLEGEL 298 as Chaya. Captain Francis LIGHT, quoted above part 6, between Chantebon and Sangora (sic) listed "Chia—Province West of Siam—produces Cotton, Dyes, Birdsnest, Salt Fish, Dryed Shrimps,—Manufactures Silk and Cotton Clothes—Plundered and destroyed by the Burmers 1787" (C. E. WURTZBURG, "A Brief Account of the several countries surrounding Prince of Wales's Island...", *J. Mal. Br. R. A. S.*, vol. 16 part 1 (July 1938). 123-126). W. LINEHAN, "A History of Pahang," *J. Mal. Br. R. A. S.* 14 part 2 (June 1936). 9 refers to Jaiya or Chaiya as near Ligor.

JIH-LO-HSIA-CHIH 日羅夏治. Unidentified. *Wan-li* 106.84b.

JIH-LO 日落. Unidentified. *Wan-li* 107.88b.

    BRETSCHNEIDER 2.314.

JIH-PÊN-KUO see Japan

***JOHORE**: Jou-fo 柔佛. Ctry., So. Malay penin. *Chia-ch'ing* 31.3b.

    GROENEVELDT 135.

JUI KUO see Sweden

JUNG 戎. "Western barbarians." Unidentified. *Wan-li* 107.87b.

    Tao-i chih-lüeh (Wang 30) has a Jung on the Malay Peninsula.

JURFATTAN see Cananore

KA-LA-PA see Java

K'AN-PA-I-T'I see Coyampadi

KAN-PA-LI see Coyampadi

KAN-SHIH 幹失. Unidentified. *Wan-li* 107.87b.

    TING Chien 2.29 line 4.

KAN-SSŬ-LA see Portugal

KARAKHODJO: Huo-chou 火州. Tn., E. of Turfan, Sinkiang, *Wan-li* 107.88.
  P: 1900: ancient Kao-ch'ang; BRETSCHNEIDER 2.186-8.

KASHGAR: Ha-shih-ha-êrh 哈失哈兒. Tn., Sinkiang. *Wan-li* 107.87b.
  P: 3224.

KASHMIR: K'o-shih-mi-êrh 克失迷兒. *Wan-li* 107.87b.
  FÊNG (2) 18.

KELANTAN: Chi-lan-tan 急蘭丹. Ctry., E. coast Malay penin. No. of Trengganu. *Wan-li* 106.84b.
  ROCKHILL (1) 65, 121; CHANG Wei-hua 109; KUWABARA 7.86: same as Ki-lan-i-tai 闌亦帶 of the Yüan period.

KHODJEND: (1) Huo-chan 火占. Tn., in Kokand, C. Asia. *Wan-li* 107.87b.
  P: 2414.
  (2) Sha-liu-hai-ya 沙六海牙. *Wan-li* 107.87b.
    TING Chien 2.29b: Sha-lu-hai-ya 鹿, ancient name for above; confirmed by BRETSCHNEIDER 2.253, who calls it Shahrokia.
  ?(3) Huo-t'an 火壇. *Wan-li* 107.87b.
    TING Chien 2.29b; no confirmation found.

KHORASSAN: Hei-lou 黑婁. Afghanistan. *Wan-li* 107.88b.
  BRETSCHNEIDER 2.272-3; FÊNG (2) 13: same as Herat.

KHOTAN: (1) Yü-t'ien 于闐. Tn., in Sinkiang. *Wan-li* 107.88b.
  Ancient name of Khotan, mod. Ho-t'ien 和; cf. P: 2058.
  ?(2) A-tuan 阿端. *Wan-li* 107.87b.

KIRGHIZ (Cossacks): Ha-sa-k'o 哈薩克. Tr., No. C. Asia.
  B863a. Divided into Eastern (Tso 左) and Western (Yu 右).

K'O-CHIEH 克肌. Unidentified. *Wan-li* 107.87b.
  Cf. TING Chien 2.29b.

KO-CHIH see Cochin

**KOREA: (1) Kao-li 高麗. (Koryŏ) pre-Ming; (2) Chao-hsien 朝鮮. *Wan-li* 105.80; *K'ang-hsi* 72.3b; *Yung-chêng* 104.4; *Ch'ien-lung* 56.1; *Chia-ch'ing* 32.2; *Kuang-hsü* 39.2.

K'O-SHIH-MI-ERH see Kashmir

KOYAMPADI see Coyampadi

KUANG-NAN see Quang-nam

199

KUCHA: K'u-hsien 苦先. Tn., Aksu district, Sinkiang. *Wan-li* 107.87.
 Ts'ên Chung-mien 152-153; H: 55F3.
K'U-CH'A-NI 窟察尼. Unidentified. *Wan-li* 106.84b.
K'U-HSIEN see Kucha
KU-LI see Calicut
KU-LI-PAN-TSU see Pansur
KU-MA-LA 古麻剌. Ctry. Unidentified. *Wan-li* 106.83b.
K'UN-CH'ÊNG see Kunduz?
K'UNG-KA-ERH 控噶爾. Unidentified. Hung Liang-chi 50.21.
KUO-SA-SSǓ 果撒思. Unidentified. *Wan-li* 107.87b.
KUNDUZ?: K'un-ch'êng 坤城. Possibly the Tn. and Ctry. in N. E. Afghanistan? *Wan-li* 107.87b.
 Ting Chien 2.28b; cf. H: 60B3.
LACON see Ligor
LAMBRI: (1) *Nan-p'o-li* 南渤利. Ctry., No. tip of Sumatra, mod. Achin. *Wan-li* 106.84b.
 Groeneveldt 44, 89; Rockhill (1) 67.
(2) Nan-wu-li 巫 same place; cited as different country in Ming History [Pelliot (1) 327; (2) 288].
LAN-PANG 覽邦. Unidentified. *Wan-li* 105.83.
 Ting Chien 15: island group east of Singapore.
LAO-CHUA see Laos
**LAOS (Lao-chua): Nan-chang 南掌. Ctry., No. Indo-Chinese penin. *Ch'ien-lung* 56.1; *Chia-ch'ing* 31.2b; *Kuang-hsü* 39.2b.
 Ch'ing t'ung-k'ao 296.28: Nan-chang is the name first used in the Chia-ching period (1522-65) for the Lao-chua 老撾 tribes, situated between the borders of Annam, Siam, and Yunnan; cf. H: 56B4: Laotien. Mayers no. 329 states that Lao-chua is the designation attributed in Chinese literature to the Shan tribes, q. v.; Chang Ch'êng-sun 69: Lao-chua is the popular name, Nan-chang the official one (kuo-hao). Cf. Soulié and Tchang, "Les barbares soumis du Yunnan," *BEFEO* 8.155-6.
LA-SA 刺撒. Tn., Arabia or Africa. *Wan-li* 106.84b.
 Rockhill (1) 616: probably on Somali coast of Africa; Wu Han 168: the *Wu-pei-chih-t'u* 武備志圖 puts La-sa in Arabia N. W. of Aden. Cf. Pelliot (2) 287 n. 3.

LIEN-KUO see Denmark

***LIGOR** (Lacon): Liu-k'un 六崑 (or 坤). Ctry., on E. coast Malay penin. No. of Sungora (now in Siam). *Chia-ch'ing* 31.3b.

    KUWABARA (1) 280; CHANG Wei-hua 109. ROCKHILL (1) 109 identifies Lo-wei 羅衞 as "Ligor (?)."

LIU-CH'ÊN 柳陳. Tn., E. of Karakhodjo, Sinkiang. *Wan-li* 107.88.

    BRETSCHNEIDER 2.31: Lukchak; FÊNG (2) 24: Lukchun.

****LIU-CH'IU** 琉球. Ctry., E. China sea. *Wan-li* 105.81; *K'ang-hsi* 72.10; *Yung-chêng* 104.16b; *Ch'ien-lung* 56.1; *Chia-ch'ing* 31.2; *Kuang-hsü* 39.2.

    ROCKHILL (1) 64: N. W. Formosa; PELLIOT (1) 332 n. 7: much debated by Japanese scholars as to whether this is mod. Ryukyu Is. or Formosa. Ming sources distinguish Greater (Ta) and Lesser (Hsiao) Liu-ch'iu, e.g. WU Han 149. Presumably Liu-ch'iu throughout the Ch'ing period is the modern Ryukyu Is., although earlier the name referred to Formosa, cf. WADA 131.

LIU-K'UN see Ligor

LIU-SHAN see Maldive Is.

LU-MI see Rum

LÜ-SUNG see Philippines

MA-CH'ÊN see Banjermassin

MALACCA: Man-la-chia 滿剌加. Ctry., S. W. coast Malay penin. *Wan-li* 106.83b.

    Many variants: Ma-la-chia 馬, Ma-liu-chia 嘛六甲.

MALDIVE ISLANDS: Liu-shan 溜山. S. W. of Indian penin. *Wan-li* 106.84b.

    ROCKHILL (1) 82,387.

MA-LIN see Melinde

***MANG-CHÜN-TA-LAO** 莽 (GILES 7667) 均達老. ? *Chia-ch'ing* 31.3b. Possibly for Magindanao i.e., Mindanao? (cf. WADA 135, 157, 160-161 where various forms are given; none are the same as this).

MAN-LA-CHIA see Malacca

MARINDUQUE?: Ho-mao-li 合貓里 or Ho-mao-wu 物 or 務. P. I., So. of Luzon. *Wan-li* 106.84b.

    WADA 156 quoting CHANG Hsieh, *Tung-hsi-yang k'ao*: same as Mao-li-wu (Marinduque); probably in fact indicating the adjacent island of Camarine, according to WADA 157.

MA-YEH-WÊNG see Billiton

MECCA see Arabia (T'ien-fang)

MEDINA: Mo-tê-na 默德那. Tn., Arabian coast of Red Sea. *Wan-li* 107.88b.

MEI-(MI)-LO-CHÜ see Molucca

MELINDE: Ma-lin 麻林. Tn., E. coast of Africa, No. of Mombasa. *Wan-li* 106.84b.
> ROCKHILL (1) 83.

MIEH-K'O-LI see Nieh-k'o-li

MIEN-TIEN see Burma

MINDANAO see Mang-chün-ta-lao?

MOGADISHO (Mogedoxu, etc.): Mu-ku-tu-tz'ŭ 木骨都束. Tn., E. coast Africa. *Wan-li* 106.84b.
> GROENEVELDT 44.

MOLUCCA: Mei-lo-chü 美洛居.
> Correct form for 芙 Fu-lo-chü.
> HUNG Liang-chi 50.5: 芙; Cf. *Ch'ing i-t'ung chih* 356.7 美.
> WADA 161; WU Han 183.

MO-TÊ-NA see Medina

MU-KU-TU-TZ'Ŭ see Mogadisho

NAN-CHANG see Laos

NAN-P'O-LI see Lambri

NAN-WU-LI see Lambri

NIEH-K'O-LI 乜克力. Tr., E. of Hami, Sinkiang? *Wan-li* 107.87b.
> TING Chien 2.2b; cf. BRETSCHNEIDER 2.178.

NISHAPUR: Ni-sha-wu-erh 你沙兀兒. Tn., in Persia, province Khorassan. *Wan-li* 107.87b.
> P: 4555, 4665.

OIRAT: Wa-la 瓦剌. Tr., Mongols. *Wan-li* 107.85.
> BRETSCHNEIDER 2.159-173 confuses Oirat with the later Oëlot.

*****PAHANG**: P'êng-hêng 彭亨. Ctry., E. coast Malay penin. *Wan-li* 105.82b.
> ROCKHILL (1) 65: P'êng-k'êng; WU Han 149: another Ming name P'ên-hêng 湓.

PAI 白. Unidentified. *Wan-li* 107.87b.
> BRETSCHNEIDER 2.315: probably the city of this name in E. Turkestan. Cf. also under Shan below.

PAI (PO)-HUA 百花. Unidentified. *Wan-li* 105.82b. Cf. LU Tz'ŭ-yün (*Pa-hung i-shih* 2.26): same as ancient Chu-nien 注輦, mod. Coromandel.

PAI-I see Shan tribes

PAI-KA-TA: 白葛達. Unidentified. *Wan-li* 106.84b.
  TING 1.28b, 2.19 suggests that this maritime tributary is Bukhara.

PAI-YIN 擺音. Tr., unidentified. *Wan-li* 107.87b.
  Listed as in the Western Regions. Cf. also under Shan.

PA-K'O-I 八可意. Unidentified. *Wan-li* 106.84b.

P'A-LA 怕剌. Unidentified. *Wan-li* 107.87b.
  Cf. old kingdom of Pala, N. E. India, H: 39F2?

PA-LA-HSI 巴喇西. Unidentified. *Hsü wên-hsien t'ung-k'ao* 239.24b.

PALEMBANG: (1) San-fo-ch'i 三佛齊. E. Sumatra, anc. Srivijaya. *Wan-li* 105.82b.
  GROENEVELDT 62, 73. KUWABARA 7.17 and FÊNG (4) 228 agree in identifying it with Palembang.
(2) Chiu-chiang 舊港, later name (for a smaller area?)
  ROCKHILL (1) 66; FÊNG (1) 11.

PA-LI-HEI see Balkh

PANG-KO-LA see Bengal

PANSUR: Ku-li-pan-tsu 古里班卒. W. coast of Sumatra near Bārūs (Baroes). *Wan-li* 106.84b.
  FUJITA (WANG 60): identifies Pan-tsu as given in *Tao-i chih-lüeh* with Pin-su 賓窣, and the "Pansur, Fansur" of the Arabs, ku-li meaning "island" (cf. ibid. 63b quoting GERINI).

PA-TA-HEI-SHANG see Badakshan

***PATANI**: Ta-ni 大泥 (also Ta-nien 年). Ctry., So. of Sungora, E. coast Malay penin. (now in Siam). *Chia-ch'ing* 31.3b.
  CHANG Wei-hua 109; WANG Kuo-wei 43b: also by error identified by Ming writers with Brunei (P'o-ni). WADA 128 n. 3 suggests this was because the name P'o-ni came through the western (hsi-yang) trade route. KUWABARA 7.83 suggests the identity of Patani (Ta-ni) with the Ta-li 大力 country of the Yüan period.

PA-TAN-SHA see Badakshan

P'ÊNG-CHIA-NA see Bengal

P'ÊNG-HÊNG see Pahang

***PHILIPPINES** (Luzon): Lü-sung 呂宋. Ctry. *Wan-li* 106.84b; *Chia-ch'ing* 31.3b.

CHANG Wei-hua 73-4: Lü-sung was the pre-Spanish name, later applied to Spain as "Great Luzon" Ta-lü-sung 大. For example see IWSM-TK 76.16 (July 1846); by contrast Hsiao-lü-sung 小 came to be used for the Philippines (Manila), e.g. *ibid.* 71.23b (May 1844). The Fukien authorities in Feb. 1847 identified Hsi-pan-ya (Spain) as Ta-lü-sung (*ibid.* 77.14b).

PIEH-SHIH-PA-LI see Bashibalik

P'O-LO see Borneo

PO-LO-ERH see Bolor

P'O-NI see Brunei

**PORTUGAL: Portugal, Spain, Italy, and France were constantly confused for one another, or not distinguished.

(1) Fo-lang-chi 佛朗機 i.e. Franks, originally derived by the Chinese from the Arabs as a term for the West in the period of the Crusades; revived for the Portuguese after 1500. Also used for the Spanish and later confused with France, see (2). Cf. CHANG Wei-hua 5-6. *Ch'ing t'ung-k'ao* 298.31b: same as Ho-lan-hsi 和蘭西, capital Pa-li-shih 巴離士 (Paris); occupied and traded at Macao (sic).

(2) Fa-lan-hsi (France) 法蘭西 or Fu-lang-hsi 弗朗. *Chia-ch'ing* 31.4: same as the Fo-lang-chi of the Ming period; occupied the Philippines (Lü-sung), lived at Macao (sic). CHANG Wei-hua 5 gives half a dozen variants of Fa-lan-hsi; Ho-lan-hsi, noted above, tends to confuse it with Holland.

(3) I-ta-li-ya (Rome or Italy, also Portugal) 意達里亞. *Chia-ch'ing* 31.3: the king, Po-na-ti-to (Pope Benedict XIII) sent tribute in 1725. Cf. *Ch'ing t'ung-k'ao* 298.6-8: a peninsula in the Mediterranean, capital Rome, etc., in 1670 and 1678 the king, A-fêng-su (Alfonso VI of Portugal), sent tribute, etc. CHANG Wei-hua 155-6: early used for Europe (Rome) and in the Ming History for Catholic missionaries. In early nineteenth century documents the Portuguese at Macao were referred to as I-ta-li-ya kuo (lit. the country of Italy), e.g. *IWSM-TK* 71.1 (Mar. 1844); but it was explained that while this name had been given the Jesuit missionaries and so applied to Macao, the country really involved at Macao was Ta-hsi-yang, see below. Meanwhile when an Italian missionary was seized it was stated in June 1848 that Italy (I-ta-li kuo) on its part had no headman in Kwangtung 查意大理國並無夷目在粵 (*ibid.* 79.17), i.e. it was an entirely new country.

(4) Ta-hsi-yang 大西洋. A general term for Europe as opposed to the Indian Ocean (Hsiao-hsi-yang), see under Western Ocean; but

also used for Portugal as a single country, e. g. *IWSM-TK* 70. 1b (Dec. 1843), 72. 3 (July 1844).

(5) Po-êrh-tu-chia-li-ya (Portugal) 博爾都嘉利亞 *Chia-ch'ing* 31. 3: the king, A-fêng-su (Alfonso VI) first sent tribute in 1670.

(6) Po-êrh-tu-ka-êrh (Portugal) 博爾都噶爾. *Chia-ch'ing* 31. 3: first sent tribute in 1727.

(7) Kan-ssŭ-la 干絲臘. *Chia-ch'ing* 31. 4: near England in the northwestern sea. CHANG Wei-hua 69: used for the Portuguese by error, being derived from "Castilla," the Spanish in the Philippines; this accords with the suggestion of PELLIOT (5) 69 n. 3 where other transcriptions for Portugal are also mentioned.

PU-HA-LA see Bukhara

PU-LA-WA see Barawa

QUANG-NAM: Kuang-nan 廣南. E. coast of Indo-China. *Wan-li* 107. 87b.

Ch'ing t'ung-k'ao 196. 30: anc. Nan-chiao 交, bounded by Annam, Champa, Burma, and Siam; MASPERO ("Royaume de Champa," *TP* 11. 195): an old capital of Champa; cf. KUWABARA 7. 19; and L. AUROUSSEAU in *BEFEO* 22. 158-160. *Hai-kuo wên-chien lu* 19b: the same as Annam.

QUILON (Kulam): Hsiao-ko-lan 小葛蘭. S. W. tip of India. *Wan-li* 106. 84.

ROCKHILL (1) 67: Hsiao-chü-nan 唄喃, Kain Colam; cf. *ibid.* 76, 83, 425.

RUM: Lu-mi 魯迷 or 密. Ctry., E. Asia Minor. *Wan-li* 107. 88.
H: 54C3; BRETSCHNEIDER 2. 306-8.

RUSSIA: Ê-lo-ssŭ 俄羅斯.

Not listed in the sources here covered; in the Ch'ing under the Li Fan Yüan (see part 3 above). BRETSCHNEIDER 2. 73-81 summarizes *Yüan History* references.

SAIRAM: Sai-lan 賽蘭. Tn., N. E. of Tashkent, C. Asia. *Wan-li* 107. 87b.

P: 5347; FÊNG (2) 31.

SAMARKAND: Sa-ma-êrh-han 撤馬兒罕. Tn., C. Asia. *Wan-li* 107. 88.

P. 5342.

SAMUDRA: (1) Hsü-wên-ta-na 須文達那. E. coast Sumatra. *Wan-li* 105. 83: "it is said to be the same as" (2). (2) Su-mên-ta-la 蘇門答剌. *Wan-li* 105. 83; *Chia-ch'ing* 31. 3b.

Translated by earlier writers as Sumatra and identified with Achin (q. v.) following Chinese sources. PELLIOT (3) 214 now concludes that it corresponds to the present village of Samudra on the Pasai River, and MILLS 6n. works out the probable location from a Chinese sailing chart as "near Meraksa about 5 miles west of the Pasai River."

SAN-FO-CH'I see Palembang

SAO-LAN: 掃蘭. ? *Wan-li* 107. 87b.
Variant for Sairam? This is another guess by Mr. TING.

SHA-LI-WAN-NI see Cananore

SHA-LIU-HAI-YA (Shahrokia) see Khodjend

SHAN TRIBES: Pai-i 擺夷. No. Indo-China penin.
MAYERS no. 329: "The Shans of the border-land between Yunnan and Burmah term themselves, and are commonly known as, Pai I 百. Chinese official writers, however, describe them as Lao Chua (Laos), and the designation Pai I is applied in the description of the tribes of Yunnan (*Nan Man Chih* 南蠻志. Book III . . .) to the aborigines of the Kuangsi frontier . . . ." SOULIÉ and TCHANG, in *BEFEO* 8.352 quoting *Nan tchao ye che*, identify the 白人 Po-jen with the 百夷 "Pai-yi" and 擺夷 "Pa-yi," all being of Thai race. J. SIGURET, *Territoires et populations des confins du Yunnan* (Peiping 1937) 137 classes the Pai-i 擺夷 as a Shan tribe in Yunnan.

SHA-TI-MAN: 沙的蠻. ? *Wan-li* 107. 87b.
Lit. "Barbarians of the desert." Cf. BRETSCHNEIDER 2. 315.

SHÊ-HEI 捨黑. Tn., So. coast Arabia? *Wan-li* 107. 87b.
TING Chien 2. 29b: in Arabia, same as Sha-ha 沙哈; cf. H: 50D4 Escier, (No. 2113) 施曷 Shih-ho, Shihr.

SHÊ-LA-CH'I 捨剌齊. Shulistan? *Wan-li* 106. 84b.
BRETSCHNEIDER 2. 127-8

SHÊ-P'O see Java

SHIRAZ: Shih-la-ssŭ 失剌思. Tn., Persia. *Wan-li* 107. 87b.
P: 5677; BRETSCHNEIDER 2. 292-4, 128

**SIAM: (1) Hsien-lo 暹羅. Ctry. *Wan-li* 105. 81b; *K'ang-hsi* 72. 16; *Yung-chêng* 104. 27; *Ch'ien-lung* 56. 1; *Chia-ch'ing* 31. 2b; *Kuang-hsü* 39. 2b. ? (2) Chiang-k'ou 港口. *Chia-ch'ing* 31. 3: a country, 160 watches from Amoy.
Hai-kuo wên-chien lu (a work completed in 1730, see under part 7

above) 1.25, in describing the sailing route from Amoy to Siam, gives its destination as Hsien-lo chiang-k'ou, translated by Schlegel 197 as "the estuary of Siam," 188 watches from Amoy; to enter port (ju-chiang) it is 40 watches more. *Hai-lu* (a work completed about 1820) 1.2 likewise refers to Hsien-lo chiang-k'ou as the end of the sea route to Siam. In the list quoted above (part 5) from the 1818 edition of the *Hui-tien*, Chiang-k'ou kuo occupies the place where one would necessarily expect to find Siam, which on its part is not listed; the identification of Chiang-k'ou kuo as identical or connected with Siam should be easily proved by further research. For example, the *Ch'ing t'ung-tien* 98.13 states that the king is named Chêng 鄭. The contemporary king of Siam had this same surname.

SO-LI see Chola

SO-LO see Borneo

SPAIN: Hsi-pan-ya 西班牙. Not formally listed in the *Hui-tien*, confused with Portugal, q. v.; see Philippines.

**SULU: Su-lu 蘇祿. Sulu Archipelago. *Wan-li* 106.83b; *Yung-chêng* 104.36; *Ch'ien-lung* 56.1; *Chia-ch'ing* 31.2b; *Kuang-hsü* 39.2b.

 ROCKHILL (1) 66; UCHIDA 32 gives variants.

SUMATRA see Samudra

*SUNGORA (Sunkla): Sung-chü-lao 宋腒勝. Ctry., on E. coast Malay penin., No. of Patani (now in Siam, mod. Sunkla). *Chia-ch'ing* 31.3b.

 CHANG Wei-hua 109: same as Sung-ch'ia 卡 or Sung-chiao 脚, Sawng Kia or Sungora; KUWABARA (1) 280.

SYRIA: Fu-lin 拂菻. E. coast of Mediterranean, incl. Palestine. (originally the Byzantine empire). *Wan-li* 106.84b.

 HERRMANN 38 distinguishes between Greater Fu-lin as the E. Roman Empire, and Sham, Smaller Fu-lin 臨, in Syria.

*SWEDEN: Jui-kuo 瑞國. *Chia-ch'ing* 31.4.

TABRIZ: T'ieh-pi-li-ssŭ 帖必力思. Tn., Persia. *Wan-li* 107.87b.

 FÊNG (2) 35.

TA-HUI 打回. Unidentified. *Wan-li* 106.84b.

T'AI-NING, district of, see To-yen

TA-NI see Patani

TA-NIEN see Patani

TAN-PA 淡巴. ? *Wan-li* 105.83. LU Tz'ŭ-yün (*Pa-hung i-shih*

207

2.26b): same as ancient Lang-ya-hsiu 狼牙修; cf. FÊNG (4) 226: Laṅkāsuka, on the northern Malay peninsula.

*TAN-TAN 單咀. *Chia-ch'ing* 31.3b (text indistinct): dependency of Johore, listed between Trengganu and Pahang. Cf. FÊNG (4) 221: 丹丹, 單單, and 旦旦 (241 n. 1) all appear to refer to the same place on the Malay peninsula. This seems more probable than the early suggestion of FERRAND 13.299-300 that Tan-tan might be "dans la partie orientale de la mer de Java."

TASHKENT: T'a-shih-kan 塔什干. C. Asia. *Ch'ing t'ung-k'ao* 299.12b.

P: 154

TIBET: Wu-ssŭ-tsang 烏思藏. *Wan-li* 108.88b; *K'ang-hsi* 73.1; *Yung-chêng* 105.1.

Also T'u-fan, Hsi-tsang, etc., cf. B: 906; and P: 2502 for variants.

TIEH-LI 碟里. Unidentified. *Wan-li* 106.84b.

T'IEH-PI-LI-SSŬ see Tabriz

T'IEN-FANG see Arabia (Mecca)

TING-CHI-NÜ see Trengganu

TOGMAK: T'o-hu-ma 脫忽麻. C. Asia. *Wan-li* 107.87b.

BRETSCHNEIDER 2.161; cf. H: 69C2 Tokmak.

TO-YEN: the districts of To-yen 朵顏, Fu-yü 福餘, and T'ai-ning 泰寧 in So. Manchuria. *Wan-li* 107.86b.

H: 55GF2

*TRENGGANU: Ting-chi-nü 丁機奴. Ctry., E. coast Malay penin. No. of Pahang. *Chia-ch'ing* 31.3b.

ROCKHILL (1) 65, 118; CHANG Hsieh 4.11b gives Ting-chi-i 宜 as a dependency of Java, adjacent to Johore; WANG Kuo-wei 29b gives Ting-chia-lu 家廬 as Tringganu; *Ch'ing t'ung-k'ao* 297.16-17: a dependency of Johore. KUWABARA 7.85 identifies it as Ting-ko-êrh 丁呵兒 of the Yüan period.

TSO-FA-ERH see Djofar

TSO-HA-SA-K'O see Khirgiz

TSO-FA-ÊRH see Djofar

T'U-LU-FAN see Turfan

TUNG-PU-LU-T'Ê see Burut

TUNG-YANG see under Western Ocean

**TURFAN (anc. Kao-ch'ang): T'u-lu-fan 土魯番. Tn., Sinkiang.

Wan-li 107.88; *K'ang-hsi* 72.8b; *Yung-chêng* 104.37b.

P: 6670.

TURGUT: T'u-êrh-ku-t'ê 土爾古特. Tr. C. Asia. *Ch'ing i-t'ung chih* 355.34.

Cf. B: 864, 903

URIANGHAI: Wu-liang-ha 烏梁海. District in E. Inner Mongolia and So. Manchuria. *Wan-li* 107.85.

P: 7182; T. C. Lin (2) 867.

WA-LA, the three princes of the, see Oirat

WÊN-LAI see Brunei

WÊN-TU-SSŬ-T'AN 溫都斯坦. Unidentified. Hung Liang-chi 50.21.

**WESTERN OCEAN COUNTRY(IES): Hsi-yang(chu)-kuo 西洋(諸)國. *K'ang-hsi* 72.18; *Yung-chêng* 104.30; *Ch'ien-lung* 56.1; *Chia-ch'ing* 31.3: at first (1690) singular, later a generic term for European countries. Cf. Chang Wei-hua 155-6: Ta-hsi-yang for Europe; Hsi-yang in the early Ming meant the So. Sea and Indian Ocean west of Borneo, as opposed to Tung-yang from Borneo east (quoting Chang Hsieh, *Tung-hsi-yang k'ao*); see also the more full (and earlier) discussion in Wada 123-5: Hsi- and Tung-yang originally referred to the trade routes along (Hsi) the Indo-Chinese-Malayan coast and (Tung) to the Philippines, Molucca, etc., respectively. Ta-hsi-yang was also used for Portugal (q. v.) in particular.

WO-NU see Japan

WU-LUN 兀倫. Unidentified. *Wan-li* 107.87b.

Cf. Rockhill (1) 238: Wu-lun 巫崙, a dependency of Java.

WU-SHÊ-LA-T'ANG 烏涉剌踢. Unidentified. *Wan-li* 106.84b.

WU-SSŬ-TSANG see Tibet

YA-CHI see Achin

YA-ÊRH-KAN see Yarkand

YA-HSI: 牙昔. Unidentified. *Wan-li* 107.87b.

Ting Chien 2.29b gives Aksu

YARKAND: (1) Ya-êrh-kan 牙兒干. Tn., Sinkiang. *Wan-li* 107.87b. (2) Yeh-êrh-ch'in (Hui-hui kuo) 葉爾欽. *Ta-Ch'ing i-t'ung chih* 355.36

Cf. Fêng (2) 41: Yeh-êrh-ch'iang 羌, Ch'ing name for Yarkand.

YEH-SSŬ-CH'ÊNG 耶思成. Unidentified. *Wan-li* 107.87b.

YING-CHI-LI see England

*YIN-TAI-MA 尹代嗎. Unidentified, near Cambodia; possibly Chantebun? *Chia-ch'ing* 31.3b: listed between Cambodia and Ligor. Cf. *Hai-kuo wên-chien lu* 196: K'un-ta-ma 崑大嗎 between Cambodia and Siam.

YÜEH-NAN see Annam
YU-HA-SA-K'O see Kirghiz
YÜ-T'IEN see Khotan

APPENDIX 1

Bibliographical note: Research on various aspects of this enormous and ramified subject has accumulated to a point where general surveys should be of value. At the same time, most of the work done has been on the Ming period, leaving a gap between it and the nineteenth century. The following modern writings relating to maritime relations and/or the tributary system, although largely concerned with the Ming or earlier periods, are selected as essential background materials for the study of the Ch'ing period. They are arranged alphabetically by author and are so cited in the article, particularly in the index of place names, section 8. For analytical purposes they may be classified under five heads:

(1) On administration: KUWABARA's masterly study of Sung and Yüan foreign trade has not been equalled for a later period; CHANG Tê-ch'ang, T. C. LIN, YANO, and UCHIDA, among others, describe the Ming organs of administration dealing with foreigners.

(2) On sea-routes and the Ming expeditions: WADA discusses the route via the Philippines and MILLS that via Malaya; GROENEVELDT, HIRTH and ROCKHILL, and ROCKHILL, among others, translate valuable texts while the expeditions under CHÊNG Ho first studied by ROCKHILL and his predecessors are dealt with in an important series of monographs by PELLIOT, DUYVENDAK, and FÊNG, which revise previous work while not supplanting it.

(3) On relations via Central Asia: BRETSCHNEIDER is still a chief work for the Ming period; the immense volume of Ch'ing materials concerning the Li Fan Yüan appear hardly to have been touched.

(4) On the Europeans: CHANG Wei-hua has done a valuable study of the sections on European countries in the *Ming History*, and CHANG T'ien-tsê a study of Macao (note PELLIOT's review); for this type of work see under table 4 below, and the bibliography given in PRITCHARD; this article does not attempt to refer to the work done on the Jesuit missions.

(5) On Ch'ing relations with neighboring states: ROCKHILL (on Korea and Tibet), CHANG Ch'êng-sun and YANO (1) (on Burma), and DEVÉRIA (on Annam, inadequate) barely enter upon this vast subject.

This cursory survey reveals many lacunae in our knowledge of Ch'ing foreign relations: Manchu administration in Central Asia; Sino-Dutch relations in the seventeenth century; tributary relations with Siam, Laos, and Liu-ch'iu; the Chinese side of foreign trade in general. Studies such as those of Prof. DUYVENDAK on the last Dutch embassy are much needed. In section 7 above we attempted to list some of the Ch'ing sources which await critical use. In the list which follows, some items are included as worthy of avoidance.

Abbreviations:

B = H. S. BRUNNERT and V. V. HAGELSTROM, *Present Day Political Organization of China*, trans. from Russian by A. BELTCHENKO and E. E. MORAN, Shanghai, 1912.

H = A. HERRMANN, *Historical and Commercial Atlas of China*, Cambridge, 1935.

P = G. M. H. PLAYFAIR, *The Cities and Towns of China, A Geographical Dictionary*, Shanghai, 1910 (1879).

IWSM-TK is used below for *Ch'ou-pan i-wu shih-mo* 籌辦夷務始末 Tao-kuang 道光 section, 80 chüan, Peiping 1930.

Atlas van Tropisch Nederland, Batavia 1938 (cf. Blad. 10b, Earlier History).

BRETSCHNEIDER, E., *Mediaeval Researches from Eastern Asiatic Sources* . . . London 1910 (1888), reprint 1937. Note that the section based on *Ming-shih* and *Ta-Ming i-t'ung-chih* appeared *with characters* in *China Review* 5 (1876-7).

CHANG Ch'êng-sun 張誠孫, *Chung-Ying Tien-Mien chiang-chieh wên-t'i* 中央滇緬 疆界問題 (Sino-Burmese Frontier Problems), *YCHP* monograph series no. 15, Peiping 1937; espec. pp. 85-91.

CHANG Hsi-lun 張錫綸, *Shih-wu-liu-ch'i shih-chi chien Chung-kuo tsai Yin-tu-chih-na chi Nan-yang-ch'ün-tao ti mao-i* 十五六七世紀間中國在印度支那及南洋羣島的貿易 (Chinese trade in Indo-China and the Southern Sea archipelago in the 15th, 16th, and 17th centuries) *Shih-huo* 食貨 2 no. 7 (Sept. 1935). 22-30. A brief survey based on the *Ming History*; interesting suggestions and bibliography.

CHANG Tê-ch'ang 張德昌, *Ming-tai Kuang-chou chih hai-po mao-i* 明代廣州之海舶貿易 (Maritime trade of Canton in the Ming period), *CHHP* 7 no. 2 (June 1932). 1-18. English version: " Maritime Trade at Canton during the Ming Dynasty," *The Chinese Social and Political Science Review* 17 (1933). 264-282. See also note 88 below.

CHANG T'ien-tsê 張天澤, *Sino-Portuguese Trade from 1514 to 1644, a synthesis of Portuguese and Chinese sources*, Leyden 1934. Equally important review by PELLIOT (5).

CHANG Wei-hua 張維華, *Ming-shih Fo-lang-chi Lü-sung Ho-lan I-ta-li-ya ssŭ-chuan chu-shih* 明史佛朗機呂宋荷蘭意大里亞四傳註釋 (A Commentary of [sic] the four chapters on Portugal, Spain, Holland and Italy in the History of the Ming Dynasty), *YCHP* monograph series no. 7, Peiping 1934. A valuable study which makes good use of the findings of PELLIOT and others.

DEVÉRIA, G., *Histoire des relations de la Chine avec l'Annam-Vietnam du XVIe au XIX siècle, d'après des documents chinois*, Paris 1880. Not of much use.

DUYVENDAK, J. J. L., (1) *Ma Huan re-examined*, Amsterdam 1933.

———, (2) The true dates of the Chinese maritime expeditions in the early fifteenth century, *TP* 34 (1939). 341-412.

———, (3) The last Dutch Embassy to the Chinese Court (1794-95), *TP* 34 (1938). 1-137.

———, (4) The last Dutch Embassy in the " Veritable Records," *TP* 34 (1938). 223-227.

DUYVENDAK, J. J. L., (5) Supplementary Documents on the last Dutch Embassy to the Chinese Court, *TP* 35 (1940). 329-353.

"Embassies to the court of Peking . . .," *The Chinese Repository* 14 (1845). 153-6. Extracts from *Chia-ch'ing hui-tien* 31, which reproduce, with some inaccuracies, part of the data presented in tables 2 and 3 below.

FÊNG Ch'êng-chün 馮承鈞, (1) *Ying-yai shêng-lan chiao-chu* 瀛涯勝覽校注 [Critical notes on the Ying-yai shêng-lan (1451)] Shanghai 1935. Reviewed by PELLIOT (3); our citations are from introduction.

———, (2) *Hsi-yü ti-ming* 西域地名 (Place names in the Western Regions), pub. by Hsi-pei k'o-hsüeh k'ao-ch'a-t'uan 西北科學考察團, n. p. 1930. A useful list but gives only general source references.

———, (3) *Hsi-yü nan-hai shih-ti k'ao-chêng i-ts'ung* 西域南海史地考證譯叢 (Collected translations of critical studies of historical places in the Western Regions and the Southern Sea); and *ibid.* . . . . *hsü-pien* (supplement), both Commercial Press 1934. Translates 25 articles, 17 of them by Prof. PELLIOT; a useful collection, even though translated.

———, (4) *Chung-kuo nan-yang chiao-t'ung shih* 中國南洋交通史 (History of Chinese intercourse with the Southern Sea), Shanghai 1937. An annotated collection of sources, up into the Ming period. Perhaps the most useful single work so far available.

FERRAND, G., "Le K'ouen-louen et les anciennes navigations interocéaniques dans les mers du sud," *JA* ser. 11, tome 13 (1919). 239-333, 431-492, tome 14. 5-68, 201-241. Based on pre-Ch'ing bibliography, like most items here listed; strikingly illustrates the phonetic problems presented by Asiatic place names.

FUJITA Toyohachi 藤田豐八, *Tōsei kōshō shi no kenkyū* 東西交涉史の研究 (A study of the history of relations between East and West), 2 vols. Tōkyō 1932-33. Vol. 2 contains a useful index of place names. See also under WANG Kuo-wei.

GROENEVELDT, W. P., *Notes on the Malay Archipelago and Malacca, compiled from Chinese sources*, n. p. 1876. Includes translated extracts from the *Ming History*, *Tung-hsi-yang k'ao*, etc.

HIRTH, F., and ROCKHILL, W. W., trans., *Chau Ju-kua: his work on the Chinese and Arab trade in the twelfth and thirteenth centuries, entitled Chu-fan-chi*, St. Petersburg 1911. Like the preceding item, must of course be used in conjunction with the more recent work of PELLIOT, DUYVENDAK et al.

HOU Hou-p'ei 侯厚培 *Wu-k'ou t'ung-shang i-ch'ien wo-kuo kuo-chi mao-i chih kai-k'uang* 五口通商以前我國國際貿易之概況 (General condition of our country's international trade before the opening of the treaty ports, i. e. before 1843), *CHHP* 4 no. 1 (June 1927). An early study, now quite superseded by other work.

JAMIESON, G., "The tributary nations of China," *China Review* 12 (1883). 94-109. Translates extracts from *Chia-ch'ing hui-tien* 31 and *Chia-ch'ing hui-tien shih-li* 392-3 which require careful and extensive checking. Used as the basis for the chapter "China and her tributaries" (reprinted from the *National Review*, June 1884) in R. S. GUNDRY, *China and Her Neighbors*, London 1893.

K. (pseudonym), "Audiences granted by the Emperors of China to western envoys," *China Review* 3 (1874). 67-83. A pot-pourri quoting chiefly western sources; no longer of value.

Kuo Yu-i 郭有義, trans., Momose Hiroshi 百瀬弘, Ming-tai Chung-kuo chih wai-kuo mao-i 明代中國之外國貿易 (China's foreign trade in the Ming period), *Shih-huo* 4 no. 1 (June 10, 1936). 42-51. Japanese original in *Tōa Tōa* 東亞 8 no. 7 (1935). 95-110.

Kuwabara Jitsuzō 桑原隲藏, On P'u Shou-kêng, a man of the Western Regions..., *Memoirs of the Research Department of the Tōyō Bunko*, no. 2 (Tōkyō 1928). 1-79; 7 (1935). 1-104.

Lin, T. C., (1) Manchuria in the Ming Empire, *Nankai Social and Economic Quarterly*, 8 no. 1 (April 1935). 1-43.

——, (2) Manchurian Trade and Tribute in the Ming Dynasty: a study of Chinese theories and methods of control over border peoples, *ibid.* 9 no. 4 (Jan. 1937). 855-892.

Mayers, W. F., *The Chinese Government* ..., 3d edition, revised by G. M. H. Playfair, Shanghai 1897 (1878).

Mills, J. V., Malaya in the Wu-Pei-Chih Charts, *J. of the Malayan Branch of the R. A. S.*, 15 part 3 (Dec. 1937). 1-48. A work of great value, on a subject first developed by Phillips. Conclusions given in part in Duyvendak, Sailing Directions of Chinese Voyages, *TP* 34 (1938). 230-237.

Momose Hiroshi see Kuo Yu-i, trans.

Morrison, Rev. R., *A View of China for philological purposes* ..., Macao 1817, 80-86, gives a rather miscellaneous list of 30 tributaries " as they stand on the records of the Board of Rites and Ceremonies "; exact source not stated. An interesting compilation rather than a translation, including the principal maritime tributaries of the early Ming.

Pauthier, G., *Histoire des relations politiques de la Chine avec les puissances occidentales* ..., Paris 1859. Translates, not impeccably, the section on tributary ritual in the 1824 edition of the *Ta-Ch'ing t'ung-li*, noting certain differences with the edition of 1756 previously translated by Pauthier as " Documents officiels chinois sur les ambassades étrangères, envoyés près de l'empéreur de la Chine," *Revue de l'Orient* 2 (1846). 1-22.

Pelliot, P., (1) Les Grands Voyages Maritimes Chinois au Debut du XVe Siècle, *TP* 30 (1933). 237-452.

——, (2) Notes Additionelles sur Tcheng Houo et sur ses voyages, *TP* 31 (1935). 274-314.

——, (3) Encore à propos des voyages de Tcheng Houo, *TP* 32 (1936). 210-222.

——, (4) L'Ambassade de Manoel de Saldanha à Pékin, *TP* 27 (1930). 421-424. Gives evidence for 1670 as the date rather than 1667.

——, (5) Un ouvrage sur les premiers temps de Macao, *TP* 31 (1934). 58-94. A review of Chang T'ien-tsê, giving new material as well as corrections.

Pritchard, Earl H., *The Crucial Years of Early Anglo-Chinese Relations, 1750-1800*, Pullman 1936; pp. 403-430 give a useful bibliography of western materials on early modern relations and includes a list of Chinese materials.

For other items relating to European embassies, Russian relations, and the like, see under table 4 above.

Rockhill, W. W., (1) Notes on the Relations and Trade of China with the Eastern Archipelago and the Coasts of the Indian Ocean during the Fourteenth Century, *TP* 14-16 (1913-1915). passim; sep. pub. Leiden 1915.

Rockhill, W. W., (2) *China's intercourse with Korea from the XVth century to 1895*, London 1905.

———, (3) *The Dalai Lamas of Lhasa and their relations with the Manchu Emperors of China, 1644-1908*, Leyden 1910; from *TP* 11 (1910) 1-104.

———, (4) Diplomatic Missions to the Court of China: the Kotow question, *American Historical Review* 2 (1897). 427-442, 627-643. Revised and extended as *Diplomatic Audiences at the Court of China*, London, 1905.

Schlegel, G., Geographical Notes, *TP* 9 (1898). 177-200, 273-298. Not reliable but has a few useful references.

Ting Ch'ien 丁謙, Ming-shih ko wai-kuo chüan ti-li k'ao-chêng 明史各外國傳地理考證 (A critical study of the geography of the *Ming History* chapters on foreign countries), in the *Chê-chiang t'u-shu-kuan ts'ung-shu* 浙江圖書館叢書 (Collectanea of the Chekiang Library), ts'ê 8 (1915). Certain of Mr. Ting's errors are indicated in Chang Wei-hua 102-103 and in Wada 157. His work contains a plethora of unsupported guesses; it is cited below in section 8 only for suggestive value.

Ts'ên Chung-mien 岑仲勉, Ming-ch'u Ch'ü-hsien A-tuan An-ting Han-tung ssŭ-wei k'ao 明初曲先阿端安定罕東四衞考 (A study of the four districts of Ch'ü-hsien ... at the beginning of the Ming period), *Chin-ling hsüeh-pao* 金陵學報 6 no. 2 (Nov. 1936). 151-172.

Uchida Naosaku, see Wang Huai-chung trans.

Wada Sei (和田清), "The Philippine Islands as known to the Chinese before the Ming Period," *Memoirs of ... the Tōyō Bunko (The Oriental Library)* no. 4 (Tōkyō 1929). 121-166. Makes extensive critical use of Chang Hsieh, *Tung-hsi-yang k'ao*.

Wang Huai-chung 王懷中, trans., Uchida Naosaku 內田直作 Ming-tai ti ch'ao-kung mao-i chih-tu 明代之朝貢貿易制度 (The system of Court tribute and trade in the Ming period), *Shih-huo* 3 no. 1 (Dec. 10, 1935). 32-37. Published originally in *Shina kenkyū* 支那研究 37 (1935). 91-101.

Wang Kuo-wei 王國維 trans., Fujita Toyohachi author, *Tao-i chih-lüeh chiao-chu* 島夷誌略校注 [Critical notes on the Tao-i chih-lüeh (Brief Gazetteer of the Island Barbarians, by Wang Ta-yüan 汪大淵 1349] in *Hsüeh-t'ang ts'ung-k'o* 雪堂叢刻 ts'ê 10. Synthesizes modern critical work on an important Yüan text.

Wu Han 吳晗, Shih-liu shih-chi ch'ien chih Chung-kuo yü Nan-yang 十六世紀前之中國與南洋 "China and South Sea Islands [sic] before 16th Century," *CHHP* 11 no. 1 (Jan. 1936). 137-186.

Yanai Watari 箭內亙. *Tōyō tokushi chizu* 東洋讀史地圖 (Far Eastern historical atlas), revised edition Tōkyō 1926.

Yano Jinichi 矢野仁一, (1) Biruma no Shina ni taisuru chōkō kankei ni tsuite 緬甸の支那に對する朝貢關係に就いて (On Burmese tributary relations with China), *Tōyō Gakuhō* 東洋學報 17 (1928). 1-39.

———, (2) *Shina kindai gaikoku-kankei kenkyū* 支那近代外國關係研究 (A study of modern Chinese foreign relations), Kyōto 1928. This volume is centered upon Ming and Ch'ing relations with the Portuguese and discusses each of their embassies.

Yü-kung pan-yüeh k'an 禹貢半月刊 "The Chinese Historical Geography, Semi-monthly Magazine" (Peiping 1934-1937). A chief repository of recent Chinese research on its subject, containing articles too numerous to list here. Cf. in particular vol. 6 no. 8-9 (Jan. 1, 1937), a special research number on the South Sea area 南洋研究專號.

For Chinese works not in this list see above under section 7.

APPENDIX 2

A note to page 177.

With the lists of tributaries from the Ch'ing editions of the *Hui-tien* may be compared certain others:

(1) a list of 57 tribes or states given by Hung Liang-chi in his *Ch'ien-lung fu-t'ing-chou-hsien t'u-chih* (see under part 7 above), ch. 50;

(2) a list of 31 tributaries in the Ch'ien-lung edition of the *Ta-ch'ing i-t'ung chih* (completed 1764), 353-356;

(3) a list of 43 such places in the revised edition of this gazetteer, *Chia-ch'ing ch'ung-hsiu i-t'ung chih* (covering material to 1820), 550-560; and

(4) a list of 32 tributaries in the *Ch'ing t'ung-k'ao* (covering the period from the beginning of the Ch'ing to 1785), 293-300. We take Hung Liang-chi's list as a framework because it is both analytically arranged and the most extensive.

Key: O = not listed. + = listed, * = not in the lists of six editions of the *Hui-tien* given above.

1. Hung Liang-chi	2. *I-t'ung chih* (1764)	3. *I-t'ung chih* (Chia-ch'ing)	4. *Ch'ing t'ung-k'ao*
Eastern border:			
Korea (Chao-hsien)	+	+	+
Liu-ch'iu	+	+	+
Japan	+	+	+
Sulu	+	+	0
Marinduque? (Ho-mao-wu)	(Ho-mao-li)	+	0
*Molucca	+	+	0
Brunei (P'o-lo, Wên-lai)	+	+	0
Southern and southeastern border:			
Annam (An-nam)	+	(Yüeh-nan)	(An-nan)
Laos (Nan-chang)	+	+	+
*Kuang-nan	0	+	+
Burma (Mien-tien)	0	+	+
*Hu-lu	0	+	+
*Chêng-ch'ien	0	+	0
*Ching-hai	0	0	0
Siam	+	+	+
Chiang-k'ou (Siam?)	0	+	+

215

1. Hung Liang-chi	2. I-t'ung chih (1764)	3. I-t'ung chih (Chia-ch'ing)	4. Ch'ing t'ung-k'ao
SOUTHERN AND SOUTHEASTERN BORDER:			
Cambodia (Tung-pu-chai)	0	(Chien-pu-chai)	+
Sungora	0	+	0
Johore	0	+	+
Achin	0	+	0
Philippines (Lü-sung)	+	+	+
Mang-chün-ta-lao	0	0	0
Java (Ka-la-pa)	(Chao-wa)	(Ka-la-pa)	+
I-ta-li-ya	0	0	+
Portugal (Po-erh-tu-ka-erh-ya)	0	0	+
Portugal (Fo-lang-chi)	+	0	+
Western Ocean	+	+	0
Lambri	+	+	0
Champa	+	+	0
Cambodia (Chên-la)	+	0	0?
Brunei (P'o-ni)	+	+	0
*Billiton	+	+	0
Palembang (San-fo-ch'i)	+	0	0
WESTERN AND NORTHWESTERN BORDER:			
*Eastern Burut	0	0	+
*Western Burut	0	0	+
*Andijan	0	0	+
Badakshan	0	0	+
*Bolor	0	0	+
*Afghanistan	0	0	+
Bengal (Pang-ka-la)	+	+	0
Syria (Fu-lin)	+	+	0
Calicut	+	+	0
Cochin	+	+	0
Ceylon	+	+	0
Chola (Hsi-yang-so-li)	+	+	0
*Wên-tu-ssŭ-t'an	0	0	0
*K'ung-ka-erh	0	0	0
England	0	+	+
Portugal (Kan-ssŭ-la)	0	0	+
Holland	+	+	+
Sweden	0	+	+
Denmark	0	+	+
*Tashkent (following Badakshan)	0	0	+
NORTHERN BORDER:			
*Russia	+	+	+
*Turgut	+	0	0
*Eastern Kirghiz	0	0	+

	1. Hung Liang-chi	2. *I-t'ung chih* (1764)	3. *I-t'ung chih* (Chia-ch'ing)	4. *Ch'ing t'ung-k'ao*
NORTHERN BORDER:				
*Western Kirghiz		0	0	+
	0	Yarkand (Yeh-êrh-ch'in, Moslems)	0	0
	0	Samudra (Su-mên-ta-la)	0	0
	0	0	Pahang	+
	0	0	*Banjermassin (Ma-ch'ên)	0
	0	0	Trengganu	0
	0	0	Malacca (Ma-liu-chia)	0
	0	0	Palembang	0
	0	0	France	0

It is apparent that even officially published lists of tributaries had no fixed membership. Since countries that made contact by trade almost necessarily attained a nominal tributary status, such lists are of greater value for economic than for political history. Yet even for this purpose they hark back so plainly to the bygone glories of the Ming (e. g. Ceylon, Chola, Calicut) that their value is dubious.

APPENDIX 3

99. Author and title index to section 7.

Ao-mên chi-lüeh 9.
CHANG Ju-lin 9.
CHANG Shu-shêng 29.
CHANG Yü-shu 2.
CH'ÊN Lun-ch'iung 8.
Chia-ch'ing ch'ung-hsiu i-t'ung-chih 19
CHIANG-SHANG-CHIEN-SOU 34.
Ch'ien-lung fu-t'ing-chou-hsien t'u-chih 17.
Ch'in-ting ku-chin t'u-shu chi-ch'êng 7.
Ch'ing t'ung-k'ao 14.
Ch'ing t'ung-tien 13.
Chung-hsi chi-shih 34.
Fu-chien t'ung-chih 31.
Fu-chien t'ung-chih chêng-shih-lüeh 16
Hai-kuo t'u-chih 32.
Hai-kuo wên-chien lu 8.
Hai-lu 20.

Hai-tao i-chih 15.
Hai-wai chi-yao 23.
Ho Chang-ling 22.
Ho Ta-kêng 28.
Hsi-ch'ao chi-chêng 30.
HSIA Hsieh 34.
Hsia-mên chih 25.
HSIEH Ch'ing-kao 20.
Hsü Chi-yü 33.
Hsü Ti-shan 24.
Hua-shi i-yen 27.
Huang-ch'ao ching-shih-wên pien 22.
Huang-Ch'ing chih-kung t'u 10.
HUNG Liang-chi 17.
I-shih chi-yü 4.
JUAN Yüan 21 (2).
KU Yen-wu 1.

217

Kuang-tung t'ung-chih 21.
Kuang-yü chi 5.
LAN Ting-yüan 6.
LI Tsêng-chieh 23.
LIANG T'ing-nan 26.
LIN Tsê-hsü 27, 29, 32.
LU Tz'ŭ-yün 4.
LU Ying-yang 5.
Lun nan-yang shih-i shu 6.
Lü-sung chi-lüeh 18.
LÜ T'iao-yang 20.
Pa-hung i-shih 4.
Shih-ch'ü yü-chi 30.
Ta-Ch'ing i-t'ung-chih 11.
Ta-chung-chi 24.
T'ai-wan-fu chih 12.

T'ien-hsia chün-kuo li-ping shu 1.
T'u-shu chi-ch'êng 7.
WANG Ch'ing-yün 30.
Wai-kuo chi 2.
Wai-kuo chu-chih tz'ŭ 3.
WANG Ta-hai 15.
WEI Yüan 32.
YANG Ping-nan 20.
Yang-wu ts'ung-ch'ao 29.
YAO Ying 29.
YEH Ch'iang-yung 18.
YIN Kuang-jen 9.
Ying-huan chih-lüeh 33.
Ying-i shuo 28.
YU T'ung 3.
Yüeh-hai-kuan chih 26.